Lawrence P. Buch

PETRARCH

D1294717

PETRARCH

PETRARCH

A Humanist Among Princes

An Anthology of Petrarch's
Letters and of Selections
from His Other Works

Edited and in Part Translated by
DAVID THOMPSON

Harper & Row, Publishers
New York, Evanston, and London

WIDENER UNIVERSITY
WOLFGRAM
LIBRARY
CHESTER, PA.

DISCARDED
WIDENER UNIVERSITY

PQ
4496
.E21
1971

PETRARCH

Copyright © 1971 by David Thompson.

All rights reserved. Printed in the United States of America. No part of this book may be used or reproduced in any manner whatsoever without written permission except in the case of brief quotations embodied in critical articles and reviews. For information address Harper & Row, Publishers, Inc., 49 East 33rd Street, New York, N. Y. 10016. Published simultaneously in Canada by Fitzhentry & Whiteside Limited, Toronto.

Illustrations courtesy of the Bettman Archive, Inc.
The map of Italy ca. 1350 is by Willow Roberts.

First HARPER PAPERBACK edition published 1971

Library of Congress Catalog Card Number: 71–141051
STANDARD BOOK NUMBER: 06–131529–X

For Aaron

Contents

VAUCLUSE, ITALY, AVIGNON: 1346–53

MILAN: 1353–61

NORTHERN ITALY: 1361–74

Illustrations

Acknowledgments

The selections used in this book are acknowledged below. Translations from the texts were done by myself.

No one can work on Petrarch without falling permanently into the debt of the late Ernest Hatch Wilkins, to whose studies I have had constant recourse. I am grateful to the Indiana University Press for permission to reprint a number of translations by Morris Bishop; and to Chatto & Windus for allowing me to use a selection from William Draper's version of the *Secretum*.

Texts

1. Giovanni Boccaccio, *Opere Latine Minori,* ed. A.F. Massèra (Bari, 1928): selection 46.

2. Francesco Petrarca, *L'Africa,* ed. Nicola Festa (Firenze, 1926): selection 70.

3. Francesco Petrarca, *Le Familiari,* ed. V. Rossi (Firenze, 1937), vol. III: selections 34, 36, 39.

4. Francesco Petrarca, *Poesie Minori,* ed. Domenico de' Rossetti (Milano, 1831, 1834), vols. II, III: selections 8, 10.

5. Francesco Petrarca, *Prose,* a cura di G. Martellotti *et al.* (Milano-Napoli, 1955): selections 12, 38, 42, 45, 55, 59, 61, 64, 66.

6. Francesco Petrarca, *Rime, Trionfi e Poesie Latine,* a cura di F. Neri *et al.* (Milano-Napoli, 1951): selections 2, 9, 14, 15, 21, 22, 24, 28, 37.

English Translations

1. Morris Bishop, *Letters from Petrarch* (Bloomington, Ind. and London, 1966): selections 6, 7, 13, 16, 27, 40, 49, 51, 52, 56, 62, 63, 65. Copyright © 1966 by Indiana University Press. Reprinted by permission.

2. Mario E. Cosenza, *Francesco Petrarca and the Revolution of Cola di Rienzo* (Chicago, 1913): selections 19, 20, 31–33, 35, 44 (somewhat modernized).

3. William H. Draper, *Petrarch's Secret, or The Soul's Conflict with Passion* (London, 1911): selection 11.

4. J. H. Robinson and H. W. Rolfe, *Petrarch: The First Modern Scholar and Man of Letters* (New York and London, 1898): selections 1, 3–5, 17, 23, 25, 26, 29, 30, 41, 47, 50, 53, 54, 57, 58, 60, 67–69.

5. Jacob Zeitlin, *The Life of Solitude by Francis Petrarch* (Urbana, 1924): selections 18, 43, 48.

Preface

As the first great figure of the Renaissance, Petrarch has a singular claim to our attention; and like Erasmus and Voltaire—the only other writers who have dominated an age in comparable fashion—he holds as much interest for historians as for students of literature. This volume focuses on Petrarch's secular career, his relationships with the princes (temporal and spiritual) and men of letters of his own century. Especially full representation is accorded the correspondence with Boccaccio, whose poem on Dante is also included. I have attempted to present a fairly complete biographical portrait through a chronological arrangement of texts and through annotations which provide an additional measure of continuity. These texts have been selected with a view to illustrating, as far as possible within the compass of a single volume, every major phase of Petrarch's life and works. Several are here translated into English for the first time.

DAVID THOMPSON

Preface

PETRARCH

PETRARCH

1. To Posterity[1]

It is possible that some word of me may have come to you, though even this is doubtful, since an insignificant and obscure name will scarcely penetrate far in either time or space. If, however, you should have heard of me, you may desire to know what manner of man I was, or what was the outcome of my labors, especially those of which some description or, at any rate, the bare titles may have reached you.

To begin with myself, then, the utterances of men concerning me will differ widely, since in passing judgment almost every one is influenced not so much by truth as by preference, and good and evil report alike know no bounds. I was, in truth, a poor mortal like yourself, neither very exalted in my origin, nor, on the other hand, of the most humble birth, but belonging, as Augustus Caesar says of himself, to an ancient family.[2] As to my disposition, I was not naturally perverse or wanting in modesty, however the contagion of evil associations may have corrupted me. My youth was gone before I realized it; I was carried away by the strength of manhood; but a riper age brought me to my senses and taught me by experience the truth I had long before read in books, that youth and pleasure are vanity—nay, that the Author of all ages and times permits us miserable mortals, puffed up with emptiness, thus to wander about, until finally, coming to a tardy consciousness of our sins,

1. Written to conclude the *Epistolae Seniles* (cf. Ovid's letter to posterity, *Tristia* IV, 10). The letter is composed of an original nucleus dating from before 1367, with additions datable to 1370–71. I have altered Robinson's text somewhat, to bring it closer to Ricci's new arrangement (*Prose*, pp. 2 ff.), and corrected some mistranslations.
2. Suetonius, *Life of Augustus,* 2.

we shall learn to know ourselves. In my prime I was blessed with a quick and active body, although not exceptionally strong; and while I do not lay claim to remarkable personal beauty, I was comely enough in my best days. I was possessed of a clear complexion, between light and dark, lively eyes, and for long years a keen vision, which however deserted me, contrary to my hopes, after I reached my sixtieth birthday, and forced me, to my great annoyance, to resort to glasses. Although I had previously enjoyed perfect health, old age brought with it the usual array of discomforts.

I have always possessed an extreme contempt for wealth; not that riches are not desirable in themselves, but because I hate the anxiety and care which are invariably associated with them. I certainly do not long to be able to give gorgeous banquets. I have, on the contrary, led a happier existence with plain living and ordinary fare than all the followers of Apicius,[3] with their elaborate dainties. So-called *convivia*, which are but vulgar bouts, sinning against sobriety and good manners, have always been repugnant to me. I have ever felt that it was irksome and profitless to invite others to such affairs, and not less so to be bidden to them myself. On the other hand, the pleasure of dining with one's friends is so great that nothing has ever given me more delight than their unexpected arrival, nor have I ever willingly sat down to table without a companion. Nothing displeases me more than display, for not only is it bad in itself, and opposed to humility, but it is troublesome and distracting.

I struggled in my younger days with a keen but constant and pure attachment, and would have struggled with it longer had not the sinking flame been extinguished by death—premature and bitter, but salutary.[4] I should be glad to be able to say that I had always been entirely free from irregular desires, but I should lie if I did so. I can, however, conscientiously claim that, although I may have been carried away by the fire of

3. Proverbial gourmet from the age of Tiberius.
4. While it is tempting to see here a reference to Laura, there are chronological difficulties. The period of life described (*adolescentia*) extended from age 15 to 28; but Petrarch's attachment to Laura lasted until her death many years later. Perhaps we must simply accept this as one of those not infrequent instances where Petrarch has altered the account of his life.

DOMINVS FRANCISCHVS PETRARCHA

The Bettmann Archive

1. Petrarch in the robes of an academician, by Andrea del Castagno.

youth or by my ardent temperament, I have always abhorred
such sins from the depths of my soul. As I approached the age
of forty, while my powers were unimpaired and my passions
were still strong, I not only abruptly threw off my bad habits,
but even the very recollection of them, as if I had never looked
upon a woman. This I mention as among the greatest of my
blessings, and I render thanks to God, who freed me, while still
sound and vigorous, from a disgusting slavery which had always
been hateful to me.[5] But let us turn to other matters.

I have perceived pride in others, never in myself, and however insignificant I may have been, I have always been still
less important in my own judgment. My anger has very often
injured myself, but never others. I make this boast without fear,
since I am confident that I speak truly: While I am very prone
to take offence, I am equally quick to forget injuries, and have
a memory tenacious of benefits. I have always been most desirous of honorable friendships, and have faithfully cherished
them. But it is the cruel fate of those who are growing old that
they can commonly only weep for friends who have passed
away. In my familiar associations with kings and princes, and
in my friendship with noble personages, my good fortune has
been such as to excite envy. I fled, however, from many of those
to whom I was greatly attached; and such was my innate longing for liberty, that I studiously avoided those whose very name
seemed incompatible with the freedom that I loved. The greatest kings of this age have loved and courted me. They may
know why; I certainly do not. With some of them I was on
such terms that they seemed in a certain sense my guests rather
than I theirs; their lofty position in no way embarrassing me,
but, on the contrary, bringing with it many advantages.

I possessed a well-balanced rather than a keen intellect, one
prone to all kinds of good and wholesome study, but especially
inclined to moral philosophy and the art of poetry. The latter,
indeed, I neglected as time went on, and took delight in sacred
literature. Finding in that a hidden sweetness which I had once
esteemed but lightly, I came to regard the works of the poets

5. Though a cleric, Petrarch was the father of two illegitimate children:
Giovanni, born in 1337; and Francesca, born six years later.

as only amenities. Among the many subjects which interested me, I dwelt especially upon antiquity, for our own age has always repelled me, so that, had it not been for the love of those dear to me, I should have preferred to have been born in any other period than our own. In order to forget my own time, I have constantly striven to place myself in spirit in other ages, and consequently I delighted in history; not that the con-flicting statements did not offend me, but when in doubt I accepted what appeared to me most probable, or yielded to the authority of the writer.

My style, as many claimed, was clear and forcible; but to me it seemed weak and obscure. In ordinary conversation with friends, or with those about me, I never gave any thought to my language, and I have always wondered that Augustus Caesar should have taken such pains in this respect.[6] When, however, the subject itself, or the place or listener, seemed to demand it, I gave some attention to style, with what success I cannot pretend to say; let them judge in whose presence I spoke. If only I have lived well, it matters little to me how I talked. Mere elegance of language can produce at best but an empty renown.

My parents were honorable folk, Florentine in their origin, of medium fortune, or, I may as well admit it, in a condition verging on poverty. They had been expelled from their native city,[7] and consequently I was born in exile, at Arezzo, in the year 1304 of this latter age which begins with Christ's birth, July the twentieth, on a Monday, at dawn. My life up to the present has, either through fate or my own choice, fallen into the following divisions. A part only of my first year was spent at Arezzo, where I first saw the light. The six following years were, owing to the recall of my mother from exile, spent upon my father's estate at Incisa, about fourteen miles above Florence. I passed my eighth year at Pisa, the ninth and following years in Farther Gaul, at Avignon, on the left bank of the Rhone, where the Roman Pontiff holds and has long held the

---

6. Suetonius, *Life of Augustus,* 87.

7. Petrarch's father, a "White" Guelph, was banished by the victorious "Black" Guelphs on October 20, 1302 (nine months after the expulsion of Dante, whom he had known).

Church of Christ in shameful exile.[8] It seemed a few years ago
as if Urban V was on the point of restoring the Church to its
ancient seat, but it is clear that nothing is coming of this effort,
and, what is to me the worst of all, the Pope seems to have
repented him of his good work, for failure came while he was
still living.[9] Had he lived but a little longer, he would certainly
have learned how I regarded his retreat. My pen was in my
hand when he abruptly surrendered at once his exalted office
and his life. Unhappy man, who might have died before the
altar of Saint Peter and in his own habitation! Had his successors remained in their capital he would have been looked upon
as the cause of this benign change, while, had they left Rome,
his virtue would have been all the more conspicuous in contrast
with their fault.[10]

But such laments are somewhat remote from my subject. On
the windy banks of the river Rhone I spent my boyhood, guided
by my parents, and then, guided by my own fancies, the whole
of my youth. Yet there were long intervals spent elsewhere,
for I first passed four years at the little town of Carpentras,
somewhat to the east of Avignon: in these two places I learned
as much of grammar, logic, and rhetoric as my age permitted,
or rather, as much as it is customary to teach in school: you
know how little that is, dear reader. I then set out for Montpellier to study law, and spent four years there, then three at
Bologna. I heard the whole body of the civil law, and would,
as many thought, have distinguished myself later, had I but
continued my studies. I gave up the subject altogether, however,
so soon as it was no longer necessary to consult the wishes of
my parents.[11] My reason was that, although the dignity of the
law, which is doubtless very great, and especially the numerous
references it contains to Roman antiquity, did not fail to delight

8. The French pope, Clement V (1305–14), had moved the papal court
to Avignon in 1309.

9. Urban V (1362–70) left Avignon in April, 1367; returned there from
Rome in September, 1370; and died on December 19 of the same year.

10. Petrarch had sent metrical epistles to Urban's predecessors, Benedict
XII (1334–42) and Clement VI (1342–52), urging them to restore the
papacy to Rome.

11. Petrarch left Bologna in April, 1326, probably on receiving news of
his father's death. His mother had died some years earlier.

me, I felt it to be habitually degraded by those who practise it. It went against me painfully to acquire an art which I would not practise dishonestly, and could hardly hope to exercise otherwise. Had I made the latter attempt, my scrupulousness would doubtless have been ascribed to simplicity.

So at the age of two and twenty I returned home. I call my place of exile home, Avignon, where I had been since childhood; for habit has almost the potency of nature itself. I had already begun to be known there, and my friendship was sought by prominent men; wherefore I cannot say. I confess this is now a source of surprise to me, although it seemed natural enough at an age when we are used to regard ourselves as worthy of the highest respect. I was courted first and foremost by that very distinguished and noble family, the Colonnesi, who, at that period, adorned the Roman Curia with their presence. However it might be now, I was at that time certainly quite unworthy of the esteem in which I was held by them. I was especially honored by the incomparable Giacomo Colonna, then Bishop of Lombez,[12] whose peer I know not whether I have ever seen or ever shall see, and was taken by him to Gascony; there I spent such a divine summer among the foot-hills of the Pyrenees, in happy intercourse with my master and the members of our company, that I can never recall the experience without a sigh of regret.[13]

Returning thence, I passed many years in the house of Giacomo's brother, Cardinal Giovanni Colonna, not as if he were my lord and master, but rather my father, or better, a most affectionate brother—nay, it was as if I were in my own home.[14]

12. Some thirty miles southwest of Toulouse. Giacomo had been elected bishop in 1328. He died in 1341.

13. It was during this summer of 1330 that Petrarch formed his lifelong friendship with "Socrates" (the Flemish Ludwig van Kempen, chanter in the chapel of Cardinal Giovanni Colonna), who resided at Avignon; and with "Laelius" (a Roman, Lello di Pietro Stefano dei Tosetti), who also resided at Avignon until the cardinal's death in 1348. Many of Petrarch's letters are addressed to these two friends.

14. As a household chaplain Petrarch was an active member of the cardinal's staff from 1330 to 1337, and an occasionally active member for another ten years. This was his first ecclesiastical appointment. On his ecclesiastical career, see E. H. Wilkins, *Studies in the Life and Works of Petrarch* (Cambridge, Mass., 1955), pp. 3–32.

About this time, a youthful desire impelled me to visit France and Germany. While I invented certain reasons to satisfy my elders of the propriety of the journey, the real explanation was a great inclination and longing to see new sights. I first visited Paris, as I was anxious to discover what was true and what fabulous in the accounts I had heard of that city. On my return from this journey I went to Rome, which I had since my infancy ardently desired to visit. There I soon came to venerate Stephano, the noble head of the family of the Colonnesi, like some ancient hero, and was in turn treated by him in every respect like a son. The love and good-will of this excellent man toward me remained constant to the end of his life, and lives in me still, nor will it cease until I myself pass away.

On my return, since I experienced a deep-seated and innate repugnance to town life, especially in that disgusting city of Avignon which I heartily abhorred, I sought some means of escape. I fortunately discovered, about fifteen miles from Avignon, a delightful valley, narrow and secluded, called Vaucluse, where the Sorgue, the prince of streams, takes its rise. Captivated by the charms of the place, I transferred thither myself and my books. Were I to describe what I did there during many years, it would prove a long story. Indeed, almost every bit of writing which I have put forth was either accomplished or begun, or at least conceived, there, and my undertakings have been so numerous that they still continue to vex and weary me. My mind, like my body, is characterized by a certain versatility and readiness, rather than by strength, so that many tasks that were easy of conception have been given up by reason of the difficulty of their execution. The character of my surroundings suggested the composition of a sylvan or bucolic song.[15] I also dedicated a work in two books upon *The Life of Solitude,* to Philip, now exalted to the Cardinal-bishopric of Sabina. Although always a great man, he was, at the time of which I speak, only the humble Bishop of Cavaillon.[16] He is the only

15. Petrarch conflates his first stay in Vaucluse (1337–41) with his third (1345–47); for the *Bucolicum Carmen* and the *De Vita Solitaria* were both begun during the latter period. Petrarch began one or more major works during each of his four periods of residence at Vaucluse.

16. Philippe de Cabassoles, whose diocese included Vaucluse, was about

one of my old friends who is still left to me, and he has always loved and treated me not as a bishop (as Ambrose did Augustine), but as a brother.

While I was wandering in those mountains upon Friday in Holy Week, the strong desire seized me to write an epic in an heroic strain, taking as my theme Scipio Africanus the Great, who had, strange to say, been dear to me from my childhood. But although I began the execution of this project with enthusiasm, I straightway abandoned it, owing to a variety of distractions. The poem was, however, christened *Africa*, from the name of its hero, and, whether from his fortunes or mine, it did not fail to arouse the interest of many before they had seen it.[17]

While leading a leisurely existence in this region, I received, remarkable as it may seem, upon one and the same day,[18] letters both from the Senate at Rome and the Chancellor of the University of Paris, pressing me to appear in Rome and Paris, respectively, to receive the poet's crown of laurel.[19] In my youthful elation I convinced myself that I was quite worthy of this honor; the recognition came from eminent judges, and I

Petrarch's age, and they shared similar tastes for books and country life. Philippe became cardinal in 1368, cardinal-bishop in 1370, and died in 1372.

17. Begun in 1338 or 1339, the *Africa* was never finished; and aside from a fragment that circulated during Petrarch's lifetime, it was not published until after his death. It proved something of a disappointment to Coluccio Salutati and others after they had seen it.

18. September 1, 1340.

19. Albertino Mussato had been crowned with laurel in Padua in 1315; and Dante had been offered a crown by Bologna but had declined (see *Paradiso* XXV, 1–9 on his desire to receive the crown in Florence). For the whole complicated question see E. H. Wilkins, "The Coronation of Petrarch" (*The Making of the "Canzoniere" and Other Petrarchan Studies* [Rome, 1951], pp. 9–69), who concludes: "The sum of the matter would seem to be that Petrarch succeeded, after persistent and varied efforts, in getting two invitations to receive the laurel crown; that the specific basis for the invitations was a rather limited amount of published Latin verse, together with the knowledge that he was engaged in the writing of a grandiose epic; that he had convinced the Colonna family and Roberto de' Bardi [Chancellor at the University of Paris, and a Florentine] that he was in truth a great poet; that their sense of his poetic worth was presumably enhanced by their knowledge that he was engaged in the writing of historical works and by the obvious range of his classical scholarship; and— just possibly—that the beauty of some of his belittled Italian lyrics was in their minds" (p. 35).

accepted their verdict rather than that of my own better judgment. I hesitated for a time which I should give ear to, and
sent a letter to Cardinal Giovanni Colonna, of whom I have
already spoken, asking his opinion. He was so near that, although
I wrote late in the day, I received his reply before the third
hour on the morrow. I followed his advice, and recognized the
claims of Rome as superior to all others. My acceptance of his
counsel is shown by my twofold letter to him on that occasion,
which I still keep. I set off accordingly; but although, after the
fashion of youth, I was a most indulgent judge of my own
work, I still blushed to accept in my own case the verdict even
of such men as those who summoned me, despite the fact that
they would certainly not have honored me in this way, had
they not believed me worthy.

So I decided, first to visit Naples, and that celebrated king
and philosopher, Robert, who was not more distinguished as
a ruler than as a man of culture.[20] He was, indeed, the only
monarch of our age who was the friend at once of learning and
of virtue, and I trusted that he might correct such things as he
found to criticize in my work. The way in which he received
and welcomed me is a source of astonishment to me now, and,
I doubt not, to the reader also, if he happens to know anything
of the matter. Having learned the reason of my coming, the
King seemed mightily pleased. He was gratified, doubtless, by
my youthful faith in him, and felt, perhaps, that he shared in
a way the glory of my coronation, since I had chosen him from
all others as the only suitable critic. After talking over a great
many things, I showed him my *Africa*, which so delighted him
that he asked for it to be dedicated to him as a great favor.
This was a request that I could not well refuse, nor, indeed,
would I have wished to refuse it, had it been in my power. He
then fixed a day upon which we could consider the object of
my visit. This occupied us from noon until evening, and the

20. Petrarch began his journey on February 16, 1341. Robert was the
grandson of that Charles of Anjou (brother of Saint Louis) whom the
papacy had called in to succeed the house of Hohenstaufen in the kingdom
of Naples and Sicily. Avignon belonged to him as count of Provence (it
was sold to the papacy by his successor in 1348), and Robert himself had
lived there from 1319 to 1324.

time proving too short, on account of the many matters which arose for discussion, we passed the two following days in the same manner. Having thus tested my poor attainments for three days, the King at last pronounced me worthy of the laurel. He offered to bestow that honor upon me at Naples, and urged me to consent to receive it there, but my veneration for Rome prevailed over the insistence of even so great a monarch as Robert. At length, seeing that I was inflexible in my purpose, he sent me on my way accompanied by royal messengers and letters to the Roman Senate, in which he gave enthusiastic expression to his flattering opinion of me. This royal estimate was, indeed, quite in accord with that of many others, and especially with my own, but today I cannot approve either his or my own verdict. In his case, affection and the natural partiality to youth were stronger than his devotion to truth.

On arriving at Rome, I continued, in spite of my unworthiness, to rely upon the judgment of so eminent a critic, and, to the great delight of the Romans who were present, I who had been hitherto a simple student received the laurel crown.[21] This occasion is described elsewhere in my letters, both in prose and verse. The laurel, however, in no way increased my wisdom, although it did arouse some jealousy—but this is too long a story to be told here.

On leaving Rome, I went to Parma, and spent some time with the members of the house of Correggio, who, while they were most kind and generous toward me, agreed but ill among themselves. They governed Parma, however, in a way unknown to that city within the memory of man, and the like of which it will hardly again enjoy in this present age.

I was conscious of the honor which I had but just received, and fearful lest it might seem to have been granted to one unworthy of the distinction; consequently, as I was walking one day in the mountains, and chanced to cross the river Enza to a place called Selvapiana, in the territory of Reggio, struck by the beauty of the spot, I began to write again upon the *Africa,*

---

21. April 8, 1341. The coronation was an adaptation of the medieval academic graduation ceremony. Petrarch's oration is translated by Wilkins, *Studies,* pp. 300–313.

which I had laid aside. In my enthusiasm, which had seemed quite dead, I wrote some lines that very day, and some each day until I returned to Parma. Here I happened upon a quiet and retired house, which I afterwards bought, and which still belongs to me. I continued my task with such ardor, and completed the work in so short a space of time, that I cannot but marvel now at my despatch. I returned thence to the Fountain of the Sorgue, and to my Transalpine solitude. I had made a long stay both in Parma and Verona, and everywhere I had, I am thankful to say, been treated with greater esteem than I merited.[22]

Some time after this, my growing reputation procured for me the good-will of a most excellent man, Giacomo the Younger, of Carrara, whose equal I do not know among the rulers of his time. For years he wearied me with messengers and letters when I was beyond the Alps, and with his petitions whenever I happened to be in Italy, urging me to accept his friendship. At last, although I anticipated little satisfaction from the venture, I determined to go to him and see what this insistence on the part of a person so eminent, and at the same time a stranger to me, might really mean. I appeared, though tardily, at Padua, where I was received by him of illustrious memory, not as a mortal, but as the blessed are greeted in heaven—with such delight and such unspeakable affection and esteem, that I cannot adequately describe my welcome in words, and must, therefore, be silent. Among other things, learning that I had led a clerical life from boyhood, he had me made a canon of Padua, in order to bind me the closer to himself and his city.[23] In fine, had his life been spared, I should have found there an end to all my wanderings. But alas! nothing mortal is enduring, and

22. On May 23 Petrarch entered Parma, where Azzo, Simone, Giovanni, and Guido da Correggio had just seized power from Mastino della Scala. He stayed until January, 1342. The house he probably bought during his second stay in Parma, 1343–45, which was followed by some time in Verona. Our text here is uncertain. Ricci (*Prose*, p. 17, n. 8) assumes a large lacuna, representing this second stay in Parma and the third at Vaucluse, 1346–47. Here I stay with the vulgate text, assuming that Petrarch has conflated his two stays at Parma (cf. above, note 15).

23. Petrarch took possession of his canonry on April 18, 1349.

there is nothing sweet which does not presently end in bitterness. Scarcely two years was he spared to me, to his country, and to the world. God, who had given him to us, took him again.[24] Without being blinded by my love for him, I feel that neither I, nor his country, nor the world was worthy of him. Although his son, who succeeded him, was in every way a prudent and distinguished man, who, following his father's example, always loved and honored me, I could not remain after the death of him with whom, by reason especially of the similarity of our ages, I had been much more closely united.

I returned to Gaul,[25] not so much from a desire to see again what I had already beheld a thousand times, as from the hope, common to the afflicted, of coming to terms with my misfortunes by a change of scene.

24. Giacomo was assassinated in December, 1350, and succeeded by his son Francesco.
25. In June, 1351.

Provence and Italy: 1333-45

2. Another Crusade[1]

Charles's successor, who adorns his head with the crown of Charlemagne, has now taken up arms to humiliate Babylon and those that take their name from her.[2] (4)

And the vicar of Christ is returning to the nest with the burden of the keys and the mantle, so that if no unforeseen event deters him he will see Bologna and then noble Rome.[3] (8)

Your meek and gentle lamb[4] brings down the fierce wolves, and may whomever lawful love separates proceed this way. (11)

Console her, then, who still awaits, and Rome that laments for her own spouse; and for Jesus' sake now gird on your sword. (14)

1. *Rerum Vulgarium Fragmenta* XXVII. Written from Avignon to Orso dell'Anguillara, who in 1329 had married Agnese Colonna, sister of Giovanni and Giacomo. For the chronology and several stages of the *Canzoniere* (Petrarch's own title may be rendered "Fragments in the Vernacular"), see Wilkins, *Making.*
2. Philip VI, who succeeded Charles IV in 1328 as the first Valois king of France, was full of crusading zeal. In 1330 Pope John XXII issued a bull authorizing Philip to collect tithes for the venture; and in 1331 another granting him and his companions the usual indulgences. The king and his chivalry took the Cross at Melun on July 25, 1332. On this and other expeditions of the period, see Aziz S. Atiya, *The Crusade in the Later Middle Ages* (New York: reprinted 1965).
3. However, because of the tumultuous conditions prevailing at Rome, the pope was unable to return.
4. *Agna,* i.e., Agnese, for whose spirit in the midst of civil strife Petrarch expresses his admiration elsewhere.

3. Journey to France and Germany[1]

I have lately been travelling through France, not on business, as you know, but simply from a youthful curiosity to see the country. I finally penetrated into Germany, to the banks of the Rhine itself. I have carefully noted the customs of the people, and have been much interested in observing the characteristics of a country hitherto unknown to me, and in comparing the things I saw with those at home. While I found much to admire in both countries, I in no way regretted my Italian origin. Indeed, the more I travel, the more my admiration for Italy grows. If Plato, as he himself says, thanked the immortal gods, among other things, for making him a Greek and not a barbarian,[2] why should not we too thank the Lord for the land of our birth, unless to be born a Greek be considered more noble than to be born an Italian. This, however, would be to assert that the slave was above his master. No Greekling, however shameless, would dare to make such a claim if he but recollected that long before Rome was founded and had by superior strength established her sway, long before the world yet knew of the Romans, "men of the toga, lords of the earth,"[3] a beggarly fourth part of Italy, a region desert and uninhabited, was nevertheless styled by its Greek colonists "Greater Greece." If that scanty area could then be called great, how very great, how immense, must the Roman power have seemed after Corinth had fallen, after Aetolia had been devastated and Argos, Mycenae, and other cities had been taken, after the

1. *Epistolae Familiares* I, 4 (June 21, 1333, from Aix-la-Chapelle) and I, 5 (August 9, from Lyons), both addressed to Cardinal Giovanni Colonna. G. Billanovich (*Petrarca letterato* [Roma, 1947], pp. 47–55) considers I, 4–5 among the fictitious letters Petrarch composed in 1350–51 when he set about rearranging the *Familiares;* but see Wilkins, *Making,* pp. 311–17.

2. Cf. Lactantius, *Divinae Institutiones* III, 19, 17.

3. Virgil, *Aeneid* I, 282.

Macedonian kings had been captured, Pyrrhus vanquished, and Thermopylae a second time drenched with Asiatic blood! Certainly no one can deny that it is a trifle more distinguished to be an Italian than a Greek. This, however, is a matter which we may perhaps take up elsewhere.

To revert to my travels in France,—I visited the capital of the kingdom, Paris, which claims Julius Caesar as its founder. I must have felt much the same upon entering the town as did Apuleius when he wandered about Hypata in Thessaly.[4] I spent no little time there, in open-mouthed wonder; and I was so full of interest and eagerness to know the truth about what I had heard of the place that when daylight failed me I even prolonged my investigations into the night. After loitering about for a long time, gaping at the sights, I at last satisfied myself that I had discovered the point where truth left off and fiction began. But it is a long story, and not suited for a letter, and I must wait until I see you and can rehearse my experiences at length.

To pass over the intervening events, I also visited Ghent, which proudly claims the same illustrious founder as Paris, and I saw something of the people of Flanders and Brabant, who devote themselves to preparing and weaving wool. I also visited Liège, which is noted for its clergy, and Aix-la-Chapelle, Charles's capital, where in a marble church I saw the tomb of that great prince, which is very properly an object of veneration to the barbarian nations.[5] . . .

I did not leave Aix-la-Chapelle until I had bathed in the waters, which are warm like those at Baiae.[6] It is from them that the town is said to derive its name.[7] I then proceeded to Cologne, which lies on the left bank of the Rhine, and is noted for its situation, its river, and its inhabitants. I was astonished to find such a degree of culture in a barbarous land. The appearance of the city, the dignity of the men, the attractiveness

4. Cf. Apuleius, *Metamorphoses* I, 5.
5. The first letter concludes here with a story about Charles the Great.
6. A resort on an inlet of the Bay of Naples, noted for its sulphur springs.
7. Aquisgrana.

of the women, all surprised me. The day of my arrival happened
to be the feast of St. John the Baptist. It was nearly sunset
when I reached the city. On the advice of the friends whom
my reputation, rather than any true merit, had won for me
even there, I allowed myself to be led immediately from the
inn to the river, to witness a curious sight. And I was not disappointed, for I found the river-bank lined with a multitude
of remarkably comely women. Ye gods, what faces and forms!
And how well attired! One whose heart was not already occupied might well have met his fate there.

I took my stand upon a little rise of ground where I could
easily follow what was going on. There was a dense mass of
people, but no disorder of any kind. They knelt down in quick
succession on the bank, half hidden by the fragrant grass, and
turning up their sleeves above the elbow they bathed their
hands and white arms in the eddying stream. As they talked
together, with an indescribably soft foreign murmur, I felt that
I had never better appreciated Cicero's remark, which, like the
old proverb, reminds us that we are all deaf and dumb when
we have to do with a foreign tongue. I, however, had the aid
of kind interpreters, for—and this was not the least surprising
thing I noted there—these skies, too, give nurture to Pierian
spirits. So when Juvenal wonders that "Fluent Gaul has taught
the British advocate,"[8] let him marvel, too, that learned Germany many a clear-voiced bard sustained. But, lest you should
be misled by my words, I hasten to add that there are no
Virgils here, although many Ovids,[9] so that you would say that
the latter author was justified in his reliance upon his genius
or the affection of posterity, when he placed at the end of his
Metamorphoses that audacious prophecy where he ventures to
claim that as far as the power of Rome shall extend,—nay, as
far as the very name of Roman shall penetrate in a conquered
world,—so widely shall his words be read by enthusiastic
admirers.

8. *Satires* XV, 111.
9. Petrarch seems to mean that no copies of Virgil, but many of Ovid
were to be found at Cologne.

When anything was to be heard or said I had to rely upon my companions to furnish both ears and tongue. Not understanding the scene, and being deeply interested in it, I asked an explanation from one of my friends, employing the Virgilian lines: "What means the crowded shore? What seek these eager spirits?"[10] He told me that this was an old custom among the people, and that the lower classes, especially the women, have the greatest confidence that the threatening calamities of the coming year can be washed away by bathing on this day in the river, and a happier fate be so assured. Consequently this annual ablution has always been conscientiously performed, and always will be. I smiled at this explanation, and replied, "Those who dwell by Father Rhine are fortunate indeed if he washes their misfortunes away with him; I fear that neither Po nor Tiber could ever free us of ours. You send your ills to the Britons, by a river; we would gladly ship ours off to the Africans or Illyrians." But I was given to understand that our rivers are too sluggish. There was a great laugh over this, and then, as it was getting late, we left the spot and returned home.

During the few days following I wandered about the city, under the guidance of my friends, from morning until night. I enjoyed these rambles not so much for what I actually saw as on account of the reminiscences of our ancestors, who have left such extraordinary monuments to the Roman power in this far-distant country. Marcus Agrippa came, perhaps, most prominently before me. He was the founder of this colony, to which, in preference to all his other great works whether at home or abroad, he gave his own name.[11] He was a great builder as well as a distinguished warrior. His fame was such that he was chosen by Augustus as the most desirable son-in-law in the world. His wife, however else we may say of her, was at least

10. *Aeneid* VI, 318–19.
11. In 38 B.C. Agrippa transferred the Ubii to the left bank of the Rhine; later an altar for the Imperial cult was consecrated at their tribal capital; and in A.D. 50 Claudius founded a colony (*Colonia Claudia Ara Augusta Agrippiensium*) in honor of his wife Agrippina (a granddaughter of Agrippa).

a remarkable woman, the Emperor's only child and very dear to him.[12] I beheld the bodies of the thousands of holy virgins who had suffered together, and the ground dedicated to these noble relics—ground which they say will of its own accord reject an unworthy corpse. I beheld the Capitol, which is an imitation of ours. But in place of our senate, meeting to consider the exigencies of peace and war, here one finds beautiful boys and girls ever lifting up together their harmonious voices in nightly hymns of praise to God. There one might hear the rattle of arms, the rolling chariots and the groans of captives; but here are peace and happiness and the voice of mirth. There it was the warrior who made his triumphal entry; here it is the Prince of Peace.

I saw, too, the great church in the very center of the town. It is very beautiful, although still uncompleted, and is not unjustly regarded by the inhabitants as the finest building of its kind in the world. I looked with reverence upon the relics of the Three Kings, who, as we read, came once upon a time, bringing presents, to worship at the feet of a Heavenly King as he lay wailing in the manger. Their bodies were brought from the East to the West in three great leaps.[13]

You may perhaps think, noble father, that I have gone too far just here, and dwelt upon unimportant details. I readily admit it, but it is because I have nothing more at heart than to obey your commands. Among the many instructions you gave me, as I was leaving, the last one was that I should write to you as fully about the countries I visited and the various things I saw and heard as I should tell about them, were we face to face. I was not to spare the pen, nor to strive for elegance or terseness of expression. Everything was to be included, not simply the more picturesque incidents. In Cicero's words, you told me to write "whatever might come into the cheek." I promised to do this, and from the numerous letters which I have despatched on the way it would seem that I had kept my en-

12. Julia was noted for her culture and wit. After the death of her first husband, Marcellus, she was married to Agrippa, and then still later to Tiberius. In 2 B.C. Augustus had her banished for adultery.

13. That is, to Constantinople, thence to Milan, and finally to Cologne.

gagement. If you had desired me to treat of higher things I should have done what I could; but it seems to me in the present case that the object of my letter should be rather to instruct the reader than to give consequence to the writer. If you and I wish to appear before the public we can do so in books, but in our letters let us just talk with one another.

But to continue, I left Cologne June 30, in such heat and dust that I sighed for Virgil's "Alpine snows and rigors of the Rhine."[14] I next passed through the Forest of Ardennes, alone, and, as you will be surprised to hear, in time of war. But God, it is said, grants especial protection to the unwary. I had long known something of this region from books; it seemed to me a very wild and dismal place indeed. However, I will not undertake with my pen a journey which I have but just completed with my horse. After many wanderings I reached Lyons today. It, too, is a noble Roman colony, a little older even than Cologne. From this point two well known rivers flow together into our ocean,—the Rhone here joining the Arar, or, as the inhabitants now call it, the Saône. But I need not tell you more about them, for they are hurrying on, one led by the other, down to Avignon, where the Roman pontiff detains you and the whole human race.

This morning when I arrived here I ran across one of your servants by accident, and plied him, as those newly arrived from foreign parts are wont to do, with a thousand questions. He knew nothing, however, except that your noble brother, whom I was hastening to join, had gone on to Rome without me. On hearing this my anxiety to proceed suddenly abated. It is now my purpose to wait here until the heat too shall abate somewhat, and until I regain my vigor by a little rest. I had not realized that I had suffered from either source until I met your servant; no kind of weariness indeed is so keenly felt as that of the mind. If the journey promises to seem tedious to me I shall float down the Rhone. In the meantime I am glad to know that your faithful servant will see that this reaches you, and that you will know where I am. As for your brother, who was

14. *Eclogues* X, 47.

to be my guide, and who now (my disappointment must be my excuse for saying it) has deserted me, I feel that my expostulations must be addressed to him directly. I beg that you will see that the enclosed message reaches him as soon as may be. Farewell. Remember your friend.

4. His Aversion to Logicians[1]

It is hazardous to engage an enemy who longs rather for battle than for victory. You write to me of a certain old logician who has been greatly excited by my letter, as if I condemned his art. With a growl of rage, he loudly threatened to make war in turn upon our studies, in a letter for which, you say, you have waited many months in vain. Do not wait longer; believe me, it will never come. He retains some traces of decency, and this is a confession that he is ashamed of his style or an acknowledgment of his ignorance. The most implacable in contests with the tongue will not resort to the pen. They are reluctant to show how ill-armed they are, and so follow the Parthian system of warfare, carried on during a rapid retreat, by letting fly a shower of winged words and committing their shafts to the wind.

It is foolhardy, as I have said, to accept an engagement with these fellows upon their own terms. It is indeed from the fighting itself that they derive their chief pleasure; their object is not to discover the truth, but to prolong the argument. But you know Varro's proverb: "Through over-long contention the truth is lost."[2] You need not fear, then, that these warriors will come out into the open fields of honest discussion, whether with

1. *Epistolae Familiares* I, 7, addressed to Tommaso Caloiro of Messina. This is another of the letters which Billanovich assigns to 1351–52.
2. Actually an excerpt from the mimes of Publilius Syrus, preserved in Macrobius, *Saturnalia* II, 7, 11.

tongue or pen. They belong to the class of whom Quintilian speaks in his *Institutes of Oratory*,[3] whom one finds wonderfully warm in disputation, but once get them away from their cavilling, they are as helpless, in a serious juncture, as certain small animals which are active enough in a narrow space, but are easily captured in a field. As Quintilian goes on to say, their tergiversations indicate their weakness; they seek, like an indifferent runner, to escape by dodging.

This is what I would impress upon you, my friend; if you are seeking virtue or truth, avoid persons of that stripe altogether. But how shall we escape from these maniacs, if even the isles of the sea are not free from them? So neither Scylla nor Charybdis has prevented this pest from finding its way into Sicily? Nay, this ill is now rather peculiar to islands, as we shall find if we add the logicians of Britain to the new Cyclopes about Aetna. Is this the ground of the striking similarity between Sicily and Britain, which I have seen mentioned in Pomponius Mela's *Cosmographia*?[4] I had thought that the resemblance lay in the situation of the countries, the almost triangular appearance of both, and perhaps in the perpetual contact which each enjoys with the surrounding sea. I never thought of logicians; I had heard of the Cyclopes, and then of the tyrants, both savage inhabitants; but of the coming of this third race of monsters, armed with two-edged arguments, and fiercer than the burning shores of Taormina itself, I was unaware.

There is one thing which I myself long ago observed, and of which you now warn me anew. These logicians seek to cover their teachings with the splendor of Aristotle's name; they claim that Aristotle was wont to argue in the same way. They would have some excuse, I readily confess, if they followed in the steps of illustrious leaders, for even Cicero says that it would give him pleasure to err with Plato, if err he must.[5] But they all deceive themselves. Aristotle was a man of the most exalted genius, who not only discussed but wrote upon themes of the

3. XII, 2, 14. The second citation is IX, 2, 78.
4. *De Chorographia* III, 50.
5. *Tusculan Disputations* I, 17, 40.

very highest importance. How can we otherwise explain so vast
an array of works, involving such prolonged labor, and prepared
with supreme care amid such serious preoccupations—especially those connected with the guardianship of his fortunate
pupil[6]—and within the compass, too, of a life by no means
long?—for he died at about sixty-three, the age which all writers deem so unlucky.[7] Now why should these fellows diverge
so widely from the path of their leader? Why is not the name
of Aristotelians a source of shame to them rather than of satisfaction, for no one could be more utterly different from that
great philosopher than a man who writes nothing, knows but
little, and constantly indulges in much vain declamation? Who
does not laugh at their trivial conclusions, with which, although
educated men, they weary both themselves and others? They
waste their whole lives in such contentions. Not only are they
good for nothing else, but their perverted activity renders them
actually harmful. Disputations such as they delight in are made
a subject of mirth by Cicero and Seneca, in several passages.
We find an example in the case of Diogenes, whom a conten-
tious logician addressed as follows: "What I am, you are not."
Upon Diogenes conceding this, the logician added, "But I am
a man." As this was not denied, the poor quibbler propounded
the conclusion, "Therefore you are not a man." "The last statement is not true," Diogenes remarked, "but if you wish it to be
true, begin with me in your major premise."[8] Similar absurdi-
ties are common enough with them. What they hope to gain
from their efforts, whether fame or amusement, or some light
upon the way to live righteously and happily, they may know;
to me, I confess, it is the greatest of mysteries. Money, certainly,
does not appeal at least to noble minds as a worthy reward
of study. It is for the mechanical trades to strive for lucre; the
higher arts have a more generous end in view.

On hearing such things as these, those of whom we are speak-

6. Alexander the Great.
7. In ancient medical theory every seventh and ninth year were critical;
so the sixty-third year would be most critical of all.
8. Aulus Gellius, *Noctes Atticae* XVIII, 13, 78.

ing grow furious—indeed the chatter of the disputatious man usually verges closely on anger. "So you set yourself up to condemn logic," they cry. Far from it; I know well in what esteem it was held by that sturdy and virile sect of philosophers, the Stoics, whom our Cicero frequently mentions, especially in his work *De Finibus*. I know that it is one of the liberal studies, a ladder for those who are striving upwards, and by no means a useless protection to those who are forcing their way through the thorny thickets of philosophy. It stimulates the intellect, points out the way of truth, shows us how to avoid fallacies, and finally, if it accomplishes nothing else, makes us ready and quick-witted.

All this I readily admit, but because a road is proper for us to traverse, it does not immediately follow that we should linger on it forever. No traveller, unless he be mad, will forget his destination on account of the pleasures of the way; his characteristic virtue lies, on the contrary, in reaching his goal as soon as possible, never halting on the road.[9] And who of us is not a traveller? We all have our long and arduous journey to accomplish in a brief and untoward time—on a short, tempestuous, wintry day as it were. Dialectics may form a portion of our road, but certainly not its end: it belongs to the morning of life, not to its evening. We may have done once with perfect propriety what it would be shameful to continue. If as mature men we cannot leave the schools of logic because we have found pleasure in them as boys, why should we blush to play odd and even, or prance upon a shaky reed,[10] or be rocked again in the cradle of our childhood? Nature, with cunning artifice, escapes from dull monotony by her wondrous changes of seasons, with their varying aspects. Shall we look for these alternations in the circuit of the year, and not in the course of a long life? The spring brings flowers and the new leaves of the trees, the summer is rich in its harvest, autumn in fruit, and then comes winter with its snows. In this order the changes are

---

9. Cf. Augustine, *De Doctrina Christiana* I, 4.
10. Cf. Horace, *Satires* II, iii, 247.

not only tolerable but agreeable; but if the order were to be altered, against the laws of nature, they would become distasteful. No one would suffer with equanimity the cold of winter in summer time, or a raging sun during the months where it does not belong.

Who would not scorn and deride an old man who sported with children, or marvel at a grizzled and gouty stripling? What is more necessary to our training than our first acquaintance with the alphabet itself, which serves as the foundation of all later studies; but, on the other hand, what could be more absurd than a grandfather still busy over his letters?

Use my arguments with the disciples of your ancient logician. Do not deter them from the study of logic; urge them rather to hasten through it to better things. Tell the old fellow himself that it is not the liberal arts which I condemn, but only hoary-headed children. Even as nothing is more disgraceful, as Seneca says,[11] than an old man just beginning his alphabet, so there is no spectacle more unseemly than a person of mature years devoting himself to dialectics. But if your friend begins to vomit forth syllogisms, I advise you to take flight, bidding him argue with Enceladus.[12] Farewell.[13]

11. *Epistulae Morales* 36, 4.

12. The giant whom Jupiter buried under Aetna (cf. Virgil, *Aeneid* III, 595).

13. Robinson and Rolfe compare Petrarch's views with those expressed almost two centuries earlier by John of Salisbury: "It seemed to me pleasant to revisit my old companions on the Mount [of St. Geneviève at Paris], whom I had left and whom dialectic still detained, and to confer with them touching the old subjects of debate, that we might by mutual comparison measure our respective progress. I found them as before, and where they were before; they did not appear to have advanced a single proposition. The aims that once inspired them inspired them still; they had progressed in one point only, they had unlearned moderation, they knew not modesty; and that to such an extent that one might despair of their recovery. So experience taught me a manifest conclusion, that, while logic furthers other studies, it is by itself lifeless and barren, nor can it cause the mind to yield the fruit of philosophy except the same conceive from other sources" (J. P. Migne, *Patrologia Latina* 199, p. 869). For some affinities between Renaissance humanism and the twelfth-century variety, see Richard B. Donovan, "Salutati's Opinion of Non-Italian Latin Writers of the Middle Ages," *Studies in the Renaissance* XIV (1967), 185–201.

5. The Ascent of Mount Ventoux[1]

Today I made the ascent of the highest mountain in this region, which is not improperly called Ventosum. My only motive was the wish to see what so great an elevation had to offer. I have had the expedition in mind for many years; for, as you know, I have lived in this region from infancy, having been cast here by that fate which determines the affairs of men. Consequently the mountain, which is visible from a great distance, was ever before my eyes, and I conceived the plan of some time doing what I have at last accomplished today. The idea took hold upon me with especial force when, in re-reading Livy's *History of Rome,* yesterday, I happened upon the place where Philip of Macedon, the same who waged war against the Romans, ascended Mount Haemus in Thessaly, from whose summit he was able, it is said, to see two seas, the Adriatic and the Euxine.[2] Whether this be true or false I have not been able to determine, for the mountain is too far away, and writers disagree. Pomponius Mela, the cosmographer—not to mention others who have spoken of this occurrence—admits its truth without hesitation;[3] Titus Livius, on the other hand, considers it false. I, assuredly, should not have left the question long in

1. *Epistolae Familiares* IV, 1, to Dionigi da Borgo San Sepolcro, whom Petrarch probably met in 1333 in Paris, where Dionigi, an Augustinian friar, was professor of theology and philosophy at the University. In 1339 King Robert called Dionigi to Naples, where he died in 1342. This letter was ostensibly written from Malaucène on April 26, 1336; but Billanovich (*Petrarca letterato*, pp. 193–98) considers it fictitious and assigns it to 1352–53. For an excellent assessment of the problem, see Hans Baron, *From Petrarch to Leonardo Bruni, Studies in Humanistic and Political Literature* (Chicago and London, 1968), pp. 17–20.

2. Livy XL, 21, 2–22. Mount Haemus (now Mount Balkan, in Bulgaria) is in Thrace, not Thessaly.

3. *De Chorographia* II, 17.

doubt, had that mountain been as easy to explore as this one. Let us leave this matter to one side, however, and return to my mountain here—it seems to me that a young man in private life may well be excused for attempting what an aged king could undertake without arousing criticism.

When I came to look around for a companion I found, strangely enough, that hardly one among my friends seemed suitable, so rarely do we meet with just the right combination of personal tastes and characteristics, even among those who are dearest to us. This one was too apathetic, that one over-anxious; this one too slow, that one too hasty; one was too sad, another over-cheerful; one more simple, another more sagacious, than I desired. I feared this one's taciturnity and that one's loquacity. The heavy deliberation of some repelled me as much as the lean incapacity of others. I rejected those who were likely to irritate me by a cold want of interest, as well as those who might weary me by their excessive enthusiasm. Such defects, however grave, could be borne with at home, for charity suffereth all things, and friendship accepts any burden; but it is quite otherwise on a journey, where every weakness becomes much more serious. So, as I was bent upon pleasure and anxious that my enjoyment should be unalloyed, I looked about me with unusual care, balanced against one another the various characteristics of my friends, and without committing any breach of friendship I silently comdemned every trait which might prove disagreeable on the way. And—would you believe it— I finally turned homeward for aid, and proposed the ascent to my only brother, who is younger than I, and with whom you are well acquainted.[4] He was delighted and gratified beyond measure by the thought of holding the place of a friend as well as of a brother.

At the time fixed we left the house, and by evening reached Malaucène, which lies at the foot of the mountain, to the north. Having rested there a day, we finally made the ascent this morning, with no companions except two servants; and a

4. Petrarch's brother Gherardo was probably born in 1307; studied with him at Bologna; shared the fashionable life at Avignon; and became a monk in 1342.

most difficult task it was. The mountain is a very steep and almost inaccessible mass of stony soil. But, as the poet has said, "Remorseless toil conquers all."[5] It was a long day, the air fine. We enjoyed the advantages of vigor of mind and strength and agility of body, and everything else essential to those engaged in such an undertaking, and so had no other difficulties to face than those of the region itself. We found an old shepherd in one of the mountain dales, who tried, at great length, to dissuade us from the ascent, saying that some fifty years before he had, in the same ardor of youth, reached the summit, but had gotten for his pains nothing except fatigue and regret, and clothes and body torn by the rocks and briars. No one, so far as he or his companions knew, had ever tried the ascent before or after him. But his counsels increased rather than diminished our desire to proceed, since youth is suspicious of warnings. So the old man, finding that his efforts were in vain, went a little way with us, and pointed out a rough path among the rocks, uttering many admonitions, which he continued to send after us even after we had left him behind. Surrendering to him all such garments or other possessions as might prove burdensome to us, we made ready for the ascent, and started off at a good pace. But, as usually happens, fatigue quickly followed upon our excessive exertion, and we soon came to a halt at the top of a certain cliff. Upon starting on again we went more slowly, and I especially advanced along the rocky way with a more deliberate step. While my brother chose a direct path straight up the ridge,[6] I weakly took an easier one which really descended. When I was called back, and the right road was shown me, I replied that I hoped to find a better way round on the other side, and that I did not mind going farther if the path were only less steep. This was just an excuse for my laziness; and when the others had already reached a considerable height I was still wandering in the valleys. I had failed to find an easier path, and had only increased the distance and difficulty of the ascent. At last I became disgusted with the

5. Virgil, *Georgics* I, 145–46.
6. Perhaps an allusion to Gherardo's choice of the monastic life in contrast to Petrarch's secular career.

intricate way I had chosen, and resolved to ascend without more ado. When I reached my brother, who, while waiting for me, had had ample opportunity for rest, I was tired and irritated. We walked along together for a time, but hardly had we passed the first spur when I forgot about the circuitous route which I had just tried, and took a lower one again. Once more I followed an easy, roundabout path through winding valleys, only to find myself soon in my old difficulty. I was simply trying to avoid the exertion of the ascent; but no human ingenuity can alter the nature of things, or cause anything to reach a height by going down. Suffice it to say that, much to my vexation and my brother's amusement, I made this same mistake three times or more during a few hours.

After being frequently misled in this way, I finally sat down in a valley and transferred my winged thoughts from things corporeal to the immaterial, addressing myself as follows: "What thou hast repeatedly experienced today in the ascent of this mountain, happens to thee, as to many, in the journey toward the blessed life. But this is not so readily perceived by men, since the motions of the body are obvious and external while those of the soul are invisible and hidden. Yes, the life which we call blessed is to be sought for on a high eminence, and strait is the way that leads to it.[7] Many, also, are the hills that lie between, and we must ascend, by a glorious stairway, from strength to strength. At the top is at once the end of our struggles and the goal for which we are bound. All wish to reach this goal, but, as Ovid says, "To wish is little; we must long with the utmost eagerness to gain our end."[8] Thou certainly dost ardently desire, as well as simply wish, unless thou deceivest thyself in this matter, as in so many others. What, then, doth hold thee back? Nothing, assuredly, except that thou wouldst take a path which seems, at first thought, more easy, leading through low and worldly pleasures. But nevertheless in the end, after long wanderings, thou must perforce either climb the steeper path, under the burden of tasks foolishly de-

7. Cf. Matthew 7, 14.
8. *Ex Ponto* III, i, 35.

ferred, to its blessed culmination, or lie down in the valley of thy sins, and (I shudder to think of it!), if the shadow of death overtake thee, spend an eternal night amid constant torments." These thoughts stimulated both body and mind in a wonderful degree for facing the difficulties which yet remained. Oh, that I might traverse in spirit that other road for which I long day and night, even as today I overcame material obstacles by my bodily exertions! And I know not why it should not be far easier, since the swift immortal soul can reach its goal in the twinkling of an eye, without passing through space, while my progress today was necessarily slow, dependent as I was upon a failing body weighed down by heavy members.

One peak of the mountain, the highest of all, the country people call "Sonny," why, I do not know, unless by antiphrasis, as I have sometimes suspected in other instances; for the peak in question would seem to be the father of all the surrounding ones. On its top is a little level place, and here we could at last rest our tired bodies.

Now, my father, since you have followed the thoughts that spurred me on in my ascent, listen to the rest of the story, and devote one hour, I pray you, to reviewing the experiences of my entire day. At first, owing to the unaccustomed quality of the air and the effect of the great sweep of view spread out before me, I stood like one dazed. I beheld the clouds under our feet, and what I had read of Athos and Olympus seemed less incredible as I myself witnessed the same things from a mountain of less fame. I turned my eyes toward Italy, whither my heart most inclined. The Alps, rugged and snow-capped, seemed to rise close by, although they were really at a great distance; the very same Alps through which that fierce enemy of the Roman name once made his way, bursting the rocks, if we may believe the report, by the application of vinegar. I sighed, I must confess, for the skies of Italy, which I beheld rather with my mind than with my eyes. An inexpressible longing came over me to see once more my friend[9] and my country. At the same time I reproached myself for this double weakness, springing, as it did, from a soul not yet steeled to manly

9. Giacomo Colonna had been in Rome since 1333.

resistance. And yet there were excuses for both of these cravings, and a number of distinguished writers might be summoned to support me.

Then a new idea took possession of me, and I shifted my thoughts to a consideration of time rather than place. "Today it is ten years since, having completed thy youthful studies, thou didst leave Bologna. Eternal God! In the name of immutable wisdom, think what alterations in thy character this intervening period has beheld! I pass over a thousand instances. I am not yet in a safe harbor where I can calmly recall past storms. The time may come when I can review in due order all the experiences of the past, saying with St. Augustine, 'I desire to recall my foul actions and the carnal corruption of my soul, not because I love them, but that I may the more love thee, O my God.'[10] Much that is doubtful and evil still clings to me, but what I once loved, that I love no longer. And yet what am I saying? I still love it, but with shame, but with heaviness of heart. Now, at last, I have confessed the truth. So it is. I love, but love what I would not love, what I would that I might hate.[11] Though loath to do so, though constrained, though sad and sorrowing, still I do love, and I feel in my miserable self the truth of the well known words, 'I will hate if I can; if not, I will love against my will.'[12] Three years have not yet passed since that perverse and wicked passion which had a firm grasp upon me and held undisputed sway in my heart began to discover a rebellious opponent, who was unwilling longer to yield obedience. These two adversaries have joined in close combat for the supremacy, and for a long time now a harassing and doubtful war has been waged in the field of my thoughts."

Thus I turned over the last ten years in my mind, and then, fixing my anxious gaze on the future, I asked myself, "If, perchance, thou shouldst prolong this uncertain life of thine for yet two lustres, and shouldst make an advance toward virtue proportionate to the distance to which thou hast departed from

10. *Confessions* II, 1, 1.

11. On the divided will see Romans 7, 14–25 and *Confessions* VIII, 5, 10.

12. Ovid, *Amores* III, xi, 35.

thine original infatuation during the past two years, since the new longing first encountered the old, couldst thou, on reaching thy fortieth year, face death, if not with complete assurance, at least with hopefulness, calmly dismissing from thy thoughts the residuum of life as it faded into old age?"

These and similar reflections occurred to me, my father. I rejoiced in my progress, mourned my weaknesses, and commiserated the universal instability of human conduct. I had well-nigh forgotten where I was and our object in coming; but at last I dismissed my anxieties, which were better suited to other surroundings, and resolved to look about me and see what we had come to see. The sinking sun and the lengthening shadows of the mountain were already warning us that the time was near at hand when we must go. As if suddenly wakened from sleep, I turned about and gazed toward the west. I was unable to discern the summits of the Pyrenees, which form the barrier between France and Spain; not because of any intervening obstacle that I know of but owing simply to the insufficiency of our mortal vision. But I could see with the utmost clearness, off to the right, the mountains of the region about Lyons, and to the left the bay of Marseilles and the waters that lash the shores of Aigues Mortes, although all these places were so distant that it would require a journey of several days to reach them. Under our very eyes flowed the Rhone.

While I was thus dividing my thoughts, now turning my attention to some terrestrial object that lay before me, now raising my soul, as I had done my body, to higher places, it occurred to me to look into my copy of St. Augustine's *Confessions,* a gift that I owe to your love, and that I always have about me.[13] In memory of both the author and the giver, I opened the compact little volume, small indeed in size, but of infinite charm, with the intention of reading whatever came to hand, for I could happen upon nothing that would be other-

13. In the last year of his life Petrarch gave his copy of the *Confessions* to Luigi Marsili, an Augustinian friar who had settled in Florence and was to be an important influence on Salutati and Niccolo Niccoli. For the great importance of Augustine in this period, see P. O. Kristeller, "Augustine and the Early Renaissance," *Review of Religion* VIII (1944), 339–58.

wise than edifying and devout. Now it chanced that the tenth
book presented itself. My brother, waiting to hear something
of St. Augustine's from my lips, stood attentively by. I call him,
and God too, to witness that where I first fixed my eyes it was
written: "And men go about to wonder at the heights of the
mountains, and the mighty waves of the sea, and the wide
sweep of rivers, and the circuit of the ocean, and the revolution
of the stars, but themselves they consider not."[14] I was abashed,
and, asking my brother (who was anxious to hear more), not
to annoy me, I closed the book, angry with myself that I should
still be admiring earthly things who might long ago have learned
from even the pagan philosophers that nothing is wonderful but
the soul, which, when great itself, finds nothing great outside
itself. Then, in truth, I was satisfied that I had seen enough
of the mountain; I turned my inward eye upon myself, and
from that time not a syllable fell from my lips until we reached
the bottom again. Those words had given me occupation enough,
for I could not believe that it was by a mere accident that I
happened upon them. What I had there read I believed to be
addressed to me and to no other, remembering that St. Augustine had once suspected the same thing in his own case, when,
on opening the book of the Apostle, as he himself tells us, the
first words that he saw there were, "Not in rioting and drunkenness, not in chambering and wantonness, not in strife and
envying. But put ye on the Lord Jesus Christ, and make not
provision for the flesh, to fulfil the lusts thereof."[15]

The same thing happened earlier to St. Anthony, when he
was listening to the Gospel where it is written, "If thou wilt
be perfect, go and sell that thou hast, and give to the poor, and
thou shalt have treasure in heaven: and come and follow me."[16]
Believing this scripture to have been read for his especial benefit, as his biographer Athanasius says, he guided himself by its
aid to the Kingdom of Heaven.[17] And as Anthony on hearing

---

14. *Confessions* X, 8, 15. On the alleged date of the ascent, Petrarch was
in his thirty-second year, as was Augustine at the end of his conversion.

15. Romans 13, 13–14, quoted *Confessions* VIII, 12, 29.

16. Matthew 19, 21.

17. *Life of St. Anthony* II (quoted *Confessions* VIII, 12, 29).

these words waited for nothing more, and as Augustine upon reading the Apostle's admonition sought no farther, so I concluded my reading in the few words which I have given. I thought in silence of the lack of good counsel in us mortals, who neglect what is noblest in ourselves, scatter our energies in all directions, and waste ourselves in a vain show, because we look about us for what is to be found only within. I wondered at the natural nobility of our soul, save when it debases itself of its own free will, and deserts its original estate, turning what God has given it for its honor into dishonor. How many times, think you, did I turn back that day, to glance at the summit of the mountain, which seemed scarcely a cubit high compared with the range of human contemplation—when it is not immersed in the foul mire of earth? With every downward step I asked myself this: If we are ready to endure so much sweat and labor in order that we may bring our bodies a little nearer heaven, how can a soul struggling toward God, up the steeps of human pride and human destiny, fear any cross or prison or sting of fortune? How few, I thought, but are diverted from their path by the fear of difficulties or the love of ease! How happy the lot of those few, if any such there be! It is of them, assuredly, that the poet was thinking, when he wrote:[18]

> Happy the man who is skilled to understand
> Nature's hid causes; who beneath his feet
> All terror casts, and death's relentless doom,
> And the loud roar of greedy Acheron.

How earnestly should we strive, not to stand on mountain-tops, but to trample beneath us those appetites which spring from earthly impulses.

With no consciousness of the difficulties of the way, amidst these preoccupations which I have so frankly revealed, we came, long after dark, but with the full moon lending us its friendly light, to the little inn which we had left that morning before dawn. The time during which the servants have been occupied in preparing our supper, I have spent in a secluded part of the

18. Virgil, *Georgics* II, 490–92.

house, hurriedly jotting down these experiences on the spur of the moment, lest, in case my task were postponed, my mood should change on leaving the place, and so my interest in writing flag.

You will see, my dearest father, that I wish nothing to be concealed from you, for I am careful to describe to you not only my life in general but even my individual reflections. And I beseech you, in turn, to pray that these vague and wandering thoughts of mine may some time become firmly fixed, and, after having been vainly tossed about from one interest to another, may direct themselves at last toward the single, true, certain, and everlasting good.

6. Reply to a Jesting Letter[1]

. . . But nothing is more persistent and insinuating than your jokes. Wherever you lead, they follow. So what do you say? That I invented the beautiful name of Laura to give myself something to talk about and to engage many to talk about me! And that in fact there is no Laura in my mind except that poetic Laurel for which evidently I have aspired with long-continued, unwearying zeal; and that concerning the living Laura, by whose person I seem to be captured, everything is manufactured; that my poems are fictitious, my sighs pretended. Well, on this head I wish it were all a joke, that it were a pretense and not a madness! But believe me, no one can simulate long without great effort; to labor to appear mad, to no purpose, is the height of madness. Add that we can in health imitate the behavior of the sick, but we cannot simulate real pallor. My pallor and my pains are well known to you; so I

1. From *Epistolae Familiares* II, 9 (from Avignon, December 21, 1336), to Bishop Giacomo Colonna, who had been in Rome since August, 1333 (when Petrarch was unable to meet him in France: cf. the end of *Familiares* I, 5).

am afraid that you are insulting my illness with your Socratic comedy, which is called irony, and therein you don't yield to Socrates. But wait; my wound will ripen with time; that other Ciceronian phrase will prove true: "One day wounds, another day cures."[2] And over that Laura, whom you call simulated, that other "simulated" Augustine will perhaps prevail.[3] For, reading many weighty works and meditating long, I shall age much before I am actually old.

But where will your jokes end? What do you say? That, taken in by my fictions and completely deluded, you waited for me quite a time in Rome because I pretended a great desire to come and see you again; but that later, like a shrewd spectator of mountebanks' tricks, you opened your eyes and penetrated my devices, so that the stage-setting of my mind was laid bare. Dear God, what is this? With your calumnies you make me out to be a magician. Already I seem to myself to be Zoroaster, the discoverer of magic, or one of his followers. Or maybe I am Dardanus or Damigerus or Apollo or somebody else famous in that art. It is no small feat to make me a prestidigitator of words.

But now we have carried the joke far enough. I want you to reply to me seriously. Pass over my desire to see you, which I have grievously borne for four years, forever thinking: "Come, he will be here tomorrow; or the day after I shall go to meet him." Omit the heavy burden of my cares, which I would not share with any mortal man but you. Say nothing of my eagerness to see your illustrious father, your high-minded brothers, your virtuous sisters, and the longed-for faces of my friends. But do you count as nothing my desire to see the walls and hills of the City and, as Virgil says, "the Etruscan Tiber and the palaces of Rome"?[4] You cannot imagine how I long to gaze upon that city I have never seen, though now it is the abandoned effigy of old Rome. I blame my sloth therefor, if indeed

2. Cf. *Tusculan Disputations* III, 24, 58.
3. Giacomo had also expressed doubts about the sincerity of Petrarch's ardor for Augustine. For Augustine vs. Laura, see the debate in Book III of the *Secretum*.
4. Virgil, *Georgics* I, 499.

it were sloth and not necessity. Seneca seems to exult, writing
to Lucilius from the very villa of Scipio Africanus, and he
counts it as no small matter to have seen the place where that
great man passed his exile, where he left his bones, denied to
his native city.[5] If this happened to a Spaniard, what do you
think I, an Italian, would feel, not at the villa of Liternum
or at Scipio's tomb, but at the city of Rome, where Scipio
was born and educated, where, as victor and defendant, he
triumphed with equal glory?[6] Where lived not he alone, but
innumerable men whose fame shall never fade? No other city
was ever like that city, none will ever be. It was called even
by its enemies "the city of kings." Of its inhabitants we read:
"Great is the fortune of the Roman people, great and terrible
its name." Its unexampled greatness, its incomparable sover-
eignty, present and future, were sung by divine poets.

But I shall not here prolong the praise of Rome. That is
too great a thing to be treated with a hasty pen. I have touched
upon it here that you may know that I prize very highly the
sight of that queen-city, of which I have read so much and
have written so much myself; and perhaps I shall write much
more, unless hurrying death cuts short my enterprises. But put
aside these classical associations; still how sweet it is for a
Christian spirit to gaze on that city like an earthly Paradise,
underlaid with the sacred flesh and bones of the martyrs and
bedewed with the precious blood of slaughtered witnesses to
the faith; how sweet to see the pictured face of our Savior,
universally worshipped, and his footsteps, preserved in hardest
stone, to be adored by all people! There one may see literally
fulfilled in brilliant light the words of Isaiah: "And the children
of them that afflict thee shall worship the steps of thy feet."[7]
How sweet to tour the tombs of the saints, to wander through
the halls trodden by the Apostles, with happy thoughts in mind,
with all the uneasy worries of my present life behind on the
shore at Marseilles. Since this is so, why do you call me lazy,
knowing well that my trip depends on the approval of others?
I had entrusted myself utterly to you—a small but lifelong gift.

5. Cf. Seneca, *Epistulae Morales* 86, I, 3.
6. Seneca, like several other writers of his time, was from Spain.
7. Isaiah 60, 14.

But you chose that I should serve another—if "another" is the right word for such a like-minded brother as yours. I am not resentful; if there is any fault, pardon yourself or pardon your brother.

At the end of your letter, perhaps being afraid that I should be offended by your funny jokes (for even the gentlest caress of a lion may crush small animals), you spread a drop of unguent balm where you think you may have wounded me. You urge me sweetly to love you, or actually to return your love. What can I say? Joy as well as pain checks a flow of words. One thing you know well, though I keep it hid. I am not so stonyhearted that I need encouragement for such a noble, such a fitting affection. Would that in my love I did not need rather a curb than a spur! Thus I should have passed my youth more tranquilly, and more tranquil would be my young manhood! I ask you only this, not to feign that I have been false. Farewell.

7. First Impressions of Rome[1]

What may you expect from Rome, after my long letter from the mountains?[2] You thought I would write something fine when I should reach Rome. No doubt I have accumulated a lot of matter to write about later, but at present I am so overwhelmed and stunned by the abundant marvels that I shouldn't dare to begin. But this I shouldn't conceal: the reverse of your predictions has taken place. For I remember that you used to

1. *Epistolae Familiares* II, 14 (March 15, 1337), to Cardinal Giovanni Colonna.
2. Because the country around Rome was infested by brigands and by roving bands of supporters of the Orsini, Petrarch had gone first to Capranica, some distance from the city, where Giovanni and Giacomo's brother-in-law had a castle. From Capranica he had written to Giovanni in January about the beauty of the countryside and the ubiquity of weapons: even the plowman wore armor, while the fisherman used a sword instead of a pole to dangle his bait.

discourage me from making the journey, arguing that my ardor would cool on seeing a ruined city, falling short of its reputation and of my expectation based on my reading. I too, though afire with desire, was willing to defer my visit, fearing that the sight of actuality would bring low my imaginations. Present reality is always hostile to greatness. But, remarkable to state, this presence has diminished nothing but has increased everything. Rome was greater than I thought, and so are its remains. Now I wonder not that the world was ruled by this city but that the rule came so late. Farewell.

8. The Hundred Years' War Begins[1]

If you wish to hear reports of the western world
Receive this brief account of how things stand.
The rest lies hid by fate; but come the hour
Of battle, bringing chiefs together, and troops,
Then who's oppressed by fortune, to which side   5
The final victory goes, all this I'll tell—
For now, let us survey the initial moves.
   Harsh Germany assembles countless bands;
Rich Britain opens up her endless wealth;
Brabant arouses her unconquered people,   10
And likewise Flanders, scene of constant war.
Seeking the first libations of the war,
All neighboring Hainaut clatters in the field.
By manifold commotion Gaul is shaken;
And bordering realms tremble at bloody Mars,   15
While kings are drawing all their strength together.
As when a whirlwind agitates the sea,
Which icy Boreas and rainy Auster
Rush on and lash, and Eurus dread to fleets,

1. *Epistolae Metricae* I, 12, written in 1339 to Mastino della Scala, lord of Verona.

The cliffs and rocks roar; sailors seek   20
Safe haven; and the dolphins flee the deep.
That is not all: but now the surging storms
Strike upon distant far-resounding shores.
Not otherwise, as winds stir the calm sky,
The West now rages. Long devoted to peace   25
The common people are confused and scared.
The cities rise; wrath calls both young and old;
All distant shores are boiling with fierce tumult.
In short: all are agreed on arms
Who lie between the ocean and the Latin Alps.   30
The end is fate's; but great things are prepared.
    May this the season be for our deliverance!
Unhappy Italy, restless home of troubles,
As it fought always while the world had peace,
May it now rest while fortune tosses them.   35

9. The Tower of Parma[1]

A mighty structure built by a victor's hand,
I rise to the stars, remarkable inside and out.
Correggio's splendor, the prince with whom Parma
    gleams,
Azzo, valiant in war, wants me as safeguard.

---

1. An epigram in rhymed hexameters, to be engraved on a tower built by Azzo da Correggio. After his coronation Petrarch stayed with the Correggi from May of 1341 through January of the next year.

Quite a few years later (probably late in 1360) Petrarch dedicated the *De Remediis Utriusque Fortunae* (*Phisicke against Fortune, as well Prosperous as Adverse,* as Englished in 1579 by Thomas Twyne) to Azzo, who had by then experienced great extremes of fortune and misfortune. This work had an enormous vogue in the Renaissance, being translated into numerous languages. Selections in modern English are now available in *The Italian Philosophers: Selected Readings from Petrarch to Bruno,* eds. Arturo B. Fallico and Herman Shapiro (New York: Modern Library, 1967); and *Petrarch: Four Dialogues for Scholars,* ed. Conrad Rawski (Cleveland, 1967).

May his friends view me securely and his enemies
    tremble:
Let them learn to surrender and sue for peace.

10. The *Roman de la Rose*[1]

This little book, which Gaul, renowned in speech,
Exalts to heaven and equals to the best,
Will testify how much our eloquence
Surpasses other tongues (Greek I except,
If we're to follow Cicero and fame).   5
The Gaul here tells the common folk his dreams:
What zeal can do, and love; what fire swells
A young man's breast; the old woman's sport,
The maddened lover's stratagems, a glance's banes;
The toil and grief and respite mixed with toil;   10
What laughter and laments to shun; how frequent tears
Bedew infrequent joys. Could there be given
A wider, richer field for eloquence?
And yet he dreams as he relates his dreams:
Awake he seems no different from asleep.   15
    How much better your fellow citizen
Set forth love's pathos in his splendid tale
Where Dido expires on a Phrygian sword!
Or Verona's bard;[2] or Sulmo, fruitful nest
Of loves, and known for amorous song;[3]   20
Or her bard's leader,[4] gift of Umbria—
Not to speak of others antiquity
Or recent times brought forth in Italy.
    But don't take this less gladly or disdain

1. *Epistolae Metricae* III, 30 (probably 1342 or 1343), to Guido Gonzaga, lord of Mantua.

2. Catullus, whose poems had been rediscovered only recently.

3. Ovid, author of the *Amores* ("Loves"), proudly declared: *"Sulmo mihi patria est"* (*Tristia* IV, 10, 3).

4. Propertius, who was born at Assisi.

My gift; for nothing better could be given   25
To one in search of foreign vernacular works—
Unless all Gaul and Paris are deceived.

11. Preface to the *Secretum*[1]

Often have I wondered with much curiosity as to our coming
into this world and what will follow our departure. When I was
ruminating lately on this matter, not in any dream as one in
sickness and slumber, but wide awake and with all my wits
about me, I was greatly astonished to behold a very beautiful
Lady, shining with an indescribable light about her. She seemed
as one whose beauty is not known, as it might be, to mankind.
I could not tell how she came there, but from her raiment and
appearance I judged her a fair Virgin, and her eyes, like the
sun, seemed to send forth rays of such light that they made
me lower my own before her, so that I was afraid to look up.
When she saw this she said, Fear not; and let not the strange-
ness of my presence affright you in any wise. I saw your steps
had gone astray; and I had compassion on you and have come
down from above to bring you timely succor. Hitherto your
eyes have been darkened and you have looked too much, yes,
far too much, upon the things of earth. If these so much
delight you, what shall be your rapture when you lift your
gaze to things eternal!

When I heard her thus speak, though my fear still clung
about me, with trembling voice I made reply in Virgil's words;[2]

> What name to call thee by, O Virgin fair,
> I know not, for thy looks are not of earth
> And more than mortal seems thy countenance.

1. Written between October, 1342, and March, 1343, this work com-
memorates the major spiritual crisis of Petrarch's life and is an important
complement to the *Canzoniere*.
2. *Aeneid* I, 327–28.

I am that Lady, she answered, whom you have depicted in your poem *Africa* with rare art and skill, and for whom, like another Amphion of Thebes, you have with poetic hands built a fair and glorious Palace in the far West on Atlas's lofty peak.[3] Be not afraid, then, to listen and to look upon the face of her who, as your finely-wrought allegory proves, has been well known to you from of old.

Scarcely had she uttered these words when, as I pondered all these things in my mind, it occurred to me this could be none other than Truth herself who thus spoke. I remembered how I had described her abode on the heights of Atlas; yet was I ignorant from what region she had come, save only that I felt assured she could have come from none other place than Heaven. Therefore I turned my gaze towards her, eagerly desiring to look upon her face; but lo, the eye of man is unable to gaze on that ethereal Form, wherefore again was I forced to turn them towards the ground. When she took note of this, after a short silence, she spoke once more; and, questioning me many times, she led me to engage with her in long discourse. From this converse I was sensible of gaining a twofold benefit, for I won knowledge, and the very act of talking with her gave me confidence. I found myself by degrees becoming able to look upon the face which at first dismayed me by its splendor, and as soon as I was able to bear it without dread, and gaze fixedly on her wondrous beauty, I looked to see if she were accompanied with any other, or had come upon the retirement of my solitude[4] alone; and as I did so I discerned at her side the figure of an aged man, of aspect venerable and full of majesty. There was no need to inquire his name. His religious bearing, modest brow, his eyes full of dignity, his measured step, his African look, but Roman speech, plainly declared him to be that most illustrious Father, Augustine. Moreover, he had so gracious a mien, and withal so noble, that one could not possibly imagine it to belong to any other than to him. Even so I was on the point of opening my lips to ask, when at that moment I heard the name so dear to me uttered from the lips of Truth herself.

3. No such description exists in the text that has come down to us.
4. We are to imagine the scene as Vaucluse.

Turning herself to him, as if to intervene upon his deep meditation, she addressed him in these words: "Augustine, dear to
me above a thousand others, you know how devoted to yourself this man is, and you are aware also with how dangerous
and long a malady he is stricken, and that he is so much nearer
to Death as he knows not the gravity of his disease. It is needful, then, that one take thought for this man's life forthwith,
and who so fit to undertake the pious work as yourself? He has
ever been deeply attached to your name and person; and all
good doctrine is wont more easily to enter the mind of the
disciple when he already starts with loving the Master from
whom he is to learn. Unless your present happiness has made
you quite forget your former sorrow, you will remember that
when you were shut in the prison of the mortal body you also
were subject to like temptation as his. And if that were so, most
excellent Physician of those passions yourself experienced, even
though your silent meditation be full of sweetness to your mind,
I beg that your sacred voice, which to me is ever a delight, shall
break its silence, and try whether you are able by some means
to bring calm to one so deeply distressed."

Augustine answered her: "You are my guide, my Counsellor,
my Sovereign, my Ruler; what is it, then, you would have me
say in your presence?"

"I would," she replied, "that some human voice speak to the
ears of this mortal man. He will better bear to hear truth so.
But seeing that whatever you shall say to him he will take as
said by me, I also will be present in person during your discourse."

Augustine answered her, "The love I bear to this sick man,
as well as the authority of her who speaks, make it my duty
to obey." Then, looking kindly at me and pressing me to his
heart in fatherly embrace, he led me away to the most retired
corner he could find, and Truth herself went on a few steps in
front. There we all three sat down. Then while Truth listened
as the silent Judge, none other beside her being present, we held
long converse on one side and the other; and because of the
greatness of the theme, the discourse between us lasted over
three days. Though we talked of many things much against the

manners of this age, and on faults and failings common to mankind, in such wise that the reproaches of the Master seemed in a sense more directed against men in general than against myself, yet those which to me came closest home I have graven with more especial vividness on the tablet of my memory. That this discourse, so intimate and deep, might not be lost, I have set it down in writing and made this book; not that I wish to class it with my other works, or desire from it any credit. My thoughts aim higher. What I desire is that I may be able by reading to renew as often as I wish the pleasure I felt from the discourse itself. So, little Book, I bid you flee the haunts of men and be content to stay with me, true to the title I have given you of "My Secret"; and when I would think upon deep matters, all that you keep in remembrance that was spoken in secret you in secret will tell to me over again.

To avoid the too frequent iteration of the words "said I," "said he," and to bring the personages of the Dialogue, as it were, before one's very eyes, I have acted on Cicero's method and merely placed the name of each interlocutor before each paragraph.[5] My dear Master learned this mode himself from Plato. But to cut short all further digression, this is how Augustine opened the discourse. . . .

12. King Robert of Sicily[1]

What will posterity say? By what atonements will our listlessness be expiated among our great-grandchildren? Pursuit of lust and avarice proceeds apace; almost all the exertion of mortals looks in this direction. If there is anyone who seems to

5. *De Amicitia* I, 3. For an important discussion of the *Secretum,* see Hans Baron, *From Petrarch to Leonardo Bruni,* pp. 51–101.

1. *Rerum Memorandarum Libri* ("Books of Memorable Things") I, 37. This was begun as a treatise on the cardinal virtues, and if completed would have been enormous. After a section devoted to general statements there are groups of examples, first ancient Roman, then ancient non-Roman (usually Greek), and finally (but not always) modern. Before leaving

have applied his spirit to studying the liberal arts, on the day
he first enters the schools he is already thinking about pecuniary
reward. I call these men not so much studious as mercenary,
and grant them no more than I do to those who plow sea or
land, except that the latter have their hands and bodies for
sale, the former their tongues and talents—and are all the more
detestable, for serving with the fairer part of man. But why do
I waste time on hateful and useless laments? Why do I not
rather search my memory (which is full of ancient examples,
devoid of modern), if there was ever anything sufficiently efficacious to redeem the shame of our age? To the shades of our
ancestors and the tongues of our successors—let them not scoff
—I think no stronger shield can be opposed than the name of
Robert, king of Sicily. He had arrived at his high estate not
after studious toil, as we see in the case of many, but was
born in a royal palace—indeed, if it may be said, was a king
even before he was born, since not only his father but his pater-
nal and maternal grandfathers and great-grandfathers were
kings—was reared in splendid circumstances, and as a boy-king
overcame many obstacles. Although born in our age, and moreover surrounded in the course of his life by grave dangers, as
fortune varied (he even spent considerable time in prison),[2]
he could never be drawn from his studies by fortune's threats
or insults or blandishments, or by the lassitude of the times.
Day and night, afoot and seated, he always wanted books near
him, whether he was engaged in the occupations of peace or
war, or in the care of his body. All his conversation was about
lofty matters. And what I have said about Caesar Augustus[3]
he always observed with great diligence, even though he had
much less and in fact absolutely no occasion, so that he embraced the talents of his age with royal favor, not just as a

Provence in September, 1343 (on his mission to Naples), Petrarch had
completed the introductory book, on solitude and study being conducive to
virtue, and part of the second. Book II was completed in Naples, Book III
and most of Book IV during his second stay in Parma (1344–45); but after
his flight from the besieged city he made only a brief attempt to resume
the work in Verona, then abandoned it for good.

2. From 1288 to 1295, as the hostage of James II of Aragon, who was
king of Sicily from 1285 to 1295.

3. *Rerum Memorandarum* I, 13, 6–7.

patient listener but even as an applauder and a kindly patron.
This was his life right to the end. He was never ashamed to
learn anything, this old philosopher and king, nor was he loath
to share his knowledge; he always said that one becomes wise
by learning and teaching. The extent to which he burned with
a love for letters is indicated by a speech of his that I heard
with my own ears. One day, talking with me about many things,
he asked why I had avoided him so long; I answered, truthfully,
that the dangers of land and sea, plus the various hindrances
of fortune, had prevented me from fulfilling my desire earlier;
then somehow the king of the French was mentioned.[4] To
Robert's question whether I had ever been in that king's court
I responded that this thought had never entered my mind. He
smiled and asked why. "Because," I said, "it has not pleased me
to be useless to an unlettered king and burdensome to myself
besides. It is more pleasant for me to keep the compact I have
made with my poverty than to try the thresholds of kings where
I wouldn't understand, or be understood by, anyone." Then he
added that he had heard the king's eldest son[5] did not slight
the study of letters. I replied that I had heard the same thing,
but that it was so annoying to his father that they said he considered his son's teachers enemies. Whether it is true I do not
affirm now, nor did I affirm it then; but I said that was the
report, and that it had cut off all thought, however slight, of
my going there. Hearing this that noble spirit bellowed, and a
shudder ran over his whole body. After a short silence, with
his eyes fixed on the ground, and, as his face showed, not without indignation at the transaction—I remember the details as
if it were all before my eyes—he raised his head and said to
me: "Thus is the life of men, thus their various judgments and
inclinations and desires. But I swear that letters are sweeter
and far dearer to me than my kingdom; and if I had to lack
one or the other, I should more calmly be without my diadem
than without letters." O speech truly philosophic and worthy
the veneration of all learned men, how much you pleased me!

4. Philip VI of Valois, king of France from 1328 to 1350.
5. Who succeeded Philip in 1350 as John II (1350–64).

What a spur you added to my own studies and how deeply and firmly you have clung to my heart!

This is enough about the king's studies. What shall I say about his learning? Certainly those who through hatred or the habit of disparagement detract from his virtues do not deny him the title of being knowledgeable. Extremely well acquainted with the sacred Scriptures, a renowned alumnus of philosophy, an outstanding speaker, he had an unbelievable knowledge of natural science. Poetry he touched upon only summarily, and in old age he was sorry for this neglect, as I often heard him say.

I find no way to end the discussion I have undertaken except by boasting somewhat about myself. I had come to Naples aroused by glorious reports of his reputation and to see that unique wonder of our age. As one who had heard greater things than true about me, he was happy at my coming. I should go on at length if I recounted the details. It seemed right for me at last to owe to him especially the laurel of poetry, which I had desired from my tender years, for I thought that I would have no more illustrious surety for so unaccustomed a gift. When I had told him this, that regal spirit, as one who took no pleasure except from lofty and glorious actions, bore witness to his joy with kind words and the serenity of his exalted brow. For the rest, during the examination itself, where that high-minded genius condescended to my littleness, when about the art of poetry and the different goals poets set themselves and the properties of the laurel itself I had said some things that touched his heart, in the hearing of many he deigned to pay me this tribute: he affirmed that he would have devoted no small part of his time to the study of poetry if he had known from youth what he had heard from me.[6]

But I now begin to see that what I always thought has happened to me: I am gradually carried away whenever there occurs to me the sweet memory of that soul, which departed to adorn heaven at the age best for him but untimely for me and for his realm.[7] Perhaps other historians will insert in their

6. Robert may have been especially impressed by the second part of Petrarch's Oration, which discussed the allegorical nature of poetry.

7. He was sixty-five years old when he died in 1343.

writings others worthy of memory, and it will be with my approbation. For my part, although I know a king should not be unaccompanied, nevertheless—and I say it with grief and indignation—in this age I have not found a companion suitable for him.

13. Lawlessness and Bloody Games in Naples[1]

I had hoped to acquit myself of my troublesome duties. I should have succeeded, I think, if that poisonous serpent had not swayed the minds of those already disposed toward pity. A Psyllian,[2] tasting his venom, would not have recognized it sooner than I did on hearing him. I tried to oppose him, but I fear that the harm is lethal. I shall try again, however, as long as any hope remains. Perhaps I should have got a decision, even though unfavorable, if at the approach of night the Council had not been forced to dissolve, sending its members home, because of the incurable plague of this city. For though Naples is very outstanding in many ways, it suffers this one dark, obscene, inveterate evil: the streets by night are as perilous as deep forest ambushes. The streets are the resort of young

1. *Epistolae Familiares* V, 6 (December 1, 1343), to Cardinal Giovanni Colonna. The Pipini had engaged in a rebellion, which was suppressed in 1341. The three brothers who headed the family were thrown into prison and their lands confiscated. A relative secured the aid of the Colonna family; Cardinal Colonna in turn secured the interest of the pope; and they decided to send Petrarch to Naples with a letter urging release of the prisoners. Petrarch found a sorry state of affairs when he arrived in September, 1343. Since Robert's granddaughter Joan was a minor, his will had provided for a regency council consisting of the queen dowager, three nobles, and Philippe de Cabassoles (who had been in Naples for some time) as vice-chancellor—the only champion of justice, in Petrarch's view, but able to do little in such a den of thieves.
2. A Libyan people who lived among serpents (cf. Lucan IX, 893 ff.).

nobles, armed to the teeth, unrestrained by home training, the authority of the magistrates, or the majesty of king and country. Their wanton boldness under the cover of night, without witnesses, is hardly surprising, since the infamous gladiatorial games are celebrated in this Italian city with worse than barbarian savagery in the full light of day, with royalty and the common people looking on. In these human blood is shed like that of cattle; and often, to the applause of maddened spectators, unhappy sons are massacred under the eyes of their wretched parents. It is regarded as the height of infamy to withdraw one's throat from the sword, as if one were fighting for one's country or for eternal life.

Yesterday, all unwitting, I was taken to a place near the city, called Carbonaria, "the Furnace"; a very appropriate name, for that smoky smithy of ferocity blackens and befouls the workers at the anvil of death. The Queen and her young consort, Andrea, were present. (He is a lad of spirit and may prove himself, if he ever attains the long-deferred crown.)[3] The whole Neapolitan militia was there, very well accoutred and outfitted; the common people swarmed in. I was impressed by the great concourse and by the intentness of so many eminent men, and I watched closely, expecting to see something grand. Then suddenly an immense outburst of applause rose to heaven, as if at something very delightful. I looked around, and there at my feet lay a very handsome youth transfixed by a sword. I shuddered with horror, and giving my horse the spur, I fled from that evil, hellish spectacle, inveighing against the companions who had tricked me into attending, the cruelty of the spectators, and the players at the game. This plague, my good Father, has been passed on from the elders to the younger, ever growing worse, and has now reached the point where a license to commit crime bears the name of honor and freedom.

But more of this later. It is a horrible business, and I have spent too many words on it and on the citizens devoted to it. You won't be surprised that your friends, victims of avarice,

3. Queen Joan's consort, Andrew of Hungary, was murdered in September, 1345.

still lie prisoners in this city, where it is a game to kill guiltless
men. Though Virgil called Naples "sweet,"[4] he would now say
it surpasses Bistonia in infamy—"Alas, flee these cruel lands,
flee this greedy shore."[5] These words I shall now apply to myself and to this city. Unless you hear otherwise, expect that I
shall leave within three days, even if my mission is not finished,
first for North Italy, then for France and for you, who gladden
my days, who make every journey sweet—unless it is by sea.
Farewell.[6]

14. The Death of Mago[1]

Here the young Carthaginian,[2] gasping and tormented by the
growing pain of his wound and the nearness of harsh death, saw
that his final hour was at hand and began: "Alas, what an end
for a lofty fortune! How blinded the mind is by prosperity!
Behold the madness of the powerful, to rejoice in a precipitous
position. That state lies subject to innumerable storms, and
those raised to high estate end by falling in ruin. Ah, the quak-

4. *Georgics* IV, 563–64.

5. *Aeneid* III, 44. Warning to Aeneas by Priam's son, Polydorus, who had
been entrusted to the King of Thrace and murdered for the sake of the gold
sent with him.

6. At about the time Petrarch left Naples a letter to the pope reported
that his mission had been unsuccessful. He did have some worthwhile experiences in Naples, though, including a tour of the northern shore of the
Bay (an area full of classical associations for him) with Barbato da Sulmona. But he could find no one to guide him to Scipio's villa at Linternum.

1. *Africa* VI, 885–918. Written perhaps on the occasion of King Robert's
death, this was the only portion of the poem in circulation during Petrarch's
lifetime. While on his mission to Naples, after many refusals he finally gave
a copy to Barbato da Sulmona, who then—contrary to Petrarch's firm instructions—promptly proceeded to make the verses public.

2. Hannibal's brother Mago, wounded in an encounter with the Romans,
was recalled by the Carthaginian Senate but died off Sardinia on the return
voyage. Livy notes his death very briefly at **XXX**, 19, 5; the rest is Petrarch's invention.

ing summit of great honors, and the false hopes of men, and empty glory overlaid with false blandishments! Alas, how uncertain is our life, devoted to unceasing toil, and how certain is the day of death which we never sufficiently foresee! Alas, man is born on earth to a harsh lot! All other living creatures have their repose; man is restless, and, troubled through all his years, hastens the road to death. Death, best of things, you alone reveal our errors, and you shatter the dreams of life when it is over. Poor me, I see now how many things I acquired in vain, and how many labors I undertook of my own accord and could have left untouched. Though destined to die, man seeks to mount to the stars, but death teaches the place for everything ours. What use has it been to bear arms against powerful Latium, torches against dwellings, to disturb the world's covenants and embroil cities in mournful tumult? Or what advantage is there in having raised lofty palaces with gold on their marble walls, when through an unlucky star I was going to perish this way under an open sky? Dear brother, what enterprises is your spirit preparing, unaware—alas!—of harsh fate, and unaware of me?" He spoke; then his spirit went forth free into the air, to look down at an equal distance from on high at Rome and the city of Carthage, departing fortunately before its time, so as not to see her great overthrow and the dishonor remaining for her glorious arms, and his brother's griefs together with his country's.[3]

3. Petrarch's verses were the target of many criticisms, against which he defended himself in a long letter to Boccaccio (in 1363). To the charge that Mago's words were appropriate only to a Christian, Petrarch replied: "What, in Christ's name, what there is Christian, and not rather human and common to all peoples?" (*Prose*, p. 1050).

15. Italia Mia[1]

My Italy, although talking does not serve to heal the mortal wounds which I see so thick on your fair body, it pleases me at least that my sighs are such as the Tiber hopes for, and the Arno, and the Po, where I now sit heavy with grief.[2] Ruler of heaven, I ask that the pity which led you to earth may turn you to your dearly beloved country: see, gracious Lord, what cruel war springs from what slight causes. Open, Father, and soften and untie the hearts that fierce and haughty Mars hardens and locks up. Make your truth be heard there—whatever I may be—through my tongue. (16)

You, in whose hands fortune has put control of our fair country, no pity for which seems to constrain you, what are so many foreign swords doing here? Why is the verdant earth colored with the blood of barbarians? A vain error deludes you; you see little and think you see much, for you seek love or faith in venal hearts.[3] He who possesses the most forces is most entangled by his enemies. O deluge gathered from what wild desert to inundate our gentle fields! If this happens to us by our own hands, who will there now be to save us? (32)

Nature provided well for us when she placed the shield of

1. *Rerum Vulgarium Fragmenta,* CXXVIII. In Wilkins's view, "perhaps the greatest of all his *canzoni,*" and certainly one of the most famous.
2. Petrarch was probably at this time at Parma, in the valley of the Po. By the autumn of 1344 the position of the Correggio brothers had become so precarious that Azzo sold the lordship to Obizzo d'Este, the Marquis of Ferrara, whom the people of Parma welcomed in November. However, Azzo had earlier promised, in return for support, to turn Parma over to the Visconti; consequently, in December the city was besieged by troops of the Visconti, the marquis of Mantua, and certain allies of his.
3. In the siege of Parma, foreign mercenaries were employed, not for the first, and certainly not for the last, time in Italian warfare (cf. Machiavelli's incessant complaints about this practice).

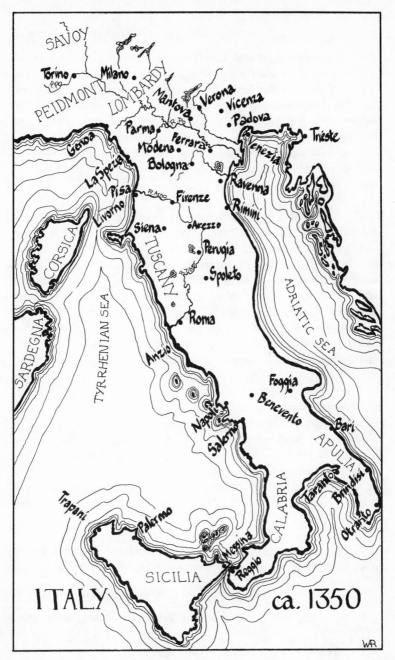

2. Italy ca. 1350.

the Alps between us and the German frenzy,[4] but blind greed, clashing with its own good, has now so contrived as to cause sores on the healthy body. Now within a single cage wild animals and tame flocks nestle together in such a way that the better always suffers; and to our greater grief, this is from the descendants of the people without law, whose side (as we read) was so laid open by Marius that the memory of the deed is still alive,[5] when thirsty and tired he drank as much blood as water from the river.[6] (48)

I'll say nothing of Caesar, who on every shore where he sent our iron made the grass bloody from their veins. Now it seems —I know not through what evil star—that heaven hates us, thanks to you to whom so much was entrusted. Your divided wills lay waste the most beautiful part of the world. What sin, what judgment, what destiny causes you to oppress your poor neighbor, and to pursue his afflicted and scattered fortunes, and to seek your forces in foreign countries, and to be pleased that blood is shed and souls sold for a price? I talk to say the truth, not out of hatred or scorn for others. (64)

After so many proofs are you still unaware of the deceit of the Bavarian, who raising a finger trifles with death?[7] But your blood rains more freely, for a different rage lashes you on. For a few hours think of yourselves and you will see how dear he who holds himself cheap holds others. Noble Latin blood, remove from yourself these harmful burdens; do not make an idol of an empty name; for that the fury from up there, a backward people, overcomes us in intelligence, is no natural thing but our own fault. (80)

Is not this the ground that I first touched? Is not this my nest, where I was so sweetly nurtured? Is not this the homeland

4. Cf. Pliny, *Natural History* III, 23: "Nature gave Italy the Alps as a wall against the onset of the barbarians."
5. In 102 B.C. Marius annihilated the Teutones at Aquae Sextae (Aix-en-Provence).
6. Florus III, 3.
7. I.e., surrenders and lives to "fight" another day.

in which I trust, the benign, devout mother that covers both my parents? For the love of God, let such thoughts sometimes move you, and look with pity on the tears of the grieving people, that for repose puts its hope in you alone, after God; and provided you just show some sign of pity, *vertù* will take arms against fury and the battle will be brief, for the ancient valor is not yet dead in Italian hearts. (96)

Lords, look how time flies, and how life flees and death is at our shoulders. You are here now; think of your departure, for the soul, naked and alone, must arrive at that uncertain path. In passing through this valley may it please you to put down hatred and disdain, winds contrary to the serene life, and let the time which is spent in causing others pain be converted to some more worthy act of hand or mind, to something praiseworthy, to some honorable pursuit. In this way one is glad here below and finds the way to heaven open. (112)

Song, I enjoin you to tell your meaning courteously, for you must go among haughty people, and their wills are already full of the worst old habits ever hostile to the truth. You will try your luck among the magnanimous few to whom the good is pleasing. Say to them: "Who will give me assurance? I go crying: Peace, peace, peace." (122)

16. His Escape from Besieged Parma[1]

I am of a mind to share with you my toils and fortunes, as is my custom. War has come to Parma, as you know. We are surrounded, pressed within the limits of a single city, by a large army, not from Liguria alone but from all Italy. It is not that

1. *Epistolae Familiares* V, 10 (from Bologna, February 25, 1345), to Barbato da Sulmona.

our men lack the spirit to fight—we have proved that often by our vigorous sorties—but the enemy's strategy is not to allow us peace or war; he trusts to conquer by mere persistence, weakening our spirits by the tedium of a long siege. Thus with various ups and downs the besieger sometimes becomes the besieged. The outcome is not yet certain. Anyway, the issue is fiercely fought, and unless I am much mistaken the day of decision is near at hand. My mind wavers, inclining toward compromise, trying to fend off both empty hope and useless fear.

In this state of affairs the siege, not the least of war's calamities, has oppressed us not for a few days but for many months. In the circumstances, I have been longing for liberty, that liberty which I always earnestly entreat and ardently embrace, though it flee me over land and sea. I had long been possessed by the desire for Vaucluse, my transalpine Helicon, since my Italian Helicon was ablaze with the wars. But what could I do? The road to the west had become impassable, so I looked to the east. Although this region swarmed with enemy troops, it seemed safer than the long roundabout way through Tuscany.

To cut it short, at sunset on 23 February I ventured forth from the city with a few companions. We succeeded in dodging the hostile pickets. About midnight we got near Reggio, held by the enemy. Suddenly a band of marauders burst out of ambush, threatening us with death. It was no time for deliberations; the time, the place, the ring of enemies were too terrifying. Few in number, unarmed, unprepared, what could we do against so many armed men, practised in violence? Our only hope lay in flight under cover of darkness. "The comrades scatter, and black night covers them,"[2] as Virgil puts it. I too fled, I confess, escaping death and the whistling arrows.

But when I thought that I had got safe—when, pray, is man ever safe?—my trusty horse stumbled into a hole or against a tree trunk or a rock; I couldn't tell what in that black, cloudy night. I was thrown to the ground, shattered and almost unconscious. But I assembled my wits and stood up. Fear gave me strength to remount my horse—though for some time now I

2. *Aeneid* IV, 123.

haven't been able to raise my hand to my mouth. Some of my companions turned back to Parma, but some, after their vain wanderings, remained fixed in purpose. Our two guides, tired, fearful, and totally lost, forced us to halt in a retired spot, where to add to our terror, we could hear the voices of sentinels on unidentifiable walls. Add to this a heavy rain mixed with hail; amid the lightning flashes our fear of a dreadful death increased.

The story is much too long to recount in detail. We spent that really hellish night in the open, lying on the ground, while the swelling and pain of my injured arm increased. No grassy turf invited us to sleep, no leafy boughs or rock cave gave us shelter. We had only bare earth, foul weather, Jupiter in anger, and the fear of men and wild beasts, and I had my injuries into the bargain. You will perhaps be surprised and sympathetic to learn that there was one comfort in our distresses; we stationed our horses across the path, and used their backs as shelter against the storm. Though before they were shying and nervous, now they became quiet, as if they were aware of their own sorry pass; and so they did us a double service. Thus in toil and terror we reached daybreak. When the dim, dubious light revealed to us a way among the underbrush we left that ominous region in all haste. Received within the walls of a friendly town called Scandiano, we learned that a large force of horse and foot had been lying in wait outside the walls to seize us, and shortly before our arrival had made off, driven by the storm. Now go and deny the power of Fortune, which can turn wise counsel to disaster and our errors to salvation! I am joking, dear Barbato. You know my judgment of Fortune; that is a formidable name. In any case, our straying was advantageous, and so was the storm; our misfortunes saved us from worse.

So when it was day I revealed for the first time my wounds to my companions; they were moved to tears. And since it did not seem safe to stay there, I had my arm temporarily bound up, and took a mountain path to Modena, and the next day I went on to Bologna. From there I am dictating (contrary to my custom) this letter, to inform you of my own case and of the general situation. My body will receive all the care humanly possible; cure is certain, though it will be slow. The doctors expect recovery by summer; I look for aid from Almighty God. In the meantime my stiff right arm will not obey orders, but my mind is strengthened by adversity. Farewell.

17. To Marcus Tullius Cicero[1]

Your letters I sought for long and diligently; and finally, where I least expected it, I found them. At once I read them, over and over, with the utmost eagerness. And as I read I seemed to hear your bodily voice, O Marcus Tullius, saying many things, uttering many lamentations, ranging through many phases of thought and feeling. I long had known how excellent a guide you have proved for others; at last I was to learn what sort of guidance you gave yourself.

Now it is your turn to be the listener. Hearken, wherever you are, to the words of advice, or rather of sorrow and regret, that fall, not unaccompanied by tears, from the lips of one of your successors, who loves you faithfully and cherishes your name. O spirit ever restless and perturbed! in old age—I am but using your own words[2]—self-involved in calamities and ruin! what good could you think would come from your incessant wran-

---

1. *Epistolae Familiares* **XXIV**, 3. This collection closes with a book of letters addressed to Cicero, Seneca, Varro, Quintilian, Livy, Asinius Pollio, Horace, Virgil, and Homer (see Mario E. Cosenza, *Petrarch's Letters to Classical Authors,* Chicago, 1910). Like Azzo da Correggio, Petrarch took refuge in Verona, where he discovered in the cathedral library a volume containing the sixteen books of Cicero's *Letters to Atticus* (along with Cicero's correspondence with his brother Quintus and with Brutus), which he copied and which gave him the inspiration to form collections of his own letters. On Cicero's significance for Petrarch, see Hans Baron, "Cicero and the Roman Civic Spirit in the Middle Ages and Early Renaissance," *Bulletin of the John Rylands Library* **XXII** (1938), 72–97, esp. pp. 85–88.

While in Verona Petrarch must have become acquainted with Dante's son, Pietro, to whom he addressed a metrical epistle (see Wilkins, *Studies,* pp. 33–47).

2. From the *Epistle to Octavian* 6 (wrongly attributed to Cicero).

gling, from all this wasteful strife and enmity? Where were the peace and quiet that befitted your years, your profession, your station in life? What Will-o'-the-wisp tempted you away, with a delusive hope of glory; involved you, in your declining years, in the wars of younger men; and, after exposing you to every form of misfortune, hurled you to a death that it was unseemly for a philosopher to die?[3] Alas! the wise counsel that you gave your brother, and the salutary advice of your great masters, you forgot. You were like a traveller in the night, whose torch lights up for others the path where he himself has miserably fallen.[4]

Of Dionysius[5] I forbear to speak; of your brother and nephew, too; of Dolabella[6] even, if you like. At one moment you praise them all to the skies; at the next fall upon them with sudden maledictions. This, however, could perhaps be pardoned. I will pass by Julius Caesar, too, whose well-approved clemency was a harbor of refuge for the very men who were warring against him. Great Pompey, likewise, I refrain from mentioning. His affection for you was such that you could do with him what you would. But what insanity led you to hurl yourself upon Antony?[7] Love of the republic, you would probably say. But the republic had fallen before this into irretrievable ruin, as you had yourself admitted. Still, it is possible that a lofty sense of duty, and love of liberty, constrained you to do as you did, hopeless though the effort was. That we can easily believe of so great a man. But why, then, were you so friendly with Augustus? What answer can you give to Brutus? If you accept Octavius, said he, we must conclude that you are not so anxious to be rid of all tyrants as to find a tyrant who will be well-disposed toward yourself.[8] Now, unhappy man, you were to take the last false step, the last and most deplorable. You began to speak ill of the very friend whom you had so lauded, although he was not doing any ill to you, but merely refusing to prevent

3. Cicero was murdered by Antony's henchmen.
4. Cf. Ennius, quoted by Cicero, *De Officiis* I, 16, 51; and Dante, *Purgatorio* XXII, 67 ff. (Statius' tribute to Virgil).
5. A freed slave, teacher to his son Marcus.
6. Husband of Cicero's daughter, Tullia.
7. Cicero's *Philippics* are a series of fierce attacks on Antony.
8. *Ad Brutum* I, 16, 7 (letter from Brutus to Cicero).

others who were.[9] I grieve, dear friend, at such fickleness. These shortcomings fill me with pity and shame. Like Brutus, I feel no confidence in the arts in which you are so proficient.[10] What, pray, does it profit a man to teach others, and to be prating always about virtue, in high-sounding words, if he fails to give heed to his own instructions? Ah! how much better it would have been, how much more fitting for a philosopher, to have grown old peacefully in the country, meditating, as you yourself have somewhere said,[11] upon the life that endures for ever, and not upon this poor fragment of life; to have found no fasces, yearned for no triumphs, found no Catilines to fill the soul with ambitious longings!—all this, however, is vain. Farewell, forever, my Cicero.

Written in the land of the living; on the right bank of the Adige, in Verona, a city of Transpadane Italy; on the 16th of June, and in the year of that God whom you never knew[12] the 1345th.

9. Again, Petrarch is referring to the pseudo-Ciceronian *Epistle to Octavian*.
10. *Ad Brutum* I, 17, 5.
11. *Ad Atticum* X, 8, 8.
12. Cf. Dante, *Inferno* I, 131: "By that God whom you did not know" (Dante's words to Virgil).

Vaucluse, Italy, Avignon: 1346-53

18. Few Busy Men Are Worthily Employed[1]

And so, to dismiss the matter once for all, in my opinion practically every busy man is unhappy, and the man who is employed in the service of another is doubly unhappy because he has only his pains for his reward. Now I am not unaware that there have been, and perchance still are, very active men of saintly nature who themselves go the way of Christ and lead straying souls along the same path. When this happens I acknowledge that it is a great and immeasurable good, a double blessing to be contrasted with the twofold misery of which I have said so much. For what is there more blessed, more worthy of a man, and more like divine goodness than to serve and assist as many as require help? Whoever is able to do so and does not, has repudiated, I think, the glorious duty of humanity and proved false to the name as well as the nature of man. If it should be proved that this is possible, I shall freely subordinate my private inclination to the public welfare and, abandoning the place of retirement in which I consulted only my own humor, I shall venture forth where I can be of use to the world, following the advice given by our Cicero. "It is more in accord with nature," he says, "to emulate the great Hercules and undergo the greatest toil and trouble for the sake of aiding or saving the world, if possible, than to live in seclusion, not only

---

1. From *De Vita Solitaria* I, iii (Zeitlin, pp. 125–26), written in 1346. The first book contrasts city life with the life of solitude, the second is devoted to examples of men and women who loved solitude.

free from all care, but revelling in pleasures and abounding in wealth, while excelling others also in beauty and strength. Thus Hercules denied himself and underwent toil and tribulation for the world, and, out of gratitude for his services, popular belief has given him a place in the council of the gods. The better and more noble, therefore, the character with which a man is endowed, the more does he prefer the life of service to the life of pleasure."[2] So says Cicero, and I yield an unconstrained assent, if things are as he says. But it is my view of the matter that the force of a general truth is not destroyed by a very few exceptional instances. There are many who profess to believe that employment is of general advantage and holier than any kind of retirement. I know. But how many, I ask you, do we see who carry out what they profess? There may be a few or there may be a great many; show me one and I shall hold my peace. I do not deny that there are learned and eloquent men who maintain the opposite view with great subtlety. But it is not so much a question of cleverness in arguing as of conduct. They go about the cities and deliver long harangues in public about vices and virtues. I could barely refrain from inserting here the satirist's biting tooth in a way which would be decidedly to the point,[3] but I recalled to whom I was addressing myself and decided to sacrifice a vanity of style rather than be wanting in true respect. Yet these earnest persons, you observe, say many useful things which often are of advantage to their hearers. I grant it, but the physician is not necessarily in good health when he helps the patient with his advice; in fact, he often dies of the very ailment which he has cured in others. I do not disdain the careful choice and artful composition of words contrived for the salvation of men, and I honor the useful work regardless of the character of the workman, but this is a school of life and not of rhetoric, and our thoughts are now fixed not on the vain-glory of eloquence but on the secure repose of the soul.

2. *De Officiis* III, 5, 25. Cf. Theodor E. Mommsen, "Petrarch and the Story of the Choice of Hercules," *Medieval and Renaissance Studies*, pp. 175–96.

3. Juvenal, *Satires* II, 20–21: *"de virtute locuti/ clunem agitant."*

19. Exhortation to Cola di Rienzo and to the Roman People[1]

I am somewhat undecided, O noble soul, whether I should first congratulate you on the achievement of such great glory, or the citizens of your rescued city for your services in their behalf and for the most happy recovery of their liberty. Both do I congratulate in equal measure. Both together shall I address, nor shall I distinguish in my words those whom I see so inseparably linked by fate itself. But what terms shall I employ in the midst of such sudden and unhoped-for joy? With what vows can I fitly set forth the emotions of my exultant soul? Hackneyed words are become utterly unfit; new ones I dare not attempt. I shall steal myself away from my occupations for a short time; and, though it were most proper to robe my thoughts in the Homeric dress, lack of leisure obliges me to present them in a more irregular and more disordered fashion.

Liberty stands in your midst. There is nothing dearer, nothing more earnestly to be desired; and never are these facts more clearly understood than when liberty is lost. Enjoy this great boon, this realization of your dreams of many years. Rejoice in it, but do so with moderation, with discretion, and with calm. Give thanks to God, the Dispenser of such gifts, who has not yet forgotten his most Holy City, and could no longer behold enchained in slavery her in whom he had placed the empire of the world. Therefore, you brave men and descendants of brave men, if sane thinking has reasserted itself together with liberty,

1. *Epistolae Variae* XLVIII (summer, 1347). The Roman soldiers under Stefano Colonna being absent from the city, on Sunday, May 20, Cola addressed the populace on the Campidoglio and was proclaimed Tribune. Petrarch had met Cola in 1343 when he led an embassy to Clement VI to justify a revolt that had resulted in the overthrow of the senators.

let each one of you choose death itself to the loss of liberty.
Without liberty life is mockery. Keep your past servitude constantly before your eyes. In this way, unless I err, your present
liberty will be somewhat dearer to you than life itself. In this
way, if at any time it should become necessary to part with
the one or the other, there will be no one (provided a drop of
Roman blood still flows in his veins) who will not prefer to
die a freeman rather than to live a slave. The fish which has
once slipped from the barb lives in constant fear of whatever
stirs among the waters. The lamb which has been snatched
from the jaws of the wolves trembles at the greyish dogs, even
from a distance. The winged creature which has extricated itself
from the bird-lime dreads even the harmless boughs. You, too,
believe me, had been baited with the blandishments of vain
hopes; you, too, had been rendered helpless by the tenacious
power of pernicious habit; you, too, had been encircled by
bands of famishing wolves.

Consider all things with minds alert. Make sure that whatever you plan, whatever you do, savor of liberty. Let all your
cares and vigils be directed to this one end; let all your deeds
tend thereto. Whatsoever is achieved with other purpose, esteem
it an irreparable loss of time—a delusion and a snare. Drive
from your hearts the ill-deserved love which, through a long
subjection, you may have conceived for your tyrants. Expel all
memory of this unworthy affection. Even the slave bends the
neck to his haughty master for the time being, and the caged
bird makes sweet music for its jailer. But the former will throw
off his shackles when the occasion offers; and if an outlet be
given, the latter will take wing with eager flight.

O most illustrious citizens, you have been living as slaves—
you whom all the nations were wont to serve. Though kings
were wont to kneel at your feet, you have lain passive beneath
the tyranny of a few. But that which makes the cup of grief
and shame full to overflowing is the thought that you have had
as tyrants strangers and lords of foreign birth. Enumerate the
ravishers of your honor, the plunderers of your fortunes, the
destroyers of your liberty. Think of their separate origins. The
valley of Spoleto claims this one; the Rhine, or the Rhone, or

some obscure corner of the world has sent us the next.[2] That one, who was but recently led in the triumph with hands fastened behind his back, has, from a captive, suddenly become a citizen; nay, not merely a citizen but a tyrant. Little marvel is it, therefore, if to such as these, when they meditate upon their former country, on the disgrace of their own former slavery and on the fields drenched with their life-blood, the city of Rome, its glory and its liberty, yea, the very blood which flows in your veins, should be a source of hatred.

Much more do I marvel at this: whence it was that you, armed Romans though you were, drew your long patience, or whereupon they based their insufferable pride. What superior qualities do they possess that they should be so highly self-complacent? What air do they breathe? What virtues own? No group of men ever existed who were more sadly lacking in these. Is their pride based on their over-abundant wealth, which can never appease their hunger except it be attended with thoughts of theft and plunder? Is it based on their great power, which will cease to be the moment you assert yourselves men? Is it possible that they can glory in the splendor of their name and origin, or in their purloined and perchance transient abode in this city? What grounds have they for boasting of their Roman stock? And yet they do make this boast most impudently. They have falsely declared themselves Romans for so long a time that, as if falsehood legalized their claims, they now esteem themselves real Romans. Forsooth, the name of Roman citizens has become low and base in their eyes. They no longer style themselves Roman citizens, but, Princes of the Romans! I scarcely know whether such pretensions are to be received with laughter or with tears. But I am the less indignant at this, when I behold that they have lost sight of even their human origin. They have lately reached that stage of insanity as to wish themselves to be considered gods and not men.

Oh unutterable shame! In that very city in which Caesar Augustus, the ruler of the world and the lawgiver of the nations, by special edict forbade that he be called a god,[3] in that same

2. The Orsini and the Colonna.
3. Suetonius, *Life of Augustus* 53.

city, today, beggarly thieves judge themselves unpardonably
offended if they be not addressed as gods. Oh wretched whirligig
of fortune! Oh unheard-of change of times! Let us dispel the
darkness, let us remove all errors, let us attain the truth.
Whether or not these lords, who are entirely devoid of reason,
are worthy the name of men, let those decide who desire to
establish hair-splitting definitions of terms. Whether they are
to be your masters, I leave to you yourselves to decide, O
Romans, provided that you keep clearly in mind that, at the
same time and in the same city, they cannot be lords and you
free men. The one fact, however, which is within my province
to decide is that they surely are not Romans. Of all these who,
as you remember, were so fastidious of their empty titles of
nobility, no matter whence they came, no matter what ill wind
blew them hither or what barbarian country turned them loose,
even though they roamed about in your Forum, though they
ascended the Capitol attended by hordes of armed retainers,
and though they trod (with proud step) upon the ashes of
illustrious Romans—of all of these, I say, there was not one
who was not an alien. As says the satirist, there was not one
but that "with whiten'd feet,/ Was hawk'd for sale so lately
through the street."[4] And still truer are the words of another
poet:[5]

> Our war no interfering kings demands,
> Nor shall be trusted to barbarian hands:
> Among ourselves our bonds we will deplore,
> And Rome shall serve the rebel sons she bore.

Would that you too had this consolation in your misery, that
you were slaves to but one man, whether fellow-citizen or king,
and not subject to many foreign robbers at once!

All too true is that which is reported to have been said by
Hannibal, formerly the most renowned enemy of the Roman
race: "It is easier to censure past events than to correct them."[6]

I do not desire to goad you further, nor to reproach you with

4. Juvenal I, 111.
5. Lucan VIII, 354–56.
6. Livy XXX, 30, 7.

bygones. I wish, rather, to offer you wherewith to screen your blushes. Even your ancestors were ruled by kings—and by kings who were not always of Roman origin, but also, at one time, of Sabine, at another of Corinthian, and indeed (if we are to believe tradition) of servile origin.[7] But evil fortune must come to an end as well as good fortune. The restorer of the liberty of the early Romans and the restorer of your liberty were alike unexpected. Each age produced its Brutus. There are now three of the name of Brutus celebrated in history. The first is he who exiled the proud Tarquin; the second, he who slew Julius Caesar; the third, he who has visited with exile and with death the tyrants of our own age. Our third Brutus, then, is the equal of both of theirs, in that in his own person he has united the causes of the double glory which the other two divided between them. He is, however, more like the earlier Brutus in disguising his nature and in concealing his purpose. Like him he is young in age,[8] but of a far different temper; and if he assumed the false exterior of that other Brutus, it was in order that, biding his time beneath this false veil, he might at last reveal himself in his true character—the liberator of the Roman People.[9]

To the valor of that ancient Brutus, Livy, prince of historians, bears testimony; to that of the present Brutus, your own experience. The former Brutus was scorned by kings; the present, by tyrants to whom he afterward became a source of fear. You have read of the former; with your own eyes you have seen the latter disdained by his fellow-citizens, men who esteemed nothing noble except it were unjust and arrogant. They spurned, they trampled upon the lowliness of this man, beneath which, however, a great soul lay concealed. I hereby testify in his behalf that he has ever had close at heart the end which he has at last attained. But he was awaiting a favorable opportunity. The instant this presented itself he was quick to take advantage of it. In restoring your liberty, he has presented you with as great a boon as the elder Brutus did present his fellow-citizens,

7. Ancus Martius, Tarquinius Priscus, and Servius Tullius. Petrarch's sources for all these statements are Livy, Eutropius, Florus, and Seneca.

8. Cola was born in 1313.

9. Cf. Livy I, 56, 7–8.

when he held on high the dagger which he had drawn from the heart of Lucretia. There is the difference, however: the patience of the early Romans was taxed by one shameful crime, whereas yours had yielded only after countless deeds of shame and countless intolerable wrongs.

These barons in whose defense you have so often shed your blood, whom you have nourished with your own substance, whom you have raised to affluence to the detriment of the state revenues, these barons have judged you unworthy of liberty. They have gathered the mangled remnants of the state in the caverns and abominable retreats of bandits. They have felt no shame that their crimes were known abroad. They have been restrained neither by pity for their unhappy country, nor by love for it. They have irreverently pillaged the temples of the Lord; they have seized the strongholds, the public revenues, and the regions of the city. They have forcibly divided the different magistracies among themselves—the one cause in which they have united in an amazing and ferocious league of crime, though at all other times restless men and full of civil discord, and disagreeing entirely in their plans and conduct of life. And lately, neither commiseration nor pity for their unhappy city has prevented them from venting their rage upon the bridges and the walls of the city and upon the undeserving stones. In fine, after the palaces of ancient Rome had sunk into ruin, either through age or the hand of man, palaces which were once the homes of noble Romans; after the triumphal arches had been dismantled, arches which, perhaps, commemorated the conquest of the barbarians' ancestors; these haughty barons have not been ashamed to seek filthy lucre in the base sale of the fragments that had survived the lapse of ages and the barons' own ungodliness.[10] And oh my present grief! oh sin unpardonable! It is with your marble columns, O Romans, with the porticoes of your churches, to which but recently the most devout believ-

---

10. In a metrical epistle written to Clement VI in 1342 (II, 5), Petrarch represents widowed Rome as saying: "My wounds are as numerous as my churches and fortified palaces; the walls of the city, thickly strewn with ruins, reveal but the remnants of a stately and lamentable city, and move all spectators to tears."

ers hastened from all quarters of the globe, it is with the statues pilfered from your sepulchers, in which the sacred ashes of your fathers rested, it is with these that (to leave other things unmentioned) indolent Naples is being adorned! Gradually the ruins themselves will be no more—eloquent memorials of the greatness of the ancients. And you, so many thousands of brave men, have not uttered a syllable of protest in the face of a few freebooters rioting about as if in a captured city. You have been not even slaves, but as so many sheep. You have kept your peace while your common mother was being torn asunder. Small wonder, then, that they drew lots for the distribution of plunder!

We marvel and are indignant that disasters such as these should have befallen peaceful Athens; that she should have been stripped of her marks of honor, bereft of her illustrious children, and subjected to the rule of the Thirty Tyrants. But that this could have come to pass in the city of Rome, the conqueror of cities and the mistress of the world, even now exalted and ennobled as the seat of the Empire and the home of the Holy See; that Rome could remain subject to the lusts and the caprices of tyrants only slightly more numerous than those who held sway at Athens (and perchance even fewer in number)—that such things could be, no one, up to this day, had considered sufficient cause for righteous indignation and displeasure. Who of your tyrant lords, pray, has ever been content with mere servile obedience on your part? Who of them has not insisted, rather, on submission, despicable and vile? Slaves of superior ability, even the beasts of the field are spared by their owners, not out of consideration for them, but because of the loss which might be incurred through harsh treatment. Have you ever been spared? What baron has not torn each and every one of you from the arms of your beloved wives, and has not sent you abroad in the cold and darkness of a winter's night, when the rain fell in torrents and the lightning threatened, exposing you to the perils of death? What one of them has not led you in his train over snow-covered peaks and through slimy marshes, as if you had been so many purchased slaves?

You seem to have awakened at last from your heavy sleep.

If you feel any shame, any grief for your past savage condition of life, sharpen your intellects and be ready for every emergency. Do not suffer any of the rapacious wolves whom you have driven from the fold to rush again into your midst. Even now they are prowling restlessly around, endeavoring through fraud and deceit, through false howlings and alluring promises, to regain an entrance to that city whence they were violently expelled. May the winds sweep away the omen, which is so dire that my soul trembles at the mere thought—how much more, then, at a possible realization! But unless you take care, . . . do not suppose that they will return to the city as famishing as they left it. Their hunger will be far more ravenous, and will have become more and more furious through lapse of time. They now thirst in equal degree for the blood of both the flock and the shepherd. Your liberty and the glory of your deliverer they reckon as their dishonor and disgrace. Have faith in yourselves. Rise against your enemies. They will be but a contemptible handful if you stand united.

I love much, hence I fear much; for the same reason I dare much, for love makes bold the weak. I know full well, alas, that at the time of the early Republic (of which I made mention above) there were some who favored the tyranny of the few as against the freedom of all. This treason was committed, moreover, not by men of obscure birth, but by the most illustrious youths, indeed, by the sons of the liberator himself, youths who had been rendered forgetful of their better selves by the bonds of intermarriage, by long usage, and by familiar intercourse. All were punished with death by the father, who, though perhaps wretched in his bereavement, was most fortunate in the possession of a courageous heart; and who deemed it a more sacredly appointed duty to bereave himself of his children than his country of liberty.[11] I fear the recurrence of this treason today, the more so that the hearts of men are now more easily tampered with and more changeable. I fear there will be many, yea, very many, who, through intermarriage with the tyrants or through their long and wretched period of servi-

11. Livy II, 5, 5–8.

tude, are persuaded that the cup of the slave is sweeter than the abstinence of the freeman; who believe that they have attained a great and noble end if they are greeted on the streets, or are summoned hastily by their lords and plagued with lewd commands; who, finally, famishing and filthy parasites that they are, seat themselves at the unrighteous board of their tyrants and greedily gulp down whatever escapes the capacious gullets of their lords. This, and nothing else, is the compensation of these unfortunates; this the only reward for their hazards and their toils.

But you, O man most brave, you who have buttressed with your patriotic shoulders the immense weight of the tottering state, gird yourself, and watch with equal vigilance against such citizens as against the most bitter enemy. O you younger Brutus, keep ever before your eyes the example of the first Brutus. He was Consul; you are Tribune. If we should compare the two offices, it would be found that the Consuls performed many acts hostile to the welfare of the Roman plebs; indeed (and I shall speak out bravely), they many times treated it harshly and cruelly. But the Tribunes were always and constantly the defenders of the People. If, then, that Consul slew his own sons because of his love of liberty, realize what is expected in all circumstances of you, a Tribune. If you do not spurn the advice of a loyal friend, give no heed to considerations of either birth or affection. Remember that he whom you have felt to be an enemy of freedom cannot possibly be a stancher friend to you than to himself. Such a man endeavors to deprive both you and liberty of that which is most dear.

It was of the city of Rome that Sallust was speaking when he said: "In so large a state many and various are the inclinations of men."[12] How numerous, indeed, are those who today, in that same city, for a small sum would sell themselves and the entire state, and would prove traitor to all law, both human and divine! Divine Providence has already shown distinct marks of favor in our behalf, in that the greater portion of the

12. *Catilina* 51, 35.

people is of one mind and has shaken off the lethargy which was crushing it. Even in its affliction the name of the Roman people inspires respect and awe. Great are its resources, great its riches, if both be managed wisely. The Roman people has exceeding power of itself, provided only it desire to be united. A beginning has, indeed, been made; the desire now exists. All who now harbor contrary sentiments are not to be reckoned in the number of citizens, but in that of enemies. The state must be relieved of these as a body would be freed of its poisonous secretions. Thus the state, though diminished in numbers, will be stronger and healthier. Be prudent, be brave, and strength will not fail you in protecting the liberties of the city or in re-establishing its ancient sway.

What inspiration, in truth, is not to be derived from the memory of the past and from the grandeur of a name once revered throughout the world? Who does not wish Rome the best of fortune in her endeavors to attain her rightful empire? Both God and men champion so just a cause. Italy, which but recently lay listless and enfeebled, with head bowed to earth, has now risen to her elbow. If you Romans show perseverance in your undertaking, if the glad reports of your doings continue to prevail, shortly joyful hopes will spring in the hearts of men. All who can will rush to your assistance; those who are prevented by circumstances, will at least second your aims with their vows and prayers. On the other hand, the betrayers of their country will be punished by the sword of the avenger in this world, and in the lower world will they undergo the tortures which they have deserved, tortures with which they are threatened not merely by the learned men of today, but also by those of antiquity. These traitors are those whom Maro has placed in the circle of most dire punishments:[13]

> This to a tyrant master sold,
> His native land for cursed gold,
> Made laws for lucre and unmade.

With such men as these, or rather (to speak as I truly feel),

---

13. Virgil, *Aeneid* VI, 621–22.

with such wild beasts, all sternness is benevolence, all pity is inhuman.

You, O extraordinary man, have opened for yourself the path to immortality. You must persevere, if you desire to reach the goal. Otherwise, remember that the more illustrious the beginning, the more ignoble the end. Many dangers beset him who travels this road, many intricate and troublesome questions will present themselves. But courage delights in obstacles; patience, in adversity. We are born for the accomplishment of a glorious task. Why should we sigh, then, for indolent inactivity? Consider, too, that many tasks which seem difficult when first essayed become most easy after further application. And yet, why should I discourse on the nature of things, when we owe much to our friends, still more to our parents, but everything to our country? You will be obliged to clash with the hostile lances of civil enemies. Rush fearlessly to the combat, inspired by the example of Brutus himself, who met in battle the son of the Proud King and slew him, though he himself fell covered with wounds. He thus pursued even into the regions of Tartarus him whom he had driven out from the city.[14] You, however, will be victorious and will survive their death uninjured. But if you must fall, if you must sacrifice your life for your country, while the shades of your enemies hasten to the regions of darkness, you will gain heaven, whither your courage and your goodness have prepared the way for you, leaving behind on earth the monuments of enduring fame.

What better can we hope for? Romulus founded the city; this Brutus whom I so frequently mention gave it liberty; Camillus restored both. What difference, then, O most illustrious man, exists between these and you? Romulus surrounded a small city with weak ramparts; are you not encircling with mighty walls the very greatest of the cities which are or have been? Brutus rescued liberty from the clutches of a single man; are you not reclaiming a freedom usurped by many tyrants? Camillus restored the city from a devastation of recent occurrence, from ashes that were still smoking; are you not

14. Florus I, 10, 8; Livy II, 6, 7–9.

restoring old ruins that had long been despaired of? Hail, then, our Camillus, our Brutus, our Romulus! Or, if you prefer to be addressed by some other name, hail, author of Roman liberty, of Roman peace, of Roman tranquillity. The present age owes it to you that it will die in liberty; to you posterity will owe that it is conceived in liberty.

I had resolved, illustrious man, to beg of you two favors, briefly and easily asked, but far-reaching and most beneficial in their effect. You have, of your own accord, anticipated me in one of these; it will suffice, then, to have asked you for the other. I hear the following reports of you: that, every day since your accession to the rule of the Republic, at dawn and before attending to any transactions of either public or private nature, it is customary for you to receive the Sacrament of our Lord's Body, with sincerest devotion and after a most searching examination of conscience. This is doubtless as it should be for the wise man who regards the frailty of the flesh and the brevity of life, and who beholds the manifold dangers that threaten on all sides. That most illustrious of Rome's generals[15] would have followed the same course, I believe, had he lived in these days. For he was as duly observant of his sacred duties as his age permitted, an age shrouded in darkness and deprived of the knowledge of heaven.

It remains for me to ask, therefore, that you should not deprive your mind of its nourishment, neither when reclining, nor lying sleepless upon your couch, nor when administering to the needs of the flesh, nor when enjoying a moment of relaxation from your labors. Read whenever you have any spare moments; if you can not do so with convenience, have others read to you. In so doing you will be imitating that most worthy Augustus, of whom it is written that "after retiring to bed, he never slept more than seven hours, nor were they seven hours of unbroken sleep; for, within that period, he would awaken three or four times, and if unable to regain his interrupted slumbers, would summon to his assistance his readers or story-tellers." Of the same Augustus is it said that he was so eco-

---

15. Scipio Africanus; cf. Livy XXVI, 19.

nomical a steward of his time that he either read or wrote even while eating and drinking.[16] For one in your present circumstances, what could be read or heard to greater advantage than the deeds of your ancestors, of whom no city has had a greater number? You have native instances of all the virtues. And, surely, in the work of that famous and venerable Cato the Censor, we read that the Romans were wont to sing the praises of their heroes to the sound of the trumpet.[17] On this I do not insist; and yet even this, as occasion warrants, will cause the eye to flash and stir the heart to emulation. I shall be content if the annals and the history of Rome are frequently read in your presence. And with this I have said enough in your regard.

But you, O citizens, now for the first time truly deserving the name of citizens, be fully convinced that this man has been sent to you from heaven. Cherish him as one of the rare gifts of God. In his defense hazard your lives. For he too could have lived his life in slavery together with the rest. He too could have submitted to the yoke which so great a people was enduring without a murmur. If such an existence had seemed too burdensome to him, he could have fled far from the sight of the unhappy city and could have escaped the shower of abuse and insults by voluntary exile, as we know to have been the case with certain prominent citizens. It was only love of country that kept him back. He deemed it sacrilege to abandon it in such condition. In the city he resolved to live; for this city to die. He took pity on your misfortunes. You see to what dangerous heights he has risen. Give him now your support, lest he fall. Recollect, how often you drew the sword in defense, not of your property, but of theirs. In fine, recollect how often you fought to decide who of them should be the most powerful, and who should display the greater licentiousness in plundering, pillaging, butchering, killing and slaying. You who have dared so much for unworthy lords and in the pursuit of shameful servitude, it is but fitting that you

16. Suetonius, *Life of Augustus* 78, 79.
17. Cicero, *Tusculan Disputations* I, 3.

should now nobly dare in your own behalf and in the defense
of liberty, liberty for which men have rid Rome of its kings
and have deprived the Caesars of their lives. Tell me, Romans:
if you did not endure the unbounded license of the Roman
kings and emperors, will you so patiently tolerate the san-
guinary rage and the insatiable greed of foreign-born robbers?
I do not think that God is so deaf to the prayers of the devout.
To live with these tyrants is sadder far than to die without
them. Dare do something for your children, for your wives, for
the hoary heads of your fathers and mothers, for the graves
of your ancestors.

There is nothing which should not be hazarded in behalf of
the Republic. It was patriotism that compelled the Decii to
offer their devoted lives to their country; that urged Marcus
Curtius to leap, full-armed and mounted, into that yawning
chasm in the earth; that urged Horatius Cocles to oppose his
own body, firm as a wall, to the Etruscan legions, to await until
the bridge had been destroyed, and then, though heavily laden
with arms, to plunge headlong into the Tiber's tide. It was love
of country that made Gaius Mutius Scaevola inflict upon his
erring right hand a penalty which struck admiration and fear
in his very enemies. Love of country drove Attilius Regulus
back to the tortures of his angered executioners, though he
could have remained safe at home. The same noble cause made
the two Scipios die in Spain, and block with their dead bodies
(when no other means remained) the path of the Carthaginians.
The son of one of these Scipios preferred to die in poverty
and obscurity rather than to impair in the slightest degree the
liberty of the people. The son of the other, though a private
citizen, crushed the turbulent measures of Tiberius Gracchus
with death. Patriotism induced many other Romans to employ
the same redress against disturbing citizens. And as a last
instance, I shall recall Marcus Cato the Younger, who received
a surname from the city of his death, and who laid violent
hands upon himself rather than behold the face of his tyrant
(remarkable and unique man though he was), or witness the
enslaving of his country.

It is interesting to rehearse the names of these men, and particularly so in the presence of those citizens from whose blood have sprung not merely individuals, but entire families of the same firm and united resolve. Of this let the Cremera bear witness, the scene of the memorable and at the same time pitiful end of three hundred and six Fabii. And not only families, but legions and entire armies have deemed it dear to rush upon death in defense of country. I desire, moreover, that these deeds be read on that very Capitol (as I conjecture) from whose summit that bold Manlius was hurled headlong, Manlius who but recently had been guardian of that hill and who suffered death for this one reason: that he was suspected of plotting against that liberty which he had previously defended, and of desiring an issue not in accord with his excellent beginning. One and the same Rock bore witness both to his great glory and to his death, and served as an everlasting warning to all who should attempt similar treason.

Let no one falsely suppose that those who keep vigilant watch over their liberties, and who have hitherto championed the cause of the abandoned Republic, are performing a duty rightfully belonging to others. It is their own cause they are defending. Let each man be convinced that only in this way will his interests be safe. It is only thus that the merchant gains peace, the soldier glory, the husbandman plenty, the devout their religious services, the scholar leisure, the old rest, the boys rudiments of learning, the maidens nuptials, and the matrons honor. Only in this way, finally, will all find happiness.

O citizens of Rome, strain every nerve, bring to bear every public and private resource to the advancement of the public and the private welfare. Let all other cares give way to this. If you neglect this care, all your other deeds will be of no avail. If, on the contrary, you devote all your energies to it, even though you may seem to accomplish nothing, nevertheless will you perform to the full your duties as citizens and as men. Let every vestige of civil fury be effaced from your midst, I beseech you. Let the flames which had been fanned among us by the breath of tyrants be extinguished by the warnings and the guarded kindness of your deliverer. Take upon yourself this friendly rivalry: not who is to be the more powerful, but who is to be the better citizen, and the more patient; who is to evince the deeper love of country, the greater humility toward his neighbors and the more implacable hatred for the tyrants. Enter upon this contest with your Tribune: as to whether he will show greater foresight in the honest administration of government than you readiness in obeying. And if, perchance, love (than which there is nothing stronger) prove insufficient to bring your hearts into harmonious accord, then may considerations of common interest avail you. Be united by this bond at least. Cling to each other tenaciously, peaceably. Wield not the arms handed down to you by your fathers except against the enemies of the commonwealth. Offer as most pleasing sacrifice to the ashes of your dead the exile, the destitution, and the punishment of the barons. The dead will rejoice in such deeds; and had they foreseen the future, they would surely have breathed their last with greater resignation and peace of mind.

But I fear that I have detained you by my words longer than is fitting, especially at a time when there is far greater need of action. Neither my calling, alas, nor my lot permit me to assist you in deed. Hence I send you my words, the one means of assistance at my disposal. I confess that at first I was roused by the glorious reports to envy you your great honor. I heaped countless reproaches upon my lot which had deprived me of taking active part in so joyous a consummation. But I was not entirely excluded. Over lands and seas there came to me my due share of happiness. Hastily I seized my pen, that, in the midst of such great and such remarkable harmony of a delivered people, my voice too might be heard though from a distance—that I too might perform my duty as a Roman citizen. Moreover, this subject which I have now treated in prose, I shall, perhaps, attempt in the near future, but in different measures, provided you will not deceive my hopes and wishes, and will not deny me perseverance in your glorious undertaking. Crowned with the chaplet of Apollo, I shall ascend the lofty and inspiring Helicon. There, at the brim of the Castalian font, I shall recall the Muses from their exile, and shall sing resounding words in abiding memory of your glory, words that will ring throughout the ages. Farewell, you bravest of men! Farewell, you best of citizens! Farewell, most glorious City of the Seven Hills.

20. Vaucluse[1]

I have long, and with difficulty, been sailing the stormy seas of this Curia which calls itself Roman. I have grown rather old in the service, but am still an awkward and inexperienced sailor. Consequently I recently fled from the troubled waters of Avignon, and sought the haven which, as ever, offers me the quiet of solitude—that Enclosed Valley which receives its name from its very nature. This retreat is fifteen miles distant from that most boisterous of cities and from the left bank of the Rhone. Though the intervening distance is so short, still the two places are so utterly different that, whenever I leave here for that city, I seem to have encircled the globe from the farthest west to the extreme east. The two places have nothing in common except the sky: the men have a different nature, the waters are of a different quality, the land brings forth a different vegetation.

Here I have the Fountain of the Sorgue, a stream which must be numbered among the fairest and coolest, remarkable for its crystal waters and its emerald channel. No other stream is like it; none other is so noted for its varying moods, now raging like a torrent, now quiet as a pool. I am astonished, therefore, that Plinius Secundus should have placed this fount among the wonders of the province of Narbonne; for as a matter of fact it is situated in the province of Arles.[2] This is the country-seat where, beyond the confines of Italy, I am detained by the inexorable claims of necessity. And yet the

---

1. *Epistolae Variae* XLII (late summer, 1347), to Cola di Rienzo.
2. Pliny, *Natural History* XVIII, 22 (51), 190.

spot is most suitable for my studies. The hills cast a grateful
shadow in the morning and in the evening hours; and at noon
many a nook and corner of the vale gleams in the sunlight.
Round about, the woods lie still and tranquil, woods in which
the tracks of wild animals are far more numerous than those
of men. Everywhere a deep and unbroken stillness, except for
the babbling of running waters, or the lowing of the oxen
browsing lazily along the banks, or the singing of birds. I
should speak of this more at length, were it not that the rare
beauties of this secluded dale have already become familiar
far and wide through my verses.

Hither then, as I was saying, I fled with great longing, both
to give my mind and my ears rest from the distracting whirl
of the city, and also to put the finishing touches to some work
I had in hand, the thought of which, in its unfinished condition,
weighed heavily upon me. The very aspect of the forest urged
me to compose a poem dealing with the wild woodlands. To
that pastoral poem, therefore, which I had sung during the
preceding summer in that same valley, I now added a chapter.[3]
Or rather, inasmuch as in matters of poetry we should ever
employ poetical terms, I should say that I now added an
eclogue. The laws of this species of poetry forbade me to choose
for a background any other than a sylvan scene. Hence I wrote
a pastoral in which the interlocutors are two shepherds, two
brothers, and forwarded this poem to you, who are so devoted
a scholar, intending that it should serve as a relief from your
numerous cares.

The nature of these compositions is such that, unless the
author himself provide the key, their meaning cannot, perhaps,
be divined. In fact, they are likely to remain quite unintelligible.
I shall not oblige you, who are straining every nerve in solving
most serious questions of state, to misspend any energy over
the words of even one of these alleged shepherds. And that
your divine intellect may not be engaged even for one instant
in unraveling these trifles of mine, I shall briefly disclose to
you the substance of what I have written.

3. Eclogue V.

The two shepherds represent two classes of citizens living in the same city, but entertaining widely divergent sentiments concerning that same Republic. One of them is named Martius, that is to say, warlike and restless, or perhaps he is named after Mars, whom tradition makes the father of him who founded our race. This Martius is affectionate toward his mother and has compassion for her. His mother, indeed, is Rome. The second shepherd is his brother Apicius, a name once borne by him who was master-connoisseur of the art of cooking. Apicius (as you see) must therefore typify that class of men totally given over to idleness and to the pursuit of pleasure. The scene represents the two shepherds in heated conversation on the love due to their aged mother, and especially on the question of restoring her ancient homestead (which, of course, is the Capitolium), and the bridge by which she was wont to visit her farms (which, again, is the Mulvian). The bridge spans a stream descending from the lofty summits of the Apennines, the Tiber. This river, whose course is there outlined, leads to the ancient orchards, and to the abodes of Saturn, in other words, to the ancient city of Orte, and to Sutri. It leads also to the shaded valleys of Tempe, by which is meant Umbria, in which are Narni and Todi and many other cities; and, further south, it enters Etruria, whose people (as you well know) are descended from the Lydian race.[4]

The shepherd who is mentioned in the following passage —he who caught the thieves on the bridge and slew them—is Marcus Tullius Cicero, who (as you know) seized the Catilinarian conspirators on the Mulvian Bridge.[5] Rightly is he styled shepherd, because he was Consul; rightly is he styled acute and keen, because of his supremacy in the field of eloquence. The woods for which the ruined bridge is a menace, and the diminished flock dwelling therein alike symbolize the Roman people. The women and the children, for whom Apicius has abandoned his mother and whom alone he cherishes, are the lands and their feudal dwellers. The caverns are the fortified palaces of these lords, relying upon which they scoff at

4. Pliny III, 5 (8), 50.
5. Cicero, *In Catilinam* III, 2, 5–6 and III, 3, 6.

the sufferings of the citizens. Apicius does not wish the Capitolium to be strengthened; on the contrary, he proposes that it be rent in two, so that this faction and that may alternately reign supreme. His brother strives to bring about a union, and in referring to the riches of their mother, à propos of restoring the Capitolium, he means to emphasize the fact that Rome is still a power, if only her children be of one mind. For (he says) Rome nourishes both sheep and bullocks, representing, naturally, the needy populace and the wealthier portion of the people. Among the remnants of their former fortune Martius mentions also a quantity of hidden salt, by which we may simply understand the revenues from the tax on salt, which I hear are quite considerable. However, understand by it rather the practical wisdom of the Romans which has too long lain dormant from dread of the tyrants.

While the brothers are thus engaged in debate, a winged messenger arrives. This is Rumor, than whom (to quote Virgil) "no evil thing is swifter."[6] This courier declares their cares vain and their altercations useless, announcing that they have both been disowned by their mother, and that, with the mother's consent, their younger brother rebuilds the old homestead and rules the forests; announcing, furthermore, that their brother thereby imposes silence upon them while he himself sings sweetly to the flocks and the herds, that is to say, while he himself promulgates just laws and abolishes the unjust. In these verses I have veiled (under the figures of wild animals) either the names, or the natural dispositions, or the armorial bearings of certain of the tyrants.[7] Thus far you have proved yourself to be the youngest of the three brothers. Everything else is clear. Farewell, O illustrious man, and keep me in your thoughts.

6. *Aeneid* IV, 174.
7. The bear must represent the Orsini, but the other animals have had different claimants, among them the Colonna, the Tebaldi, the Conti, the Gaetani, and the Savelli.

21. Luchino Visconti[1]

Live fruitful, noble wood, through many years
Mindful of your great lord; rise, fertile shoots,
And stretch up to the sky your fruited boughs.
Protect with shade the grassy earth beneath,
While Leo roars and summer's drought returns,   5
And keep away the sun's excessive rage.
The snows have now dissolved, winter is gone;
The flowery Ram pursues the rainy Fishes.
As spring begins change garb and dress in green,
And for the season assume a joyous look: 10
So orders he who deigns now to request
A part of you, and may deign someday (grow!)
To pluck with noble hand your heavy fruits—
That great man Italy regards with honor,
He whom the lofty Alps forthwith obey.   15
The Apennines plow for him; the regal Po,
Foaming, divides his rich fields with its stream,
And stupefied to see on lofty towers
His crowned serpents, venerates him as lord.
The Adriatic and the wide Tyrrhenian   20
Hold him in dread, whom the transalpine realms
Revere and want as chief. Crimes with harsh bands
He snares and with the reins of law restrains;
With justice rules the peoples; and is third

---

1. *Epistolae Metricae* III, 6. Sent on March 13, 1348. At this time Petrarch was canon of the cathedral in Parma, which was in the possession of Luchino Visconti (co-ruler of Milan, along with his brother, the archbishop Giovanni). Luchino had written asking Petrarch for some verses and some scions from his fruit trees.

To bring a golden age to weary Italy.[2]   25
He has carried to Milan the art of Rome:
"To spare the subject and war down the proud."[3]

22. *Rotta e l'alta colonna è 'l verde lauro*[1]

Shattered is the lofty column and the verdant laurel that
created shade for my weary thoughts. I have lost what I do
not hope to find again from Boreas to Auster, or from the In-
dian sea to the Mauritanian. (4)

You have taken from me, death, my double treasure, which
made me live in joy and walk proudly; and neither earth nor
empire can compensate for the loss, nor Oriental gem nor the
power of gold. (8)

But if it is with the will of destiny, what can I do but have
a sorrowful soul, and eyes ever moist and head bent? (11)

Our life which is so fair in appearance, how swiftly it loses
in a morning that which is acquired in many years at great
pain! (14)

2. Cf. Virgil, *Aeneid* VI, 792–94.
3. *Aeneid* VI, 853 (the line concluding Anchises' statement of Rome's
mission).
1. *Rerum Vulgarium Fragmenta*, CCLXIX. Laura died April 6, Cardinal
Giovanni Colonna July 3, 1348, the year of the Black Death (cf. the opening pages of Boccaccio's *Decameron*, which is set at that time).

23. Laura[1]

Laura, who was distinguished by her own virtues, and widely celebrated by my songs, first appeared to my eyes in my early manhood, in the year of our Lord 1327, upon the sixth day of April, at the first hour, in the church of Santa Clara at Avignon; in the same city, in the same month of April, on the same sixth day, at the same first hour, in the year 1348, that light was taken from our day, while I was by chance at Verona, ignorant, alas! of my fate. The unhappy news reached me at Parma, in a letter from my friend Ludovico,[2] on the morning of the nineteenth of May, of the same year. Her chaste and lovely form was laid in the church of the Franciscans, on the evening of the day upon which she died. I am persuaded that her soul returned, as Seneca says of Scipio Africanus, to the heaven whence it came. I have experienced a certain satisfaction in writing this bitter record of a cruel event, especially in this place where it will often come under my eye, for so I may be led to reflect that life can afford me no farther pleasures; and, the most serious of my temptations being removed, I may be admonished by the frequent study of these lines, and by the thought of my vanishing years, that it is high time to flee from Babylon. This, with God's grace, will be easy, as I frankly and manfully consider the needless anxieties of the past, with its empty hopes and unforeseen issue.

1. Written on the first guard leaf of Petrarch's *Virgil*, where he recorded his bereavements.
2. Socrates.

The Bettmann Archive

3. Portrait of Laura, by Boccaccio Boccacino.

24. A Florentine in Naples[1]

If the glorious sight of the field he has cultivated pleases the farmer, while he measures with his eye the golden ears of corn, his riches, nevertheless on a pleasant hill the same man notes with greater delight the lofty oak and the leafy beech and the elm clothed with vines. If the general renown of his flock makes a shepherd proud, yet he is happier to distinguish from the whole crowd a great bullock playing in a grassy valley: it he cares for more than the others, stroking it, giving it a name, interlacing its horns with fragrant garlands. Consider what your glory is for me and for our people, what a splendor it is for our homeland! We see you bear so many harsh labors and bypass so many snares with cautious step, fearful to foes and dear to friends. Neither with fierce threats nor with treacherous blandishments can Fortune move you from your glorious endeavor: you are one man she admires as much amid sad as amid happy circumstances. At last weary Sicily has entrusted to you the sails and rudder of her bark: thus a steersman is always chosen when the storm is at its worst, a general when the war is uncertain. Chosen under a doubtful lot for noble ventures, live mindful of yourself and of us. What torches will be lit by your inborn virtue, O our hope, and by my concern to please first you, then the good and the throng of those who love you!—among whom deign to number your poet.

1. *Epistolae Metricae* III, 14, to Niccolò Acciaiuoli, on his appointment as grand seneschal of the Kingdom of Naples (June, 1348). Niccolò had long been the mentor of Louis of Taranto (who became Queen Joan's second husband in 1347); and it was probably he who arranged the sale of Avignon to Clement VI.

25. On the Nature of Poetry[1]

I judge, from what I know of your religious fervor, that you will feel a sort of repugnance toward the poem[2] which I enclose in this letter, deeming it quite out of harmony with all your professions, and in direct opposition to your whole mode of thinking and living. But you must not be too hasty in your conclusions. What can be more foolish than to pronounce an opinion upon a subject that you have not investigated? The fact is, poetry is very far from being opposed to theology. Does that surprise you? One may almost say that theology actually is poetry, poetry concerning God. To call Christ now a lion, now a lamb, now a worm, what pray is that if not poetical? And you will find thousands of such things in the Scriptures, so very many that I cannot attempt to enumerate them. What indeed are the parables of our Savior, in the Gospels, but words whose sound is foreign to their sense, or allegories, to use the technical term? But allegory is the warp and woof of all poetry. Of course, though, the subject matter in the two cases is very different. That everyone will admit. In the one case it is God and things pertaining to him that are treated, in the other mere gods and mortal men.

Now we can see how Aristotle came to say that the first theologians and the first poets were one and the same.[3] The

1. From *Epistolae Familiares* X, 4 (from Padua, December 2, 1348), to his brother Gherardo. For a contemporary's extensive exposition of much the same ideas, see *Boccaccio on Poetry,* ed. Charles G. Osgood (reprinted in the Bobbs-Merrill Library of Liberal Arts).

2. An allegorical eclogue which Petrarch explicates at some length in the body of this letter.

3. *Metaphysics* 2, 4, 12. Both Petrarch and Boccaccio follow the line of Mussato: see the chapter on "Poetry and Theology" in E. R. Curtius, *European Literature and the Latin Middle Ages,* trans. Willard R. Trask (New York, 1953), pp. 214–27.

very name of poet is proof that he was right. Inquiries have
been made into the origin of that word; and, although the
theories have varied somewhat, the most reasonable view on
the whole is this: that in early days, when men were rude and
unformed, but full of a burning desire—which is part of our
very nature—to know the truth, and especially to learn about
God, they began to feel sure that there really is some higher
power that controls our destinies, and to deem it fitting that
homage should be paid to this power, with all manner of
reverence beyond that which is ever shown to men, and also
with an august ceremonial. Therefore just as they planned for
grand abodes, which they called temples, and for consecrated
servants, to whom they gave the name of priests, and for magnificent statues, and vessels of gold, and marble tables, and
purple vestments, they also determined, in order that this
feeling of homage might not remain unexpressed, to strive to
win the favor of the deity by lofty words, subjecting the powers
above to the softening influences of songs of praise, sacred
hymns remote from all the forms of speech that pertain to
common usage and to the affairs of state, and embellished
moreover by numbers, which add a charm and drive tedium
away. It behoved of course that this be done not in everyday
fashion, but in a manner artful and carefully elaborated and
a little strange. Now speech which was thus heightened was
called in Greek *poetices;* so, very naturally, those who used
it came to be called *poets*.

Who, you will ask, is my authority for this? But can you not
dispense with bondsmen, my brother, and have a little faith in
me? That you should trust my unsupported word, when I tell
you things that are true and bear upon their face the stamp
of truth, is nothing more, it seems to me, than I have a right to
ask of you. Still, if you find yourself disposed to proceed more
cautiously, I will give you bondsmen who are perfectly good,
witnesses whom you may trust with perfect safety. The first of
these is Marcus Varro,[4] the greatest scholar that Rome ever
produced, and the next is Tranquillus,[5] an investigator whose

4. Cf. Augustine, *De Civitate Dei* VI, 5.
5. There is nothing to this effect in the surviving works of Suetonius.

work is characterized always by the utmost caution. Then I can add a third name, which will probably be better known to you, Isidore. He too mentions these matters, in the eighth book of his *Etymologies,* although briefly and merely on the authority of Tranquillus.[6]

But you will object, and say, "I certainly can believe the saint, if not the other learned men; and yet the fact remains that the sweetness of your poetry is inconsistent with the severity of my life." Ah! but you are mistaken, my brother. Why, even the Old Testament fathers made use of poetry, both heroic song and other kinds. Moses, for example, and Job, and David, and Solomon, and Jeremiah. Even the psalms, which you are always singing, day and night, are in meter, in the Hebrew; so that I should be guilty of no inaccuracy or impropriety if I ventured to style their author the Christian's poet. Indeed the plain facts of the case inevitably suggest some such designation. Let me remind you, moreover, since you are not inclined to take anything that I say today without authority, that even Jerome took this view of the matter. Of course these sacred poems, these psalms, which sing of the blessed man, Christ— of his birth, his death, his descent into hell, his resurrection, his ascent into heaven, his return to judge the earth,—never have been, and never could have been, translated into another language without some sacrifice of either the meter or the sense. So, as the choice had to be made, it has been the sense that has been considered. And yet some vestige of metrical law still survives, and the separate fragments we still call verses, very properly, for verses they are.

So much for the ancients. Now as regards Ambrose and Augustine and Jerome, our guides through the New Testament —to show that they too employed poetic forms and rhythms would be the easiest of tasks; while in the case of Prudentius and Prosper and Sedulius and the rest the mere names are enough, for we have not a single word from them in prose, while their metrical productions are numerous and well known. Do not look askance then, dear brother, upon a practice which you

6. VIII, 7, 2: "De poeta."

see has been approved by saintly men whom Christ has loved.
Consider the underlying meaning alone, and if that is sound and
true accept it gladly, no matter what the outward form may be.
To praise a feast set forth on earthen vessels but despise it when
it is served on gold is too much like madness or hypocrisy. . . .

26. Petrarch's Preface to His First Collection of Letters[1]

. . . Your partiality for the author will make his style pleasing (indeed what beauty of style is likely to be perceived by
an unfriendly judge?); it is vain to adorn what already delights.
If anything gratifies you in these letters of mine, I freely concede that it is not really mine but yours; that is to say, the
credit is due not to my ability but to your good will. You will
find no great eloquence or vigor of expression in them. Indeed
I do not possess these powers, and if I did, in ever so high a
degree, there would be no place for them in this kind of composition. Even Cicero, who was renowned for these abilities,
does not manifest them in his letters, nor even in his treatises,
where, as he himself says, the language is characterized by a
certain evenness and moderation. In his orations, on the other
hand, he displayed extraordinary powers, pouring out a clear
and rapid stream of eloquence. This oratorical style Cicero used
frequently for his friends, and against his enemies and those of
the republic. Cato resorted to it often on behalf of others, and
for himself four and forty times. In this mode of composition
I am wholly inexperienced, for I have been far away from the
responsibilities of state. And while my reputation may sometimes have been assailed by slight murmurs, or secret whisper-
ings, I have so far never suffered any attack in the courts which

1. From *Epistolae Familiares* I, 1 (from Padua, January 13, 1350), to
Socrates.

I must needs avenge or parry. Hence, as it is not my profession to use my weapons of speech for the defence of others, I do not frequent the tribunals, nor have I ever learned to loan my tongue. I have, indeed, a deep repugnance for such a life, for I am by nature a lover of silence and solitude, an enemy of the courts, and a contemner of wealth. It was fortunate for me that I was freed from the necessity of resorting to a weapon which I might not have been able to use if I had tried. I have therefore made no attempt to employ an oratorical style, which, even if it had been at my disposal, would have been uncalled for in this instance. But you will accept this homely and familiar language in the same friendly spirit as you do the rest, and take in good part a style well adapted to the sentiments we are accustomed to express in ordinary conversation.

All my critics, however, are not like you, for they do not all think the same, nor do they all love me as you do. But how can I hope to please everybody, when I have always striven to gratify a few only? There are three poisons which kill sound criticism: love, hate, and envy. Beware lest through too much love you should make public what might better be kept concealed. As you are guided by love, so others may be influenced by other passions. Between the blindness of love and that of jealousy there is indeed a great difference in origin, but not always in effect. Hate, to which I have assigned a middle place, I neither merit not fear. Still it can easily be arranged that you may keep and read my trifling productions for your own exclusive pleasure, thinking of nothing except the incidents in our lives and those of our friends which they recall. Should you do this, it would be most gratifying to me. In this way your request will have been satisfied and my reputation will be safe. Beyond this I do not deceive myself with the vain hope of favor. For how can we imagine even a friend, if he be not an *alter ego,* reading without weariness such a mass of miscellaneous and conflicting recollections? There is no unity in the themes or composition of the letters, and with the various matters treated went varying moods, which were rarely happy and usually despondent.

Epicurus, a philosopher held in disrepute among the vulgar

but esteemed by those better able to judge, confined his correspondence to two or three persons—Idomeneus, Polyaenus, and Metrodorus. Cicero wrote to hardly more, to Brutus, Atticus, and the other two Ciceros, his brother and son.[2] Seneca wro.e to few except his friend Lucilius. It obviously renders felicitous letter-writing a simple matter if we know the character of our correspondent and get used to his particular mind, so that we can judge what he will be glad to hear and what we may properly communicate. But my lot has been a very different one, for heretofore almost my whole life has been passed in journeying from place to place. I might compare my wanderings with those of Ulysses; and certainly were we only on the same plane in reputation and in the fame of our adventures, I might claim that he had not wandered farther or been cast upon more distant shores than I. . . .

27. Misadventures on His Journey to Rome[1]

I had hoped that with my change of situation and state of mind Fortune too would change; but I was evidently mistaken. Wherever I flee, Fate pursues me. Whether I am borne in a swift car or on a panting charger or on a speeding ship or even

2. Cicero's *Ad Familiares* had not yet been rediscovered.

1. *Epistolae Familiares* XI, 1 (from Rome, November 3, 1350), to Giovanni Boccaccio. On his way to Rome in the Year of Jubilee, Petrarch had stayed with Boccaccio at Florence, where there was a small circle of Petrarch's admirers: Zanobi da Strada, Francesco Nelli (the prior of Santi Apostoli), and Lapo da Castiglionchio. Boccaccio had already written several times in praise of Petrarch, including a life that contained numerous errors: see E. H. Wilkins, "Boccaccio's Early Tributes to Petrarch," *Speculum* 38 (1963), 79–87. Petrarch corresponded with Boccaccio until the end of his life: see E. H. Wilkins, "A Survey of the Correspondence Between Petrarch and Boccaccio," *Italia Medioevale e Umanistica* VI (1963), 179–84.

on the wings of Daedalus, grim Fate will cut me off. But to no avail; she can pinch and tweak, but as long as God guides my steps she cannot lay me low. I have already learned, with Democritus, "to thumb my nose at her in high defiance."[2] But she continues trying her tricks on me; and since in my younger days I often defeated her, she thinks she can win in my sober, tranquil age. As if a contest with a wise old man were easier! As if strength of mind decreased with living, like the body's powers! If in fact my strength of mind had not increased, I should think that I had lived in vain. But not to keep you longer in suspense, I shall tell you of her latest trick.

When I left you, I set out, as you know, for Rome, where has assembled almost the whole body of Christians in this year which all of us sinners have so longed for. To avoid the tedium of a solitary journey I found some companions. The first was a venerable cleric; the second a learned wit; the others seemed the sort who could beguile the hardest journey by their experience of travel and by their amiability.[3] I had made these dispositions very sensibly, but, as it turned out, unfortunately. So I was heading for Rome with the fervent intention of making an end of my sins; for, as Horace says, "I was not so shamed at having played as at not withdrawing from the game."[4] And certainly, I hope, Fortune could not and cannot swerve me from my purpose. Though she cast my wretched body on the reefs and spatter the rocks with my blood and brains, though perchance she remove my spirit that despises her and her doings, she cannot subdue it. She can often infect my limbs; she will never make my soul sick.

However, not to keep you in suspense, her assault on my body was no small matter. I had left Bolsena, now a poor, mean town, but once numbered among the chief cities of Etruria; and I was hurrying on, eager to see the Holy City for the fifth time; and I was turning over this thought in my mind: "How our lives slip by! How things change, and men's judgments with them! What I wrote in my *Bucolics* is true indeed: 'Youthful zeal

2. Juvenal, *Satires* X, 52–53.
3. Cf. Chaucer's pilgrims to Canterbury.
4. *Epistles* I, xiv, 36.

pleases age no more, and man's concerns are whitened with his locks.'[5] It has been fourteen years since I first came to Rome only from my desire to see its miracle. A few years later I came a second time, drawn by an immature but seductive ambition for the laurel. My third and fourth visits were prompted by sympathy for illustrious friends; I did not fear to bring them some poor comfort when they were in Fortune's disfavor. Now I am making my fifth trip to Rome; who knows if it be not the last? It should be more blest than the others as the care of one's soul is nobler than the care of the body, as one's eternal salvation is more to be desired than mortal glory."

While I was brooding thus and thanking God in silence, the horse of the old Abbot I mentioned before, which was at my left—to *sinister* indeed!—launched a kick at my mount. The kick landed at the junction of my shin and the knee, with such force that the noise, as of fractured bones, attracted many who were some distance off to see what was the matter. Feeling excruciating pain, I thought at first of stopping; but the place was too dreadful. So, making a virtue of necessity, I continued on, arriving late at Viterbo; and three days later I reached Rome. Doctors were summoned. The bone was laid bare; it was horribly white, but it was apparently not fractured. The marks of the horse's iron shoe were perfectly clear. The odor of the neglected wound was so revolting that on my word I could hardly endure it. Although our innate familiarity with our bodies is such that we can bear in them what is repulsive in others, I never learned from any corpse the lesson of my own flesh, that man is a vile, wretched animal unless he redeems the ignobility of the body with the nobility of the soul.

Well, to be brief, I have been lying here in Rome in the doctors' hands, wavering between fear and hope of recovery, for fourteen days now, which have seemed longer and more burdensome than so many years. This situation would be intolerable enough anywhere, since, more than with most people, my mind is benumbed by the body's inactivity and is quickened by moderate movement. So now my reclusion is most serious

5. *Bucolicum Carmen* VIII, 76–77.

and annoying because of my insatiable desire to revisit the queen of cities. The more I look at her, the more I am led to believe all the great things written of her.

I do find some consolation for my condition and for my pain in the thought that it may be heaven's will, that perhaps my confessor seemed too lenient and that another agent had to make up for his omissions. I sometimes thought it might be God's will to amend with his own hands one whose mind had long been limping, by making his body limp. Properly judged, this exchange was not to be considered distressing, thanks be to him who has restored to me the hope of seeing you again, sound in both body and mind. Anyway, I wrote you this lying on my cot—as my handwriting sufficiently indicates—not to make you grieve for my misfortunes, but that you may rejoice that I have borne everything philosophically and that I would bear much worse if need be.

Do you live happily, and farewell; and forget me not.

28. Exile from Florence[1]

It is sweet to journey to my homeland, sweet to flee it. An occasional host draws me there, but I withdraw in dislike for that notorious throng. What would you do, my spirit? The place we go to produces good things joined to bad, and mixes

1. *Epistolae Metricae* III, 8. To Zanobi da Strada, one of Petrarch's small circle of Florentine friends, a highly regarded writer who in 1355 was crowned poet by the emperor Charles IV. Probably written in late 1350 or early 1351. In March of 1351 Boccaccio carried to Padua a letter inscribed "To the Reverend Francesco Petrarca, Paduan canon, crowned poet, our most dear fellow citizen, from the Prior of the Arts and the Gonfalonier of Justice of the People and the City of Florence," reporting their decision to return the property confiscated from his father and asking him to live in his *patria* as professor at the new university (establishment of which had been authorized in 1349 by Pope Clement VI). On April 6 Petrarch replied that he deeply appreciated the offer of restitution; but he decided to go to Avignon, whither he had just been summoned by the Pope.

sweet with bitter. I must bear or flee them all at the same time, for distinguishing things is not easy. "He chooses flight." What, when the door is not open if I wish to return? My haughty fellow citizens have driven me into exile; he who suppresses in himself all sense of justice closes the unfriendly city to me. It is a tacit sort of exile; the wounds are concealed. You wonder at this? Who does not know about the injustice committed by a few (which is nourished by the patience of our heedless people), or my home seized by force, or the pastures of my ancestral land, and the entreaties dismissed, and the vain laments? I am disdainful, to tell the truth. Shall I be able to share your pride? Golden Rome has embraced me in her bosom and regarded as worthy of citizenship, as did Virgil's beloved Naples, by the decree of venerable Robert. What should I say of Bologna, learned in laws; or Pisa, which adorns the shore of the Tyrrhenian Sea, and Venice, a world by itself, ruling the Adriatic; and Padua, mother of history;[2] or Mantua, the Latin Smyrna, the ancient nurse of brilliant poetry;[3] or Parma, once the shield of empire, we are told, when harsh fortune oppressed the Roman leaders?[4] Why speak of the Italian cities and towns that number my name among their honored alumni, the name your Florence alone removes from its lists? But I am being carried along too far by the anger that seizes my flaming pen. Gaul wanted me, and the noble offspring[5] of Philip would not say no; even the remote Britons wanted me. I did not merit it, I confess; but in this at least I am favored by propitious stars mitigating the influence of an unlucky constellation.

Look where grief has borne me! Forgive me if my sense of injury has made me loquacious. I do not flee my homeland, but in truth it puts me to flight—an old custom of which there are famous examples: behold the numerous tombs of men forbidden

2. Livy, Petrarch's favorite historian, was from Padua. As a young man in Avignon Petrarch had produced the first scholarly edition of the portions of Livy that were then known.

3. Virgil was born in the village of Andes, in Mantuan territory; Smyrna was one of the cities that claimed Homer.

4. During the war of Modena, between Octavian and Antony, shortly after Caesar's death. In Latin *parma* is the word for a small round shield.

5. King John, who acceded to the throne of France in 1350.

to lie in native grounds![6] What citizens are buried in foreign dust! I shall take comfort, then, and having been warned, shall bear better circumstances with equanimity.

29. Exhortation to the Emperor Charles IV[1]

My letter, most serene Emperor, when it considers its origin, whence it proceeds and whither it is bound, is filled with dread at the thought of the gulf over which it must pass. Born in the shadow of obscurity, what wonder if it is dazzled by the brilliancy of your splendid name? But love casteth out fear: it will, as it ventures into the light of your presence, at least serve to bear to you the message of my faithful affection. Read, then, I pray you, Glory of our Age, read! for you need fear no empty flattery, that common affliction of kings, so irksome and hateful to you. The art of adulation is repugnant to my character; prepare rather to listen to my lamentations, for you are now to be disturbed not by compliments but by complaints.

Why do you forget us—nay, forget yourself, if I may be pardoned for so speaking? How is it that your Italy no longer enjoys your watchful care? We have long placed our hope in you, as one sent to us from heaven, who would speedily re-establish our liberty; but you have forsaken us, and, when action

6. The most famous such instance is Dante, whose remains still lie in Ravenna, where he died in exile. (A new cenotaph was built in Santa Croce in 1965, to mark the anniversary of his birth.) The most stirring part of Boccaccio's *Trattatello in laude di Dante* is his "Reproof to the Florentines" (VII), which may be read in *The Earliest Lives of Dante* (Ungar paperback).

1. *Epistolae Familiares* X, 1 (from Padua, February 24, probably 1351 but possibly 1350). After John XXII had deposed Ludwig the Bavarian, Clement VI in 1346 ordered that a new emperor should be elected. The obvious choice was John of Luxembourg, King of Bohemia (who perished later that year in the Battle of Crécy), but since John was ill, Clement suggested his son Charles. Aided by Philip of Valois, Charles won the favor of the pope and then the election.

is most essential, you occupy your time in lengthy deliberations. You will perceive, Caesar, how frankly I dare to address you, though a person insignificant and unknown. Be not offended at my boldness, I beseech you, but congratulate yourself upon the possession of a nature which can arouse this confidence in me.

To revert to the question in hand, why do you spend your time in mere consultation, as if master of the future? Do you not know how abruptly the most important matter may reach a crisis? A day may bring forth what has been preparing for centuries. Believe me, if you but consider your own reputation, and the condition of the state, you will clearly perceive that neither your interests nor ours require longer delay. What is more fleeting and uncertain than life? Although you are now at the height of manly vigor, your strength will not endure, but is slipping from you steadily and apace. Each day carries you insensibly toward old age. You hesitate and look about you; ere you are aware, your hair will be white. Can you apprehend that you are premature in undertaking a task for which, as you must know, the longest life would scarcely suffice? The business before you is no common or trifling affair. The Roman Empire, long harassed by storms, and again and again deluded in its hopes of safety, has at last placed its waning reliance in your uprightness and devotion. After a thousand perils, it ventures, under the protection of your name, to breathe once more; but hope alone cannot long sustain it. You must realize how great and how holy a burden of responsibility you have assumed. Press on, we exhort you, to the goal, with the utmost speed!

Time is so precious, nay, so inestimable a possession, that it is the one thing which the learned agree can justify avarice. So cast hesitation to the winds and, as behooves one who is entering upon a momentous task, count every day a priceless opportunity. Let this thought make you frugal of time, and induce you to come to our rescue, and show the light of your august countenance, for which we long amidst the clouds of our adversity. Let not solicitude for Transalpine affairs, nor the love of your native soil, detain you; but whenever you look upon Germany, think of Italy. There you were born, here you were nurtured; there you enjoy a kingdom, here both a kingdom and an empire; and, as I believe I may, with the consent of all nations and peoples, safely add, while the members of the Empire are everywhere, here you will find the head itself. There must, however, be no slothfulness if you would reach the desired result, for it will prove no small matter to re-unite all these precious fragments into a single body.

I well know that novelty always excites suspicion, but you are not summoned to an unknown land. Italy is no less familiar to you than Germany itself. Pledged to us by divine favor from your childhood, you followed, with extraordinary ability, the footsteps of your illustrious father. Under his guidance you made yourself acquainted with the Italian cities, the customs of the people, the configuration of the land, and mastered in this way the first principles of your glorious profession. Here, while still a boy, and with a prowess more than mortal, you gained many a famous victory. Yet great as were these deeds they but foreshadowed greater things; since, as a man, you could not look with apprehension upon a country which had afforded you, as a youth, the opportunity for such signal triumphs. You could forecast from the auspicious results of your first campaign what you might, as Emperor, anticipate upon the same field.[2]

Moreover, Italy has never awaited the coming of any foreign prince with more joy; for not only is there no one else to whom she can look for the healing of her wounds, but your yoke she does not regard as that of an alien. Thus your majesty, although you may not be aware of it, enjoys a peculiar position in our eyes. Why should I fear to say frankly what I think, and what will, I am confident, appear to you as true? By the marvellous favor of God our own national character is once more restored to us, after so many centuries, in you, our Augustus. Let the Germans claim you for themselves, if they please; we look upon you as an Italian. Hasten then, as I have so often said, and must continue to say, hasten! I know that the acts of the Caesars

---

2. John of Bohemia had made an expedition into Italy in 1329, and on withdrawing entrusted to Charles (then fifteen) his territory in the Paduan plain and in central Italy. Contemporary chroniclers agree in their praise of the young prince's efforts during 1331–33.

delight you,—and rightly, for you are one of them. The founder
of the Empire moved, it is reported, with such rapidity that he
often arrived before the messengers sent to announce his coming.[3] Follow his example. Strive to rival in deeds him whom
you equal in rank. Do not longer deprive Italy, which deserves
well of you, of your presence. Do not cool our enthusiasm by
continued delay and the despatch of messengers. It is you whom
we desire, it is your celestial countenance that we ask to behold.
If you love virtue (I address our Charles as Cicero addressed
Julius Caesar),[4] and thirst for glory—for you will not disclaim
this thirst, wise though you be—do not, I beseech you, shun
exertion. For he who escapes effort escapes both glory and virtue, which are never attained but by a steep and laborious path.
Arise then and gird up your loins, for we know you to be eager
for true praise and ready for noble toil.

You will rightly place the heaviest burdens in this mighty
undertaking upon the strongest backs, and upon those in the
prime of life, for youth is the suitable time for work, old age
for repose. Surely there is among all your important and sacred
duties none more pressing than that you should restore gentle
peace once more to Italy. This task alone is worthy of your
manly strength; others are too slight to occupy so great and
generous a spirit. Do this first, and the rest will find an appropriate time. Indeed, I cannot but feel that little or nothing
would remain to be done when peace and order were again
established in Italy.

Picture to yourself the Genius of the city of Rome, presenting
herself before you. Imagine a matron, with the dignity of age,
but with her grey locks dishevelled, her garments rent, and her
face overspread with the pallor of misery; and yet with an
unbroken spirit, and unforgetful of the majesty of former days,
she addresses you as follows: "Lest thou shouldst angrily scorn
me, Caesar, know that once I was powerful, and performed great
deeds. I ordained laws, and established the divisions of the year.
I taught the art of war. I maintained myself for five hundred
years in Italy; then, as many a witness will testify, I carried

3. Suetonius, *Life of Caesar* 57.
4. Cicero, *Pro Marcello* 8, 25.

war and victory into Asia, Africa, and Europe, finally compass-
ing the whole world, and by gigantic effort, by wisdom and the
shedding of much blood, I laid the foundation of the rising
Empire. . . .[5] At last the ocean, which I had dyed with the
blood of both my enemies and my children, was subjected to
our fleets, in order that from the seeds of war the flower of
perpetual peace might spring; and by the works of many hands
the Empire might be so established that it should endure until
thy time. Nor was I disappointed in my hopes; my wish was
granted, and I beheld everything beneath my feet. But then, I
know not why, unless it is not fitting that the works of mortals
should prove themselves immortal, my magnificent structure
fell a prey to sloth and indifference.

"I need not relate again the sad story of its decline; thou
canst behold the state to which it is reduced. Thou, who hast
been chosen to succor me when hope had well-nigh deserted
me, why dost thou loiter, why dost thou vainly hesitate and
consider? Assuredly, I never stood in more dire need of assistance, nor hast thou ever been better placed to bear aid. Never
was the Roman pontiff more mildly inclined, nor the favor of
God and man more propitious; never did greater deeds await
this doing. Dost thou still defer? Delay has always been most
fatal to great princes. Would that thou mightest be moved to
emulate the illustrious example of those who left nothing for
old age, but straightway grasped an opportunity which might
offer itself but once. Alexander of Macedon had at thine age
traversed the whole Orient, and, burning to extend his kingdom
over alien races, knocked at the gates of India. Dost thou, who
wouldst only recover thine own, hesitate to enter thy devoted
Italy? At thine age Scipio Africanus crossed into Africa, in
spite of the adverse counsels of older men, and supported with
pious hands an empire tottering upon the verge of ruin. With
an incredible display of valor he freed me from the impending
yoke of Carthage. His was a mighty task, and, by reason of its
unheard-of dangers, memorable to all generations. While war
was bitterly waging in our country he invaded the land of the

_____

5. A page omitted here reviews the gradual extension of Roman power.

enemy. Hannibal, conquerer of Italy, Gaul, and Spain (who was already contemplating, in his dreadful ambition, the dominion of the whole earth), Scipio cast out of Italy and vanquished upon his own soil. But thou hast no seas to cross nor a Hannibal to defeat; the way is free from difficulty, all is open and accessible. Should obstacles present themselves, as some fear, thy presence will shatter them as with a thunderbolt. A vast field of fresh glory spreads out before thee, if thou dost not refuse to enter it. Press bravely, confidently forward. God, the companion and present help of the righteous prince, will be with thee. The armed cohorts of the good and upright will gather about thee, demanding to regain under thy leadership their lost liberty.

"I might urge thee on by examples of another character, of those who by death or by some other insuperable check were unable to bring their glorious undertakings to an end. But we need not look abroad for instances when such excellent illustrations are to be had at home. Without searching the annals, a single example, most familiar to thee, will serve for all, that of Henry VII, thy most serene grandfather of glorious memory.[6] Had his life been spared to accomplish what his noble mind had conceived, how different would have been the fate of Italy! He would have driven his enemies to despair, and would have left me once more queen of a free and happy people. From where he now dwells in heaven he looks down upon thee and considers thy conduct. He counts the days and the hours, and joins me in chiding thy delay. 'Beloved grandson,' he pleads, 'in whom the good place their hope, and in whom I seem still to live, listen to our Rome, give heed to her tears and noble prayers. Carry out my plan of reforming the state, which my death interrupted, working thereby greater harm to the world than to me. Imitate my zeal, fruitless as it was, and mayest thou, with like ardor, bring thy task to a happier and more joyful issue. Begin, lest thou shouldst be prevented; mindful of me, know that thou, too, art mortal. Up, then; surmount the passes! Joyful at thy approach, Rome summons her bridegroom,

6. See William M. Bowsky, *Henry VII in Italy: The Conflict of Empire and City-State, 1310–1313* (Lincoln, Nebr., 1960).

Italy her savior, yearning to hear thy footsteps.[7] The hills and rivers await thy coming in glad anticipation; the cities and towns await thee, as do the hearts of all good men. If there were no other motive for thy departure, a sufficient reason would be found in the opinion of evil men, in whose eyes thou canst never linger too long, and in the belief of the good, that thy coming cannot be unduly hastened. For the sake of both, delay no longer; let the virtuous receive their reward; bring retribution upon the evil, or, if they come to their senses, grant them thy forgiveness. To thee alone God Omnipotent has granted the final glory of my interrupted purpose.' "[8]

30. Reactions to a Ciceromaniac[1]

... What could I say, I who am myself so great an admirer of Cicero's genius? I felt that the old scholar was to be envied for his ardor and devotion, which had something of the Pythagorean savor. I was rejoiced at finding such reverence for even one great man; such almost religious regard, so fervent that to suspect any touch of human weakness in its object seemed like sacrilege. I was amazed, too, at having discovered a person who cherished a love greater than mine for the man whom I always had loved beyond all others; a person who in old age still held, deeply rooted in his heart, the opinions concerning him which

7. Cf. Dante, *Purgatorio* VI, 112–14: "Come and see your Rome that weeps, widowed and alone, crying day and night: 'My Caesar, why are you not with me?' "

8. See C. C. Bayley, "Petrarch, Charles IV, and the 'Renovatio Imperii,' " *Speculum* XVII (1942), 323–41. In his reply (for stylistic help with which he turned to Cola di Rienzo, then languishing in the castle of Raudnitz) Charles answered that Rome was a burden on the Empire, that the aims of a Caesar or an Augustus were no guide in such changed times, and that besides, "doctors wish, and the Caesars learned, that everything should be tried before iron."

1. From *Epistolae Familiares* XXIV, 2 (en route, May 13, 1351), to Enrico Pulice of Vicenza.

I remember to have entertained in my boyhood; and who, notwithstanding his advanced years, was incapable of arguing that if Cicero was a man it followed that in some cases, in many indeed, he must have erred, a conclusion that I have been forced, by common sense and by knowledge of his life, to accept at this earlier stage of my development—although this conviction does not alter the fact that the beauty of his work delights me still, beyond that of any other writer. Why, Tullius himself, the very man of whom we are speaking, took this view, for he often bewailed his errors, bitterly. If, in our eagerness to praise him, we deny that he thus understood himself, we deprive him of a large part of his renown as a philosopher, the praise, namely, that is due to self-knowledge and modesty. . . .

31. Convulsions of Nature[1]

What shall I do first? Shall I voice my laments or my fears? Everywhere there is cause for grief; and all the present woes give promise of deeper woes to come. And yet, I can scarcely conceive what worse evils can possibly be expected. The world has been destroyed and brought to an end by the madness of men and by the avenging hand of God. We have sunk to such depths of misery that no new species of misfortune occurs to the mind. Whosoever, indeed, will narrate the present state of humanity to posterity—provided any descendants survive us— will seem to be recounting mere fables. Nor will it be right to wax indignant if we should be given less credence in matters which we ourselves would not believe from others. As for myself, I frankly confess that the present times, in which mankind has experienced every conceivable evil, have made me more prone to believe many things of which I had been skeptical.

1. *Epistolae Familiares* XI, 7 (dated June 11, 1351, while Petrarch was at Piacenza, en route back to Vaucluse), to Socrates.

I shall pass over those floods and hurricanes and conflagra-
tions, whereby cities that were flourishing one moment perished
root and branch the next. I shall pass over, too, those wars
raging throughout the world and attended by endless slaughter
of men. I shall touch but lightly, furthermore, upon this heaven-
sent plague, unheard of during the ages. They are matters well
known to all. The depopulated cities and the fields deprived
of their tillers bear witness to them; the face of the earth,
afflicted and well-nigh turned into a desert—aye Nature herself,
so to speak—sheds tears of sorrow. These facts, I repeat, are
abundantly known in the lands of the setting sun, as well as
in those of the rising sun; in the regions of Boreas, and in those
of Auster.

But as you know, the Alps were in many places shaken to
their very foundations recently. Thence did the earthquake
proceed; and—oh unusual and dire presage of the future!—a
great portion of both Italy and Germany were simultaneously
rocked. Evils followed which we cannot recollect without tears,
and which it is beyond our power to enumerate. Very recently
we, the insignificant few who seemed to have been snatched
from the universal shipwreck, hoped that the deathly visitation
had abated its ravages, and that the wrath of the Lord had
been appeased. But behold!—and you may perchance be still
in ignorance of this—Rome herself was so violently shaken by
the strange trembling that nothing similar to it had ever there
been known in the two thousand years and more since the
founding of the city.

The massive structures of the ancients fell in ruins, structures
that, though neglected by the citizens, brought amazement to
the stranger. That famous tower called the Torre dei Conti,
unique in the world, was rent by enormous cracks, and fell
apart; and now, with its summit lopped off, it looks down and
beholds strewn upon the ground the glory of its proud head.
Finally, that there may not be lacking positive proofs of the
divine wrath, the appearance of many churches speaks loud in
testimony. Above all, the ruined aspect of a large portion of
the Church of St. Paul the Apostle, and the fallen roof of the

Church of St. John the Lateran saddened the fervor of the
Jubilee and caused the pilgrims to shudder. With the Church of
St. Peter, however, Nature dealt more kindly.

These occurrences are unprecedented—and justly do they
deject the spirits of many. For, if the trembling of the limbs
did presage the occurrence of such dread calamities, what is
not now threatened by the trembling of the head? Aye, let those
who judge themselves of some authority fume and fret; let them
murmur their disapprobation. Nonetheless, Rome is the head
of the world. Though grown old and unkept, Rome is undoubtedly the head of all nations. The world itself would not
deny this, could it speak to me with one voice; and if the world
should not acknowledge it on good authority, it would be conquered by written proofs.

That I may not, however, be deemed a most malignant
prophet of evil in the hour of adversity, or be thought to have
created unfounded fears, I shall free myself from such charges
by citing the examples of the recent ills that have befallen us,
and also by appealing to the authority of Pliny, a writer rank-
ing among the very highest. To avoid even the suspicion of
warping his statements, I shall quote him verbatim. He says:
"Indeed, the evil is not free from complications, nor does the
danger lie only in the earthquake itself, but it is a portent of
an equal or of a greater danger. Never has the city of Rome
trembled without its being the omen of some future disaster."
These are Pliny's very words.[2] Why, therefore, should I now
remain silent? Or why repeat them? I am speaking thus to
you because you belong to those of our generation who dearly
love the Roman republic. What matters it, forsooth, where you
first drew breath? I consider your disposition rather, which our
friendship has rendered quite distinctly Italian.

Wherefore, my dear Socrates, give me your close attention.
I feel deep concern for the highest welfare of the republic, and
sad forebodings cause me to tremble not so much for Rome
as for the whole of Italy. I fear not so much the convulsions

2. *Natural History* II, 84 (86), 200.

of Nature, as indeed the upheavals of men's minds. I am terrified by many things, but above all by that ancient prophecy
uttered so long before the City was founded, and inserted not
in any minor writings but in the sacred Scriptures themselves.
Though I was then entirely absorbed in secular literature, and
not familiar with the Scriptures, I confess that when I first read
it I shuddered, and the blood in my heart grew cold and chill.
The utterance is in the final words of the last prophecy of
Balaam. I shall quote it here, to relieve you of the labor of
running through the pages. Thus, then, is it written: "They
shall come in galleys from Italy, they shall overcome the Assy-
rians, and shall waste the Hebrews, and at the last they themselves also shall perish."[3]

Some may hold that this prophecy has long since been fulfilled in the fall of the Roman Empire; but I trust that this
recent trembling of the city does not portend a second overthrow of peace and of liberty. However, steady your faltering
spirits upon the strong foundation of your virtues and your
firmness. In spite of quaking earth, may you remain unshaken
in your secure abode; may you be like unto him of whom
Horace speaks:[4]

> Should the whole frame of Nature round him break,
> In ruin and confusion hurled,
> He, unconquered, would hear the mighty crack,
> And stand secure amidst a falling world.

I wrote this letter to you while I was still at Padua, but it
was delayed in sending as late as today for want of a messenger.
It has pleased me to dispatch it to you from this city, for no
other reason than to humor this mutual friend of ours, who
refused to go to you without bearing a letter from me. For that
matter, there was no need of either messenger or letter, since
I myself am just about to follow him. When, therefore, you
read this letter, know that I am already near. You will give
me pleasure indeed, if you should come to meet me at the
Fountain of the Sorgue. Remember me always, and farewell.

3. Numbers 24, 24.
4. *Odes* III, iii, 7–8 (trans. Addison).

32. Reform of the Roman Government[1]

. . . I trust you do not doubt that the city of Rome shelters many who are nobler and better than those who only boast of a noble name, but who are a burden to heaven and to earth. I shall not refuse to call them noble, if they will act accordingly; but surely, not only I, but Rome herself denies them the name of Romans. Let us grant that they are nobles, and Romans too. Are they still to be preferred to our ancestors, the defenders of justice, the protectors of the down-trodden, the conquerors of haughty nations and the builders of empire? Though great their impudence, they will not dare to make this claim. If, then, our ancestral Romans yielded, let not the barons feel shame in likewise yielding to the plebeians, who justly demand that they shall not live in their own city as if in exile, and that they shall not be excluded from public office, as if they were a diseased member of the body politic.

In this regard, it may behoove us to remember what Aristotle says.[2] As in the case of those who straighten the plant that grows one-sided, so must you compel these nobles not only to share with the rest the senatorial and other dignities, but also

1. From *Epistolae Familiares* XI, 16 (November 18, 1351), to the four cardinals appointed by Clement VI as a commission to reform the government of Rome. Although Petrarch again assails the Roman nobility at great length, he observes at one point: "That no one may suspect my words to be prompted by even the slightest malice, it may not be inappropriate to mention here, by way of parenthesis, that, of the two families whence all this trouble arises, I do not hate the one, whereas the other (needless to say) I do not merely love, but indeed have cherished throughout a long period of almost familiar intercourse. In fact, I wish to state here that none of the princely families of this world has been dearer to me than the latter. Nevertheless the public welfare is even dearer to me. Dearer is Rome, dearer is Italy, dearer the peace and the security of the upright."

2. *Nicomachean Ethics* II, 9, 1109b5.

to surrender unconditionally and for a long period all the privileges which they have so long usurped through their own arrogance and the patient suffering of the plebeians. And you must persevere along these lines until the republic, like unto the one-sided plant, will have bent in the opposite direction and thus have returned to its proper, erect position.

These are my opinions, this I beg of you on bended knee, this venerable Rome tearfully implores of you. If you display lack of energy in restoring her liberty, she will call you to account before the tribunal of the dreadful Judge. Christ orders you to re-establish her freedom, Christ, who will stand in your midst as you deliberate, that he may shield unto the very end those whom he chose in the beginning. The apostles Peter and Paul entreat it, who inspired the Roman Pontiff to confide this sacred duty to none other than to you. Give heed to the silent prayers of these saints, and you will find it very easy to spurn the hostile wishes and the pressure of all others. Finally, consider not what may please the pride of others, but only what best becomes your own integrity, and what will be of the greatest advantage to Rome, to Italy, and to the world.

33. Avignon[1]

If I should wish to commit to writing all that my soul feels on the condition of affairs in this western Babylon, of which I so frequently become a resident either through fate or rather in atonement for my sins, I fear, O reverend Father, lest I should heighten my grief by my laments, or lest, by my inopportune and unavailing complaints, I should interrupt your most holy cares and most honorable occupations. In fine, rest

1. *Epistolae Sine Nomine* VIII (from Avignon, probably winter 1351–52), to Ildebrandino Conti, the bishop of Padua. In these "Letters Without Name" Petrarch excoriates the papacy so fiercely that a measure of discretion obviously seemed advisable.

The Bettmann Archive

4. Petrarch and Laura introduced to the emperor at Avignon. Engraving.

assured that neither my pen nor even that of Cicero could render
the subject justice. Whatsoever you have read of the Assyrian
Babylon, or of the Egyptian Babylon; whatsoever you have
read of the four labyrinths, of the threshold of Avernus and
of the forests of Tartarus and its lakes of sulphur, is but a mere
fable when compared to these infernal regions.

Here in Avignon there is Nimrod,[2] builder of turrets and at
the same time sower of dread; here there is Semiramis,[3] armed
with the quiver; here is Minos, inexorably severe; here is Rhada-
manthus; here is Cerberus, the all-devouring; here is Pasiphae,
yoked to the Bull; here, in the words of Virgil, is the

> Minotaur, of mingled race,
> Memorial of her foul disgrace.[4]

Here, finally, may you behold whatever chaos, whatever viru-
lence, whatever horror exists anywhere or can be conceived.

O you who have ever been happy in your good qualities, well
may you now be happy for your absence from Avignon. Do you
think that this city is as you once beheld it? Far different is it,
and far unlike it. The Avignon of former days was, to be sure,
the worst of cities, and the most abominable of its day. But the
Avignon of today, indeed, can no longer be considered a city.
It is the home of spooks and of goblins, of ghosts and of spec-
ters. In a word, it is now the sink of all iniquities and disgrace;
it is now that Hell of the Living sung by the lips of David so
long before Avignon was founded and known.[5]

Alas! How frequently your truly fatherly advice recurs to
my mind, your wholesome admonitions, when you said to me
as I was making preparations for my departure: "Where are
you going? What are you doing? What ambition drags you and
makes you forgetful of yourself? Do you not know what you
seek and what you abandon? Hence do I ask, what is it you
are setting about so keenly? Whither are you hastening? If I
have come to know you well, I assure you that you will repent

---

2. Pope Clement VI, who was fond of hunting.
3. Clement's mistress, the countess of Turenne.
4. *Aeneid* VI, 25–26.
5. Psalm 54, 16 [55, 15].

of your course. Do you, who have so frequently experienced the snares and fetters of the Curia, not know that, when you have once been entrapped thereby, you will not be able to release yourself at will?"

When you had concluded with these and other persuasive arguments, I had no answer to make except that I was returning to well-known afflictions because I was held fast by my love for my friends. Thus did I answer you, nor did I speak falsely. Up to this day I have not repented of that love, but I am uncertain whether I repent having lost my liberty out of love for my friends. I assure you that I am grateful for your counsels, so ill received then and now approved of at a late hour. Hitherto, my not hearkening to your words of advice has not been unattended by mortification. But I shall obey you better hereafter, if ever I escape hence. Of this I do not despair, if Christ stretch forth his hand. To this end do I bend my energies.

It was a sense of shame, Father, that forbade my writing this to you sooner; for it is shameful and unbecoming in a man to wish that which he shortly afterward no longer wishes.

34. Lombardy and Tuscany[1]

. . . Cisalpine Gaul, in which is what the people call Lombardy but the learned call Liguria, Emilia, Venetia, and whatever lies between the Alps and the Apennines and the Rubicon, Italy's ancient border—almost all this great area is oppressed by an endless tyranny. And that part of it which, looking toward the west, sits under the foot of the mountains—O the offensiveness of fortune!—has become an approach for tyrants from across the Alps. And so not even there will you find anyplace where a friend of virtue and tranquillity may enjoy com-

1. From *Epistolae Familiares* XV, 7 (April, 1352), to Stefano Colonna (great-grandson of Stefano the Elder), provost of Saint-Omer.

plete repose, except that renowned city of the Venetians, which
although it has been thus far the only sanctuary of liberty and
justice, is nevertheless now shaken by so great tumult of war[2]
—and besides, even should she regain her former peace, has
always been so much fitter for commerce than the Muses—that
I doubt whether residence there could please you.

Tuscany was once the most flourishing of lands: as Livy
recalls,[3] she had filled the whole world with the renown of her
name and works. The extent of her prosperity long before the
time of the Roman Empire is witnessed by many things, especially the fact that although countless peoples live along the
two seas that gird Italy, Tuscany alone, with everyone's consent, gave to the double sea a name that will last as long as
time. Today, her step faltering between uncertain liberty and
dreaded servitude, she is in doubt which direction she will
fall. . . .

35. Cola in Avignon[1]

What do you expect to find in this letter? Do you think that
I shall complete the mournful, and, at the same time, ridiculous
tale of my last letter to you?[2] To be sure, there is just now
nothing of greater importance to do; or rather, there are many
such tasks, but lack of time forbids me to apply myself to those
of greater importance. What little time I have is not at my own

2. Against Genoa.
3. Livy V, 33, 7.

1. *Epistolae Familiares* XIII, 6 (from Vaucluse, August 10, 1352), to
Francesco Nelli, prior of Santi Apostoli in Florence. The correspondence
between Petrarch and Nelli is surveyed by Wilkins in *Italia Medioevale e
Umanistica* I (1958), 351–58.

2. Petrarch's friends had been advancing him for the office of apostolic
secretary, a position for which he felt something less than enthusiasm. Since
there was official concern about his style—could Petrarch write low
enough?—when he received his theme he purposely disqualified himself by
writing as loftily as possible.

disposal, but is clogged with truly remarkable interruptions. Even I am constantly on the go; I find myself in the midst of turmoil and of confusion; I am here and there at once, with the result that I never really get anywhere. This is the familiar evil attending all wanderers. But recently I departed from Babylon and came to a halt at the Fountain of the Sorgue, the well-known refuge from the storms which beset me.

Here I await some traveling companions and the end of autumn, or at least that season described by Virgil, when "the days are shorter, and the heat milder."[3] In the meantime, therefore, that my stay in the country may not be altogether fruitless, I am bringing together the scattered fragments of previous meditations. My daily endeavor is, if possible, to add a little to the larger works which I have in hand, or to put finishing touches to some of the minor ones.[4] Learn from this letter, then, the task which I have set myself for today.

Poetry, a divine gift bestowed upon only a few, begins to be the common property of the mob. This is putting it mildly, for I might well say that poetry is now desecrated and degraded. There is nothing which stirs greater wrath within me; and if I have come to know your tastes, my friend, I am sure that you too can in no way tolerate such an affront. Never at Athens or at Rome, never in the times of Homer or of Virgil, was there so much prattle about poets as there is today along the banks of the Rhone. And yet I am positive that in no place and at no time was there such profound ignorance of the subject of poetry. Appease your wrath with laughter, please; and learn to be merry in the midst of sorrow.

There recently came to the Curia, or rather, he did not come, but was led here a prisoner, Cola di Rienzo, formerly the widely feared Tribune of Rome, today the most wretched of men. He has now touched the very lowest depths of misfortune; for, though he is extremely miserable, I know not whether he is by any means to be pitied. He might have died a glorious death

---

3. *Georgics* I, 312. Petrarch actually started for Italy in November, but had to turn back; he was not to escape Provence until the following spring.

4. The larger works would be the *De Viris Illustribus* and the *Familiares;* the minor, poems in Latin and Italian.

on the Capitol; but he has submitted to the chains first of a
Bohemian, and then of a Limousin[5]—to his everlasting disgrace
and in mockery of the Roman name and republic.

The constant praises and exhortations in which my pen was
so busily engaged are perhaps better known than I should wish
at present. I loved his virtues, praised his aims, and marveled
at the courage of the man. I congratulated Italy; I foresaw the
empire of the bountiful city, and anticipated the peace of the
entire world. I could not repress the joyous feelings springing
from such numerous causes, and it seemed to me that I should
partake of his glory, if I should goad him on in his course. And,
indeed, his messengers and letters to me bear witness that he
esteemed my words most potent incentives. The heat of my
enthusiasm became more intense thereat. I racked my brain
to devise means whereby I might the more inflame his already
glowing spirit. I knew full well that nothing enkindles a generous heart more readily than praises and the prospects of glory;
hence I constantly introduced words of high praise, which to
many appeared extravagant, but which to me seemed justly
deserved. I lauded the deeds already performed, and urged him
to the performance of others.

There are extant several letters which I wrote to him, letters
which even today it does not displease me to have written. I
am not accustomed to predict the future; and would that he,
too, had not been addicted to prophecy! Verily, the deeds which
he was performing and which he gave promise of performing
at the time when I wrote, were most deserving not only of my
praise and admiration, but of that of the whole human race.
I hardly think that all those letters should be destroyed for
this one false step: that he chose to live in shame rather than
to die in glory. But it is a waste of time to deliberate on the
impossible. Though great should be my desire to destroy them,
I am now powerless. They have gone forth into the world, and
are no longer subject to my control.

But to resume my story. Rienzo entered the Curia, humbled
and despised, he who once had made the wicked of this world

5. The Emperor Charles IV and Pope Clement VI.

to tremble and to fear, and who had filled the upright with the most joyful hopes and expectations. Once upon a time, he was attended by the whole people of Rome, and in his train followed the princes of the Italic cities. Today the unhappy man proceeded on his way, hemmed in on this side and on that by two guards, while the rabble eagerly rushed forward to gaze upon the face of him whose illustrious name they had heard of only. He was being sent to the Roman Pontiff by the king of the Romans! Oh strange traffic indeed! I do not dare commit to writing the thoughts which now rush to my brain. Not even this much did I intend should escape me; and so I shall continue with the story which I began.

Upon his arrival, then, the Supreme Pontiff immediately appointed three princes of the church to try his case, with instructions to discover the most suitable punishment for him who desired the freedom of the republic. *O tempora, o mores!*[6] Alas, how often is it necessary in our age, to utter these words of exclamation! In a certain sense, I admit that no penalty is too severe for Cola; firstly, because he did not persevere in his aims as steadfastly as he should have, and as the condition and the needs of the state demanded; and secondly, because, having once declared himself liberty's champion, he should not have permitted the enemies of liberty to depart in arms, when he could have crushed them all at a single blow, an opportunity which fortune had never offered to any ruler. Fatal and dreadful darkness, which often obscures the sight of men as they struggle over projects of supreme importance![7]

He was wont to style himself "severe and clement." Forsooth, if he had determined to put into practice only the second part of this title, and not that other part which was quite necessary on account of the disease of the republic; if, I say, he had determined to display only mercy to the traitors of their country, he should at least, in sparing their lives, have deprived them of all means for working injury, and especially should he have

6. Cicero, *In Catilinam* I, 1, 2.
7. Cola had arrested the Roman nobles at a banquet, then released them the next day. He also failed to follow up his victory over them on November 20, 1347.

driven them from their frowning strongholds. In this way, those who had previously been enemies of Rome would have become her citizens; or, at any rate, those who had been a source of constant fear would have become an object of contempt. I remember having written to him a well-pondered letter on that occasion. Had he heeded its substance, the republic would now be in a far different condition. Rome would not be, today, the slave of others, nor he a prisoner.

I cannot forgive this, nor do I see how his subsequent actions can very well be excused. Although he had assumed the protection of all good citizens, and the extermination of all wicked ones, it was only after a short interval that he unexpectedly changed in purpose and in manners, began to favor the wicked, and to place in these his whole trust, greatly to the dismay and the detriment of the upright. Rienzo himself may perhaps know the motives of his actions, for I have not seen him since; but surely the excuse for a misdeed, though it may always be readily framed by a man of eloquence, never can have the ring of truth. Would at least that he had not chosen the very lowest of the low! Once again did I write to him on the subject, and at a time when the republic had not yet fallen, but was already tottering.

But enough, I am speaking with too great ardor, and I dwell in sadness (as you see) on the different steps of my story. And naturally so, for I had placed in that man my last hope for the liberties of Italy. I had long known him, and cherished him; but when he began to essay that most glorious enterprise, I allowed myself to love and worship him beyond all other mortals. And, therefore, the more I hoped in the past, the more do I now grieve at the destruction of those hopes. I frankly confess that, whatever the end of it all may be, even now I cannot help admiring his glorious beginning.

But to return once more to my story. He came, but not in chains. This alone was lacking to his public disgrace; as for the rest, he was so carefully guarded that there was no hope of escape. As soon as they reached the city gate, the poor unfortunate inquired whether I was in attendance at the Curia, hoping, perhaps, that I might be of some assistance to him (which, to my knowledge, I cannot be), or else simply because he was reminded of an old friendship formerly contracted in that very city.[8] Now, therefore, the life of that man in whose hands rested the safety and the welfare of so many nations, hangs upon the nod of strangers. His life and his name are alike at stake. Do not be surprised at the outcome; men are now wavering in their opinions, and you will be sure to hear one of two sentences; either that he has been deprived of all legal rights, or else that he has been condemned to death.[9] The clay of any mortal creature, even of the most sacred and pure, can indeed be destroyed; but virtue fears neither death nor reproach. Virtue is invulnerable, and survives uninjured all calumny and attack.

And oh that he had not stained his honor by his own lethargy and change of purpose! He would have nothing to fear from the sentence pending over him except physical injury. And yet, even today his fame is not in danger among those who judge of right and of wrong, of glory and of shame, not according to the general opinion but according to certain and more reliable tests. His fame rests secure with those who measure the greatness of men by considering the noble qualities they have displayed, and not the success which has attended their undertakings.

That this is so results most clearly from the nature of the charge brought against him. No account is taken of the many errors with which all upright citizens upbraid him. He is accused for that which he did at the opening of his career, and not at all for that which signalized its close. He is not accused of embracing the cause of the wicked, nor of deserting the standard of liberty, nor of fleeing from the Capitol, although in no other place could he have lived more honorably, or died more gloriously. What, then, is the charge, you may ask? This is the one

8. Cola and Petrarch had become well acquainted at Avignon in 1343.

9. As it turned out, Cola became the weapon of Innocent VI against a second Roman tribune, Francesco Baroncelli (elected on September 14, 1353). Cola followed Cardinal Albornoz, vicar-general of Italy and the Papal States, who took possession of Rome in November. Cola himself did not enter the city until August 1, 1354. He ruled briefly as senator, then was assassinated in October.

great crime for which he is brought to trial, and if he be condemned for this, I shall consider him to have been marked not
with infamy but with eternal glory: he has dared to entertain
the hope that the republic should be restored to safety and to
freedom, and that questions of the Roman empire and the
Roman dominion should be settled at Rome. A crime, this,
worthy of the gallows and the attendant vultures, indeed! This,
surely, is the sum and substance of the accusation, and it is for
this that punishment is demanded: that a Roman citizen should
have voiced his grief at seeing his country, the rightful queen
of the universe, the slave of the vilest of men!

Now at last listen to that which first prompted me to write,
and you will have good cause for laughter after the sad recital
which has preceded. While the trial is in this unsettled state,
I learn from the letters of friends that one hope of safety still
remains—the rumor which has spread abroad that Rienzo is
a most famous poet! Consequently it seems an act of sacrilege
to do violence to a man so worthy and dedicated to so sacred
a study. The magnificent phrases which Cicero addressed to
the judges in defense of his teacher Aulus Licinius Archias are
now upon the lips of everyone.[10] Many years ago I brought
back that speech from far-off Germany, whither I had roamed
impelled by my youthful desire to visit those regions; and the
following year I sent it on to you all at Florence, who were so
eagerly expecting it. I do not stop to cite the passage; for I
can readily see from your letters that you still prize that famous
oration, and still read it with care.

What shall I say of this strange rumor? I heartily rejoice.
I deem it a cause for endless congratulation that the Muses
are held so much in honor even today. The following is even
more astonishing: that the mere mention of the Muses should
be potent enough to bring safety to one who is hated by his
very judges, men who are quite unacquainted with their re-
fining influence.

What greater victory could the Muses have scored under
Augustus Caesar, an age when they were most highly honored,

---

10. *Pro Archia,* viii.

and when, from every land, poets assembled at Rome to behold the noble countenance of him who was at once an unparalleled prince, the friend of poets, and the master of the universe? What greater tribute, I ask, could have been paid to the Muses in those days than this which we witness today: that a man undoubtedly hated (though how just or unjust the hatred I do not stop to prove), and entirely free from all guilt (yet pronounced guilty and convicted), a man who, by the unanimous vote of his judges was deemed worthy of capital punishment, that this man, I say, should be snatched from the very jaws of death by an appeal to the Muses? I repeat, I rejoice, and congratulate both him and the Muses. I congratulate him, because the Muses have been his shield; and the Muses, because of this honor so freely bestowed. I do not begrudge him that, in his hour of extreme need and when the trial has assumed such a doubtful aspect, the rumor of his being a poet should bring him salvation.

If, however, you were to ask me my private opinion, I should answer that Cola di Rienzo is a very fluent speaker, possessing great convincing powers and a decided vein for oratory; and that as a writer, though not extensive, is charming and brilliant. I suppose he has read all the poets, at least those who are generally known; but he is no more a poet for that reason than he would be a weaver for robing himself with a mantle wrought by another's hands. The mere production of verses is not sufficient to merit for the composer the name of poet. Most true are the words of Horace:[11]

> For one certainly should never say this, "I know it's
> Quite enough to give lines their six feet," or suppose
> Those true bards who, like me, write what's much more like prose.

As for Cola, never, to my knowledge, has he managed to write a single line; nor has he devoted to the subject of poetry the slightest study, and without application nothing can be well done, no matter how easy it be.

I have wished to acquaint you with these facts, that you may

---

11. *Satires* I, iv, 40–42.

grieve over the lot which has befallen the former deliverer of
a people, that you may rejoice at this unhoped-for freedom,
and thirdly, that you may, at one and the same time, weep and
laugh over the cause of his safety, even as I do now. Stop to
consider for a moment. If, under the shield of poetry, Cola escapes uninjured from such great perils (and may it so fall
out!), what dangers would Virgil not escape? If tried by the
judges of this generation, Virgil, however, would perish for
other reasons: for today he is considered not a poet, but a
sorcerer.[12] Indeed, I shall now tell you something that will increase your mirth. Even I, the most inveterate enemy that
ever was of both divination and sorcery, even I have at times
been pronounced a magician by these most worthy judges—
and all because of my intimacy with Virgil. Behold how low
our studies have fallen! Behold to what hateful and ridiculous
trifles they are reduced! . . .[13]

As for yourself, may you live happily and well. And unless
you think otherwise, when you are through reading today's
letter and yesterday's, send them on to our dear Zanobi at
Naples, so that both he and my Barbato may share our mirth
and our indignation, provided, of course, that Barbato has by
this time left his haven at Solmona and has returned to the
stormy waters of Parthenope.

12. Cf. J. W. Spargo, *Vergil the Necromancer* (Cambridge, Mass., 1934);
and Domenico Comparetti, *Vergil in the Middle Ages,* trans. E. F. M. Be-
necke (reprint: London, 1966).

13. When an apostolic secretaryship was offered Petrarch ten years later,
he wrote to Cardinal Talleyrand: "You know, in truth, how often we joked
over these accusations, and several times even in the presence of him
[Cardinal Aubert] whom my accuser had persuaded. But when at last he
[Aubert] had been raised to the papal see [as Innocent VI], then the accusation ceased to be a jesting matter, and it began to turn to wrath with
you, and to grief with me. It is not that I especially desired anything of
him, for all my desires are well known to you. But since Benedict had
judged my youth, and Clement my manhood, and since they had found me,
I do not say innocent, but at any rate averse to base studies and to in-
jurious arts, I could not but grieve that my old age had been suspected by
Innocent. Therefore, at the time that he ascended the sacred chair [Decem-
ber 30, 1352], I left Avignon not knowing whether or not I should ever
return. And though, in compliance with even his wishes, you had desired
to take me to him that I might bid him farewell, I refused, lest my magical
arts should annoy him, or lest his credulity should annoy me."

36. War Against Aragon[1]

What I was wishing for I now see happening: you are turning your victorious standards from the east to the west. Here I entreat you to press forward, brave men: pursue this patriotic, this just, this holy war which is by no means between Italians. Here I want you to employ your courage and your knowledge of military matters; here I want you to follow up the attack. The prime root of these evils must be extirpated by your axes. Here is that perjured king,[2] who cooked up legalistic pretexts when he declared war on you. You answered, with equal truth and spirit, that his pretexts were contrived with empty words, that the real cause of his madness was greed, but that he was selling his own honor and his people's blood for a poor price and would repent at a late hour what he was doing early in the day. . . .

1. From *Epistolae Familiares* XIV, 6 (February or March, 1353), to the doge and Council of Genoa.

Although Venice was allied with Aragon and with the Byzantine emperor, Genoa had won the first battle, fought a year before this in the Bosporus. Now against Aragon Genoa had formed an alliance with a powerful Sardinian rebel.

2. Peter IV of Aragon (1336–87), whose grandfather, John II (king of Sicily as well), had begun the expulsion of the Genoese and Pisans from Sardinia (1323–24)—a process that lasted almost a century.

Milan: 1353-61

37. Return to Italy[1]

Hail, land most holy, dear to God,
Safe for the good, but for the proud to fear,
Land far nobler than noble climes,
More fertile and more fair than all the rest,
Girt by a twofold sea and crowned with mountains,   5
Venerable alike for arms and sacred laws,
Home of the Muses, rich in gold and men—
On your uncommon favors art and nature
Were both intent, and gave the world its mistress.
To you I eagerly return at last   10
To dwell forever. You will give repose
For my tired life, and finally enough earth
To cover my pale limbs. With joy I see you
From the lofty hill of flowering Gebenna.
The clouds remain behind; a breeze serene   15
Blows in my face, the air's caress receives me.
I know my homeland, greet it with delight:
Hail, beautiful mother, glory of the earth.

---

1. *Epistolae Metricae* III, 24. Petrarch left Vaucluse in late May or early June of 1353, entered Italy through the pass of Mont Genèvre ("Gebenna"), and arrived in Milan at the end of June or at the beginning of July. This poem may be compared with Virgil, *Georgics* II, 136–74 (the *Laudes Italiae*).

38. Poetry Versus Medicine[1]

... I come now to the heavily armed wedges of syllogisms in which, as if in picked cavalry, you place all your hope of victory, so that here also your capability appears. Right away there is one sufficient token of your folly, when, digressing from the praises of medicine (which are many, if you did not diminish them by not so much talking as bellowing), and seized by a sudden madness, without any cause you fall furiously upon the poets and—in your usual way mixing up what you know and what you do not—force me to laugh again. In the first place, I could easily parry your calumny with a few words. You attack the poets—what is this to me? Let the poets answer, or—more fittingly—disdain you; for you are not of such consequence that you should be strongly opposed. Poetry is not in need of my help, nor do I make myself out a poet, for "I do not consider myself worthy such honor," as Virgil says.[2] And if you should say I am a poet, or if perhaps others have wished to say so, nevertheless my argument with you has absolutely nothing to do with the matter of poetry. But since you were unable to grasp this in my other letter to you, and when one's mind is tired discussions of this sort are sometimes agreeable even with fools, I shall

---

1. From the *Invective Contra Medicum,* Book III, Petrarch's most extended defense of poetry. When Clement VI was ill in 1352, Petrarch wrote advising him to remove himself from the swarm of doctors, who, being mere charlatans, were endangering his life, and to choose a reliable one. A doctor of the papal court took umbrage and had a polemical response written. When Petrarch responded in a letter, the doctor obtained aid in the composition of a pamphlet that was finished early in 1353. Petrarch's answer was composed a little before his departure from Vaucluse; then in Milan he arranged his replies into a single work, Book I of which consists of his letter, Books II–IV of his additions from 1353.

2. *Aeneid* I, 335.

not be annoyed at slogging on and hearing whatever nonsense it has pleased you to utter.

When you belch many things against the poets with that rash, sluggish, viscous and medicine-smeared tongue, as if they were adversaries of the true faith and to be avoided by the faithful and had been banished from the Church, first of all I'd like to ask what you feel about Ambrose, Augustine, Jerome, Cyprian, the martyr Victorinus, Lactantius, and other Catholic writers. Almost no lasting work of theirs is built without the lime of the poets, while on the contrary almost none of the heretics has inserted anything poetical in his works, whether from ignorance or because nothing there harmonized with his errors. The poets do mention many names of gods, but we should believe they did so in compliance with the nature of their times and peoples rather than their own judgment. The same thing was done by the philosophers, who, as we read in the *Rhetoric*,[3] do not believe that there are gods. Nevertheless, the greatest of the poets have acknowledged in their works one omnipotent, all-creating, all-ruling God, the maker of things.[4]

But you will answer that you do not know what goes on in Catholic writers, since in fact you read only Galien's *Terapentica*,[5] which you say I have not read. Receive to this that answer of the distinguished general Marius: "I have not learned Greek letters: it little pleased me to do so, since for virtue they had been of no use to those who had learned them."[6] Certainly if that *Terepentica* of yours had made you better or more learned or at least healthier, I should be sorry not to have read it. But while I behold you within and without, I thank my judgment or my fortune, through which I am clear of that reading which made you what you are, if it would have been for me what it is for you. . . .

3. Cf. Cicero, *De Inventione* I, 29, 46.
4. On this "theology of the poets," see the references cited by Hans Baron in *The Crisis of the Early Italian Renaissance* (Princeton, 1955), II, 556 ff.
5. "Galienus" was how Galen was known in the Middle Ages. The title Petrarch has in mind is Galen's *De Therapeutica ad Glauconem*.
6. Sallust, *Bellum Iugurthinum* 85, 32.

You do not admit poetry among the liberal arts, and that you can do by your authority as a master of philosophy and the arts. But Homer and Virgil beseech you at least not to exclude them from the mechanical arts, since—and you can't hide it—you are yourself a mechanic.[7] You say philosophy is yours, others say you are a mechanic. You do not receive the poets in your order? You will be cruel indeed if you will have repulsed them even from there! But, joking aside, reckon the liberal arts: will you find there—I do not say medicine, which dwells elsewhere and is sixth among the mechanical— but the name of philosophy itself? Often not being placed among great things is evidence of a certain extraordinary magnitude. I'll give you a clear historical example. (You'd be gladder, I'm sure, to listen to the tales you are accustomed to hear after dinner before the fire, about ogres and witches; but since in years you are now no boy, accustom yourself to something better if you can.) In Livy, Hannibal himself, a man very learned indeed in his art, was asked which military leaders of all peoples he estimated as the most illustrious. When he had named Alexander of Macedon first, Pyrrhus of Epirus second, and himself third (a sign not of pride but of his self-confidence, about which I have said much), he was reminded that he had passed by Africanus, by whom it was agreed he had been conquered. His response surely indicates that it was not from forgetfulness or envy that he had been silent, but as a mark of singular praise for the greatest among the great, or for the incomparable among the greatest. To quote Livy himself, "he had distinguished Africanus from the troop of generals as inestimable."[8] About which many things could be said; but enough has been said for him who understands, and too much for him who does not. . . .

7. The liberal arts were grammar, rhetoric, dialectic, arithmetic, music, geometry, and astronomy (the Trivium and Quadrivium); the mechanical were wool weaving, armor, navigation, agriculture, hunting, medicine, and theater.

8. Livy XXXV, 14, 12.

39. Unease in Milan[1]

... For my part, I don't know whether it is my fault or fortune which has deprived me of my pleasant hiding place;[2] thus far in my frequent attempts at flight I have always been betrayed by my reputation, which is more loquacious and mendacious than I should wish. So I, from my earliest years such a lover of solitude and of the woods, labor now at a more advanced age in cities and amidst the hateful multitude; and I find it unpleasant. Often there come to my mind those words of Vespasian, who is reported to have said, when on the day of his triumph he felt oppressed by the extended pomp and the tediousness of the hubbub, that he was deservedly punished for having aspired—at such a shamefully late stage—to that honor, which he had never expected and which did not befit his ancestors.[3] Dignified and temperate words, indeed. I have only one excuse, because although I should not deny that I am desirous of true praise, I do not remember having striven after this pomp which is doing me in.

I have gone this far astray in my zeal to converse; let this be at last an end of the conversation, so that you may perceive —although one labor leads to another, and amidst my labors there arise every day new causes and matter for labor—that nevertheless I think of liberty even while in bonds, of the country while in cities, of repose amidst labors, and finally (to turn inside out that well-worn saying of my Africanus) of ease while I am busy.[4] Meanwhile know that some art or nature has

1. From *Epistolae Familiares* XVII, 10 (from Milan, January 1, 1354), to Giovanni Aghinolfi, one of several friends who had reproached Petrarch for settling in Milan at the invitation of the archbishop Giovanni Visconti. (Boccaccio was especially outraged and incredulous.)
2. Vaucluse.
3. Suetonius, *Life of Vespasian* 12.
4. *"in negotiis de otio cogitare"*—cf. Cicero, *De Officiis* III, 1, 1: *"in otio de negotiis cogitare"* (a major theme of Petrarch's *De Vita Solitaria*).

granted to me that by constant strong meditation I render worthless what I cannot achieve and pleasant what I am unable to avoid. Live mindful of me, and farewell.

40. Thanks for a Manuscript of Homer in Greek[1]

. . . I rejoice in possessing such a friend as you, wherever you may be. But your living voice, which could both rouse and sate my burning thirst for learning, no longer sounds in my ears. Without it your Homer is dumb to me, or rather I am deaf to him. Nevertheless I rejoice at his mere physical presence; often I clasp him to my bosom and say with a sigh: "O great man, how gladly would I hear you speak! But death has stopped one of my ears, and hateful remoteness has blocked the other."[2] Nevertheless I am very grateful to you for your magnificent gift.

I have long had a copy of Plato;[3] it came to me from the west, rather remarkably. He was the prince of philosophers, as you know. I am not afraid that you, with your intelligence, will object, like certain scholastics, to this statement. Cicero himself would not object, nor Seneca nor Apuleius nor Plotinus, that great Platonist, nor in later times our Ambrose and Augustine. Now by your bounty the prince of Greek poets joins the prince of philosophers. Who would not rejoice and glory in housing such guests? I have indeed of both of them all that

1. From *Epistolae Familiares* XVIII, 2 (from Milan, January 10, 1354), to Nicholas Sygeros, whom Petrarch had met in Verona in 1348, when Sygeros had come west as Byzantine envoy to the papal court.
2. Petrarch laments the remoteness of Sygeros and the death of Barlaam, an Orthodox priest who had given him instruction in Greek at Avignon in 1342. On Barlaam see K. M. Setton, "The Byzantine Background to the Italian Renaissance," American Philosophical Society, *Proceedings,* 100 (1956), 40–45.
3. See Aubrey Diller, "Petrarch's Greek Codex of Plato," *Classical Philology* LIX (1964), 270–72.

has been translated into Latin from their own tongue.[4] But it
is certainly a pleasure, though no advantage, to regard the
Greeks in their own dress. Nor have the years robbed me of
all hope of making progress in your language; after all, we see
that Cato made great strides in Greek at a very advanced age.

If you want anything that I can provide, feel free to call upon
me without hesitation. You will see that I call freely upon you.
And since the success of prayer begets still bolder prayers, I
ask you to send me, if available, a Hesiod; and send me, I beg,
Euripides.

So farewell, worthiest of men. And since my name is well
known in the west, not for my merits but by the favor of men
or of fortune, may you be pleased to mention it among the illustrious men of the Oriental palace. Thus may the Emperor of
Constantinople not disdain one whom the Roman Caesar cherishes.

41. His Audience with the Emperor[1]

. . . On the fourth day after leaving Milan I arrived at Mantua, where I was received by the successor of our Caesars with
a cordiality hardly to be expected from a Caesar, and with a

4. See the articles gathered by Giovanni Gentile under the title "Le
traduzioni medievali di Platone e Francesco Petrarca," in *Studi sul Rinascimento* (Firenze, 1936), pp. 23–88. At this time Petrarch knew Homer
only through adaptations, not a genuine translation.

1. From *Epistolae Familiares* XIX, 3 (February 25, 1355), to Laelius.
Under the leadership of Giovanni Visconti, Milan was coming so close to
a hegemony of the Lombard cities that in 1352 Charles concluded an alliance with the Tuscan League, and the new pope, Innocent VI, sent Cardinal
Albornoz to Italy. In these circumstances Petrarch wrote again to Charles;
then late in 1353, having finally received the emperor's cool answer to his
first missive, he wrote once more, concluding that if all else fails, "the sword
remains." Bayley remarks: "Altogether, a piquant letter, the flavor of
which is heightened by the fact that Petrarch was residing at that time in
Milan as a protégé of those same Visconti whom he was urging Charles to
discipline" (*Speculum* XVII, 330). Charles arrived in Italy in October,
1354; Giovanni Visconti's death made a settlement reasonably easy; and
then Charles asked for an interview with Petrarch, who reached Mantua on
December 15.

graciousness more than imperial. Omitting details, I may say that we two sometimes spent the whole evening, from the time the lights were first lit until an unseasonably late hour of the night, in conversation and discussion. Nothing, in a word, could be more refined and engaging than the dignified manners of this prince. So much, at least, I know; but I must defer a final judgment upon his other traits, in accordance with the dictum of the satirist, "Trust not the face."[2] We must wait! We must, if I mistake not, take counsel of the acts of the man and their outcome, not of his face and words, if we would determine how far he merits the title of Caesar. Nor did I hesitate frankly to tell him this.

The conversation happening to descend to my works, the Emperor requested copies of some of them, especially of that one which I have entitled *Lives of Famous Men*. I replied that the latter was still unfinished, and that time and leisure were necessary to its completion. Upon asking me to agree to send it to him later, he met with an example of my customary freedom of speech when talking with persons of rank. This frankness, which I had by nature, becomes more pronounced as the years go on, and by the time I reach old age it will doubtless exceed all bounds. "I promise that you shall have it," I answered, "if your valor approves itself, and my life is spared." As he asked, in surprise, for an explanation, I replied that as far as I was concerned I might properly demand that a suitable period be granted me for the completion of so considerable a work, as it was especially difficult to set forth the history of great deeds in a limited space. "As for you, Caesar," I continued, "you will know yourself to be worthy of this gift, and of a book bearing such a title, when you shall be distinguished not in name only, and by the possession of a diadem, insignificant in itself, but also by your deeds; and when, by the greatness of your character, you shall have placed yourself upon a level with the illustrious men of the past. You must so live that posterity shall read of your great deeds as you read of those of the ancients."

2. Juvenal, *Satires* II, 8.

That my utterance met with his ready approval was clearly shown by the sparkle of his eye and the inclination of his august head; and it seemed to me that the time had come to carry out something which I had long planned. Following up the opportunity afforded by my words, I presented him with some gold and silver coins, which I held very dear. They bore the effigies of some of our rulers—one of them, a most life-like head of Caesar Augustus,—and were inscribed with exceedingly minute ancient characters. "Behold, Caesar, those whose successor you are," I exclaimed, "those whom you should admire and emulate, and with whose image you may well compare your own. To no one but you would I have given these coins, but your rank and authority induces me to part with them. I know the name, the character, and the history, of each of those who are there depicted, but you have not merely to know their history, you must follow in their footsteps—the coins should, therefore, belong to you." Thereupon I gave him the briefest outline of the great events in the life of each of the persons represented, adding such words as might stimulate his courage and his desire to imitate their conduct. He exhibited great delight, and seemed never to have received a present which afforded him more satisfaction.

But why should I linger upon these details? Among the many things we discussed I will mention only one matter, which will, I think, surprise you. The Emperor desired to hear, in due order, the history—or shall I say the romance?—of my life, from the day of my birth to the present time. Although I protested that the story was long and by no means diverting, he listened to me through it all with grave attention, and when, from forgetfulness or a desire to hasten on, I omitted some event, he straightway supplied it, seeming often to be better acquainted with my past than I myself. I was astonished that any wind was strong enough to have wafted such trifles across the Alps, and that they had caught the eye of one whose attention was absorbed by the cares of state. When I finally reached the present time in my narrative I paused, but the Emperor pressed me to tell him something of my plans for the future. "Continue," he said; "what of the future? What objects have

you now in view?" "My intentions are of the best, Caesar,"
I replied, "although I have been unable to bring my work to
the state of perfection I should have desired. The habits of the
past are strong, and prevail in the conflict with good intentions of the present. The heart opposes a new determination,
as the sea which has been driven by a steady breeze rises up
against a contrary wind." "I can well believe you," he answered,
"but my question really referred to a different matter, namely,
to the kind of life which pleases you best." "The life of solitude," I promptly and boldly answered, "for no existence can
be safer, or more peaceful and happy. It transcends, in my
opinion, even the glory and eminence of your sovereign position.
I love to pursue solitude, when I may, into her own proper
haunts—the forests and mountains. Often in the past have I
done this, and when, as at present, it is impossible, I do the
best I can, and seek such seclusion as is to be found in the city
itself." He smiled, and said, "All this I well know, and have intentionally led you step by step, by my questions, to this confession. While I agree with many of your opinions, I must de-
preciate this notion of yours."

And so a great discussion arose between us, which I did not
hesitate to interrupt by exclaiming: "Beware, Caesar, of your
course! for in this conflict your arms are by no means equal
to mine. This is a debate in which not only are you predestined
to defeat, but a very Chrysippus,[3] armed with syllogisms, would
have no chance of victory. I have for a long time meditated
upon nothing else, and my head is full of arguments and illustrations. Experience, the mistress of the world, sides with me,
although the stupid and ignorant multitude oppose my view.
I refuse to engage with you, Caesar, for I should inevitably be
declared the victor by any fair-minded person, although he
were himself a dweller in the city. Indeed, I am so absorbed
by the subject that I have recently issued a little book which
treats of some small part of it." Here he interrupted me, declar-
ing that he knew of the book, and that, should it ever fall into

3. Chrysippus (c. 280–207 B.C.), who succeeded Cleanthes as head of the
Stoa, used his training in logic and dialectic to combat Academic skepti-
cism.

his hands, he would promptly commit it to the flames. I told him, in reply, that I should see to it that it never came in his way. Thus our discussion was protracted by many a merry sally, and I must confess that, among all those whom I have heard attack the life of seclusion, I have never found one who advanced more weighty arguments. The outcome was, if I do not deceive myself, that the Emperor was worsted (if it is permissible), both by my arguments and by reason, but in his own opinion he was not only undefeated but remained clearly the victor.

In conclusion, he requested me to accompany him to Rome. This request was, he explained, his primary motive in subjecting one who held quiet in such esteem to the discomforts of this inclement season. He desired to behold the famous city not only with his own but, so to speak, with my eyes. He needed my presence, he said, in certain Tuscan cities,—of which he spoke in a way that would have led one to believe him an Italian, or possessed, at least, of an Italian mind. This would have been most agreeable to me, and the two words "Rome" and "Caesar" rang most gratefully in my ears; nothing, I thought, could be more delightful than to accompany Caesar to Rome; nevertheless I felt obliged, for many good reasons, and owing to unavoidable circumstances, to refuse him.

A new discussion ensued in regard to this matter, which lasted many days and did not end until the last adieux were said. For as the Emperor left Milan I accompanied him to the fifth milestone beyond the walls of Piacenza, and even then it was only after a long struggle of opposing arguments that I could tear myself away. As I was about to depart a certain Tuscan soldier in the imperial guards took me by the hand, and, turning to the Emperor, addressed him in a bold but solemn voice. "Here is he," he said, "of whom I have often spoken to you. If you shall do anything worthy of praise, he will not allow your name to be silently forgotten; otherwise, he will know when to speak and when to keep his peace."

But to return to our first subject.[4] I do not, as you can see,

4. Rumor had it that the Milanese had deputed Petrarch to negotiate a peace.

repudiate the honor you ascribe to me, because it is distasteful, but because truth is dearer to me than all else. I did not negotiate the peace, though I ardently desired it; I was not deputed to bring it about, but only aided with exhortations and words of encouragement. I was not present at the beginning but only at the close, since Caesar and my good fortune decreed my presence at the solemn public ratification of the treaty which followed its conclusion.

Assuredly no Italian has ever received such tributes as I have at this juncture. I have been summoned by Caesar and urged to be his companion; I have been permitted to jest and argue with him. The tyrant Dionysius, as Pliny tells us,[5] once sent a ship covered with garlands to fetch Plato, the disciple of wisdom; and as he disembarked he was received upon the shore by the prince himself, in a chariot drawn by four white horses. These things are spoken of as magnificent tributes to Plato, and as redounding to his glory. You see now, my dear Laelius, whither I am tending, and that I omit no opportunity which promises distinction. What might I not venture, who do not fear to compare myself to Plato? . . .[6]

42. *Invective Against a Certain Man of Great Rank but No Knowledge or Virtue*[1]

You were, I own, not unworthy of having your madness readily scorned by anyone in his senses; not your virtue, certainly, but your worthiness makes you worthy of being smitten

5. *Natural History* VII, 30, 10.
6. After his coronation April 5, 1355, Charles withdrew immediately, stopping at Pisa to crown Zanobi da Strada. Petrarch was unamused.
1. Written in 1355 (probably during the period March–August) against the apostolic protonotary, Jean de Caraman, a cardinal in the Curia at Avignon. Jean was grandnephew of Pope John XXII, who in 1321 had supplied his brother the money to purchase the viscountcy of Caraman.

with words, not silence. I feel pity, though, for that "worthiness" —if it should be called worthiness at all, and not rather "mockery." Those who are chosen to provoke great ridicule at spectacles are covered with gold, their heads wreathed with purple, mounted on elegantly decked-out horses, and marched around through the streets of the city. After wandering about all day and filling the people with amusement (and themselves with scorn), in the evening they are put down, stripped, and sent on their way. The same thing will happen to you—namely, in your person fortune will show the world these diversions and spectacles. Now the people has had enough of you; now, if you consider your age, the day and its diversions are at an end; now the circus director will take away the clothes you delight in and cast you aside. Then you will observe what you are and what you seem; leaving laughter behind for others, for yourself you will discover grief and misery. Moreover, this is by no means a new and unusual sort of evil; for Eutropius held the consulship and Heliogabalus was emperor—the former a vile eunuch, the latter the basest of men. The satirist's observation is based on cruel fact; such men "fortune raises to the highest rank whenever she wishes to have a laugh."[2] With you she has indeed now amused herself enough and more than enough; we beg her to put you down; the joke's now beginning to get distasteful. And do not flatter yourself that this order of yours is immune from these monstrosities—far easier for your order to be corrupted by you than for you to be adorned by it with honor. Think how many members it has had in our time who were not simply unjust or base, but even absurd and insane. However, it has a source of consolation, since among the Roman patricians (than whom nothing is more illustrious) were Catiline and Nero, and among Christ's apostles (than whom nothing is more holy) there was Judas.

I'll come to the point. I perceived beforehand, and thought it would come about thus, that if I wrote anything I should subject myself to the judgment of learned men; and I should be unbearable if I should not bear this lot common to all writ-

2. Juvenal, *Satires* III, 39–40.

ers. I could have not written—if we can do the opposite of what our whole spirit urges. However, I could no more write and escape men's judgments than I could avoid being seen if I stood in the light. But although I was heedful and apprehensive of the mishaps suffered by abilities no less than by inheritances and bodies, I was certainly not apprehensive about your judgment; or to put it better, I was not hoping for it.

In what way, by what stratagems, could you have given me and others such hope for myself as you have furnished by disparaging me? Frankly, this is how things stand: when I first heard that you were often using my name, I was in fearful suspense lest you praise me. If you were doing so, I was done for: you were leaving no opportunity for glory or the trust of others, since a base and infamous praiser is not the last sort of infamy. For what, pray, would you praise except what you grasped? And what would you grasp that was not insignificant, petty, and abject? Besides, just as there is a likeness between the understanding and the thing understood, so there is generally a certain parity and natural connection between praiser and praised. Were this the case . . . But what am I thinking? Forbear, my spirit, from shrouding yourself in these cares. I don't know what I should not prefer to be—even nothing—than similar to him.

And so, when I learned that you were using my name as a topic of disparagement, I swear to God I was affected as I should be if some great man praised me. My desire to be similar to good and learned men is no greater than my desire to be unlike the evil and unlearned. The rationale is the same: the remoter one is from vice, the nearer one is to virtue. I see then the cause of the problem: I am dissimilar to you. I could perhaps have been led by other paths, but not to another hope. I should hope and rejoice, if I were similar to the good; and I do hope and rejoice if I am dissimilar to the bad. You conferred on me more than you believed when there came to your mind that desire to revile at banquets my name, which you would certainly praise if you had discerned in me the similarity which I am speaking about. However, you will be especially worthy of a return from me, as one obliged to you for my fame, when you have transferred these insults (with which you rail at me in my absence) and these so laborious, fiery disparagements to sober and meager colloquia. Now because you praise me by censuring, I am afraid it may be ascribed to the wine rather than your judgment. Therefore, if you wish me fully praised, censure when you are sober and fasting, or after sleep as you rise from the bed where you have digested your drunkenness. That way not the fumes of wine but the blind darkness of your spirit will give some brightness to my abilities. . . .

It is time to return the discussion to me and clear myself of your charge that I am the familiar friend of tyrants—as if those who live together necessarily have everything in common, when the wicked often dwell among the good and the good among the wicked. Was Socrates not among the Thirty Tyrants of Athens, Plato with Dionysius, Callisthenes with Alexander, Cato with Catiline, Seneca with Nero? Virtue is not corrupted in the vicinity of evil; for, although slight causes often shake tender spirits, sound minds are not touched by moral contagion. This calumny, and many others with which folly and malice have shackled me (this is not the first time it has happened), I think I have previously answered in a whole volume,[3] shattering the snares of empty words. For the present, I shall say one thing—if you'd believe it, you would be astonished; if not, you would jeer—that my spirit is subject to no one, except Him who gave it to me, or anyone I am persuaded is very pleasing to Him . . . a rare sort. Let me add several kindred spirits to whom love has subjected me with a most agreeable yoke—a sway not light, but so rare that from youth to the present day I have been submissive to very few such yokes. Among them have been the lowly and the illustrious, pontiffs and kings, in such a way that their fortune and rank counted for nothing, virtue and love for everything, so that willingly was I their subject, and heavily did I grieve whenever death absolved me from such servitude. Hence I was often more subject to those of lowlier status, because I discerned in them less

3. This may have been the original core of Petrarch's letter "To Posterity."

of that fortune which I neither love nor revere, and more virtue, which I have ever resolved to revere and love in others, if I cannot in myself. Except for them, there is no man to whom my spirit is subject; so, as you see, the better part of me is free, or lacking liberty for pleasant and honorable reasons does not wish to be free otherwise, and fears and refuses to be forced. Such is my spirit.

This other, earthly part of me, though, ought to be subject to the earthly lords whose regions it inhabits. Why not, when I see that they themselves, who rule over their inferiors, submit to their superiors, and it all comes down to that saying of Caesar's, that "the human race lives for a few."[4] But indeed, even these few for whom the human race is said to live are not more dreadful to their peoples than their peoples are to them. Thus scarcely anyone is free; everywhere there is slavery and prison and nooses—unless perhaps some rare person has broken the knots with heaven's help and the force of his spirit. Turn wherever you please: no place is free from tyranny, for where tyrants are lacking the people tyrannize, and so when you seem to have escaped one you fall into the hands of many —unless perhaps you will have shown me some place ruled by a just and gentle king. Should you do so, I shall transfer my residence there immediately and migrate with all my baggage. Not love of country, not the splendor and nobility of Italy shall retain me; I shall go to India, to Persia, to the Garamantes, remotest of men, to find this place and this king. But it is vain to search for what is nowhere. Thanks to our age, which having made everything almost equal has spared us this toil. It is enough for grain merchants to take a fistful and examine it to gain an idea of the whole heap. There is no need to explore the farthest shores and penetrate the bowels of the earth: languages, modes of dress, and features vary, but desires, spirits, and character are so similar wherever you go that the satirist's words never seem to have been truer: "If you wish to know the ways of man, one house suffices."[5] There is, I own, one sacred place, where you live, where with your presence and your counsels,

4. Lucan V, 343.
5. Juvenal XIII, 159–60.

like a second Saturn or Augustus, you have restored the Golden Age. Happy the Rhone with such an inhabitant! Happy the Church with such a counsellor! Truly, I say, the place you dwell is sacred! Thus in Virgil the fire of an incurable disease is called "sacred," as is the hunger for gold and the gates of hell.[6]

At all events, you have heard what I feel about our young men: they are leaders of their homeland, not tyrants, and as free from all spirit of tyranny as you are from equity and justice.[7] So they are thus far; what they will be I do not know, for the spirit is changeable, especially the spirit of those who possess unshaken good fortune and an immutable freedom to do what they please. But whether you have falsely called them tyrants, or the passage of time will make them tyrants, or disclose what it up to now conceals—what is this to me? I live with them, not under them, in their lands, not their houses. I have nothing in common with them, except the favors and honors which they abundantly and constantly bestow upon me, as much as I allow them to. Counsels, the conduct of affairs, administering public finances—these things are entrusted to others born for them. My cares, my business, consist in nothing but leisure, silence, security, and liberty. And so while others betake themselves to the palace in the morning, I seek out the woods and my familiar places of solitude. In nothing but their liberality and benefits am I conscious of having lords. I was promised—and the promise has been kept to this day—that nothing was required of me except my presence, my staying in this flourishing city and in these delightful places. They think it confers glory on themselves and their dominion. Everyone knows these things; but to you they will seem incredible, because no such thing has ever been seen under you and your

6. *Georgics* III, 566; *Aeneid* III, 57; *Aeneid* VI, 573–74.

7. Cf. Jacob Burckhardt, *The Civilization of the Renaissance in Italy* (Harper Torchbook), I, p. 31: "The most complete and instructive type of the tyranny of the fourteenth century is to be found unquestionably among the Visconti of Milan, from the death of the Archbishop Giovanni onward (1354). The family likeness which shows itself between Bernabò and the worst of the Roman Emperors is unmistakable; the most important public object was the prince's boar-hunting; whoever interfered with it was put to death with torture; the terrified people were forced to maintain five thousand boar-hounds, with strict responsibility for their health and safety."

tyranny. No affection, no charity, no sweetness of friendship touches you; from men, as if from cattle, you seek only lucre; you make much more of a useful lion than of useless philosophy. It is hard for you to reflect upon what you know. Indeed, I shouldn't think there is a greater difference between the depth of the abyss and the highest point of heaven than between your senile, avaricious pride and their youthful mildness and magnanimity. In short, I'll have you know that they are not tyrants, and that I am completely free. And if, as human affairs go, chance should enslave me, I am minded nowhere to bear it ill, just so long as I am not under you, to whom I should far prefer Agathocles or Phalaris or Busiris.

It remains for me to snatch from your eyes the veil of one utterly false opinion, so that you may see and ponder more freely whether it makes more sense to enter unarmed into these wars of words, or to enjoy your pleasures in silence. As I see it, you hope that I will be terrified by your rank. You are mistaken: I fear only those whom I esteem highly. I do not esteem you, because you do not let me; moreover, I hate your morals and your pride, and the cause of your pride, your rank. Or could it be you have not heard in that earlier contest over fame (kindled against me by an ill will similar to yours, where, having then too been assailed by undeserved insults, I seized arms for a revenge, or more truly a defense, that was not only just but almost necessary) how completely unsparing I was to that man who was at the time dreaded throughout Italy?[8] Although he was not at the literary level he wrongly thought he was (whether because of a deeply rooted vanity or the windy compliments of sycophants), nevertheless he was, nobody doubts, more than ordinarily lettered and eloquent. In addition there was the man's power, and the mighty favor of fortune, which served his pleasure, and moreover a mind that would bear no offense, and his well-known custom of avenging himself, which was then widely suspected by neighboring princes. Relying on the aid of truth alone, I did not fear such a man, so powerful not only in pen and words, but in bonds and the sword. Shall I then fear

8. Brizio Visconti, Luchino's natural son, who had in 1344 written a fierce poem against Petrarch.

you, with your slow mind, duller pen, and well-tied tongue? You have absolutely nothing going for you, unless perhaps in place of all these things you will set against me your red hat. But will reverence for your rank restrain the force of my style? By all the gods I beseech you, where did you get the idea I was so doltish as to value not the horse but the harness? Or are you now something else from what you were when even the common people regarded you with contempt? Most precious and invaluable would be the cloth on your head, if it so quickly granted wisdom to its possessors! Believe me, though, it does not grant wisdom, but unfolds the secrets of private life and draws what is hidden into the open. I know, everyone knows—and you are not ignorant of—the means by which you reached this step. Certainly if you examine yourself, if you behold yourself, if you weigh yourself, if you judge yourself, and do not deceive yourself, you will find nothing—although you love and are greatly pleased with yourself—I repeat, you will find nothing with which you could distinguish yourself, unless you are out of your mind. You have nothing; no one is so dull as to doubt that this is the case. Everything was granted to your family and to the line from which you boast descent, which, although it is not of long standing, does nevertheless have many recent claims to renown and regard. But were he still alive, the memory of whom[9] I believe makes me hateful to you, all these things would never have been able to raise you to your present estate, where, now an old man, with him at length out of the way you have stolen in so slowly and so wretchedly that it would have been finer not to begin—although to the trade of Simon you have come as a late merchant but not a lazy one. No one sells the Holy Spirit more freely, and so no one more often. But lest I afflict you too much, I shall leave off mentioning that man whom I think you still fear after his death, and return to your family. Although its merits were a sort of stairway for your ascent, I shall take nothing away from them. But I ask you: with what sort of front, with what sort of spirit do you hold a position granted

9. Unidentified, but perhaps Cardinal Giovanni Colonna.

not to you but to your forebears? What sort of impudence is
this, what sort of madness, that you take pride in another's virtue rather than blushing for your own vices? For my part I
felt pity for this position of yours; while you suffered being
loved by me, I alone remained outside the number of those who
laughed at you. You believed you had frightened me with your
new insignia. I am not fearful, as you think; you have irritated
me, rather, and roused me. I scorned a gleaming helmet, I opposed an armed young man face to face; shall I quake with
fear at the red hat of an old man in civilian dress? . . .

43. The Solitude of Saint Ambrose (and How Women Destroy the Life of Solitude)[1]

Ambrose, having been appointed by divine will and compul-
sion to the charge of a numerous population in Milan, though
from his consciousness of so serious a duty and obligation he
did not dare to lead a life of entire solitude, whenever he could
and in what way he could he gave evidence of his desire. He
lived where the circuit of the wall now runs in a remote corner
of the city, where his holy body resides to this day and where
stands the sacred church established by him, renowned for its
sublime worship, and attended by huge throngs of people. At
that time, as may be inferred from definite indications, the
place was quite out of the way and solitary in the extreme.
Whenever he was free from his episcopal cares and eased from
the severe and endless labors which he sustained in repelling
the Arians from the church, whenever for a little while he

1. From *De Vita Solitaria* II, iv (Zeitlin, pp. 204–7). Some details of
this selection seem based on a direct acquaintance deriving from Petrarch's
years of residence in Milan; and at least one part seems datable to 1356
or shortly thereafter (see below, note 2).

could withdraw and steal away from his business, this holy man used to betake himself to a more private solitude in this quarter. There was a wood which though not far away was nevertheless suited for meditation; in the midst of it was a little house, capacious enough for a man who, though surely great, was also humble, and which, small as it was, was converted into the form of a temple with greater appropriateness than once the house of Pythagoras in Metapontum. The wood is now destroyed, but though the character of the place is changed, its name remains: it is commonly called Ambrose's Wood. It is toward the north side, which in this year—memorable for great disturbances and upheavals everywhere—was enclosed inside the city itself, within the farthest circuit of the walls, which were increased by rapid construction.[2]

In this place, as I hear, and as I might infer, he strewed the honey-filled flowers of the books, of which the taste today is most sweet and the odor most fragrant throughout the domains of the church. If I may adduce a single passage in evidence of this man's style as well as of his deeds, he says in a certain letter to Sabinus: "I shall continue to speak with you more frequently in my writings and when I am alone." Then, converting to his own use an expression of Scipio's, of which I shall speak later, he goes on to say, "For I am never less lonely than when I seem to be alone, nor less idle than when at leisure. I summon whom I wish according to my pleasure and attach to myself those whom I like best and whom I consider most congenial. No one interrupts, no one interferes. On such occasions therefore I retain you in particular and converse with you about the scriptures, and together we chop words at great length. Mary was alone when she talked with an angel and when the Holy Ghost descended upon her and the power of the All-highest overshadowed her. She was alone and she effected the salvation of the world and conceived the redeemer of all mankind. Peter was alone and he learned the mysteries by which

2. In 1356, threatened by a coalition promoted by Charles IV and headed by Giovanni II of Monferrato, Galeazzo and Bernabò Visconti extended the fortifications of Milan. I have recast this sentence, since Zeitlin's rendering was apparently based on a faulty text.

the nations throughout the world were to be made holy. Adam was alone and did not go astray, because his mind was faithful to God, but after he was joined with woman he could not stay faithful to the divine commands."[3]

If I may intrude a little on Ambrose's discourse, I would not pass over in silence what everybody knows, though many pretend not to. There is no poison as destructive to those who would follow this life as the company of woman. For the attraction of women, the more fascinating it is, the more dreadful and baleful, to say nothing of their dispositions, than which there is naught more fickle or more inimical to the love of repose. Whoever you are that desire peace, keep away from woman, the perpetual source of contention and trouble. Peace and a woman rarely dwell under the same roof. The satirist says:[4]

> Besides what endless brawls by wives are bred:
> The curtain-lecture makes a mournful bed.
> Then, when she has thee sure within the sheets,
> Her cry begins and the whole day repeats.

Nor is a concubine's bed any more peaceful; there is less fidelity and greater dishonor, but the quarrelsomeness is the same. The sentence of the famous orator is well known, "The man who does not quarrel is a celibate." And what is better than not to quarrel? And what, I pray you in the name of Jesus Christ, what, I say, is more blessed than solitude, especially at night, or than silence and peace and the freedom of your own couch? Nothing is more blessed than celibacy, but for celibacy nothing is more appropriate than solitude. Whoever you are, therefore, that would avoid strife, avoid also woman; you will hardly escape the one without running away from the other. Even though her disposition be most gentle, which is a rare thing, the very presence of a woman, her mere shadow, so to speak, is an annoyance. If I am deserving of any trust, everybody who seeks solitary peace will avoid her face and her tongue no less than, I will not say a serpent's, but than the gaze and hiss of a basilisk.

---

3. *Patrologia Latinia* 16, col. 1153 f.
4. Juvenal, *Satires* VI, 268–69.

For not otherwise than a basilisk she slays with her eyes, and infects before she touches. To whom, do you suppose, can the application be made more justly than to us of what Virgil says with as much truth as propriety in a remote connection?[5]

> With two fair eyes his mistress burns his breast;
> He looks and languishes, and leaves his rest;
> Forsakes his food, and, pining for the lass,
> Is joyless of the grove, and spurns the growing grass.

Truly, in saying that merely by a look the forces of body and mind were devoured and consumed, he might have been alluding to all whom that disease emaciates and inflames, but if in adding that the same mischief erases the memory of grass and meadows, he had said it of men as he did of horses and oxen, whom else would he seem to have meant than us who find a special pleasure in groves and meadows? Hence I proclaim that the allurements of woman should be avoided and shunned by all whose purpose it is to guard their pledge sacredly and honorably, and most particularly by ourselves. And whosoever neglects this warning, let him know that he must be banished from the paradise of solitude, for the very same reason that the first man was expelled from the paradise of delight.[6]

44. Pope John XXII[1]

Our own listlessness is responsible for the daring of these cowards.[2] They take unholy joy in our patience, and at the same time they hate us. Indeed, that you may be most pro-

5. Virgil, *Georgics* III, 215–16.
6. Based on the *De Vita Solitaria* and the *Secretum* is Charles Trinkaus's study "Petrarch's Views on the Individual and His Society," *Osiris* XI (1954), 168–98.
1. From *Epistolae Sine Nomine* XVII (October, 1357), addressed to Francesco Nelli but not sent, for fear that it fall into the wrong hands.
2. The foreign barbarians.

foundly astonished, know that they have an inward fear of those for whom they outwardly show contempt. The latter is merely feigned, the former exists in reality. There are a thousand proofs of their hatred and of their terror. I shall now relate an anecdote that will serve as a proof of both at once. Though this story was at first kept secret, ultimately it got abroad, so that it became known not only at Babylon but even in more distant lands.

The incident occurred at the time when that Supreme Pontiff had organized a decrepit expedition of the priestly soldiery with the purpose of reducing Italy to the condition of a province, and above all, of destroying the city of the Milanese. It was at the time, I repeat, when the Father of the Christians was rendered so extremely furious by his thorough and complete hatred of this Christian land and Christian city, that one would not have thought this land Italy, but Syria or Egypt; and this city not Milan, but Damascus or Memphis.

For the accomplishment of this holy and pious undertaking, the Pontiff chose one of the Fathers of the Sacred College, his own son, as many said; and, indeed, in addition to his figure, a strong resemblance and the ferocity of his character strengthened the belief. He did not equip him in the manner of an apostle, but in that of a robber; not with the signs of the virtues and with the power of working wonders, but with the ensigns of the camps and with wonderful legions. Thus equipped did he send him into these lands, not as a second Peter, but as a second Hannibal. In the war which ensued, Omnipotent God, according to his wont, humbled the proud and raised the lowly, and fought openly for the side of justice.

There was in that same troop of cardinals a certain man who likewise nourished an insatiable hatred for us. He was a man of boundless arrogance, whom I, at that time a mere boy, knew by sight and whose character I execrated with all the energy of my feeble youth. This man was dear to the Pontiff beyond all others. One day, entering the papal cabinet, he found the Pope dismayed and distressed by the reports of the war. In fact, the onslaught of the war had, contrary to expectations, been checked on the very threshold of this city, which was not then defended by walls, but, indeed, by that which constitutes the very best kind of wall, extraordinary soldiers and very brave commanders. And so, the besieged had frequently put the besiegers to flight; the prisons were full to overflowing with the hordes of captives; and the fields were being fattened by the blood of the slain.

While, therefore, matters were in this state, and since he beheld the Pope more downcast than usual, relying upon his great intimacy with the Pope, he addressed him and said: "I wonder, most Holy Father, why it is that, though you are very clearsighted in other matters, you see to but little purpose in that one question which is of especial and of highest importance to us."

At these words the Pontiff raised his head, which had been weighed down by heavy cares, and said, "Continue. What do you mean?"

Thereupon that surpassingly fine counselor replied: "I know that you desire nothing so ardently as the destruction of Italy. To this end are we devoting all our strength, our resources, our counsels; to this end have we now squandered nearly all the riches of the church. We have ventured into an inextricable labyrinth, unless another way be tried. Behold now our magnificent preparations for war! The edge of our power is being blunted at the very gates of Milan, a city which your cringing sycophants asserted to be like unto any one of our cities, but which by experience has been found to be superior to them all. If we are conquered by a single Italian city, when shall we conquer the whole of Italy? But if you wish, there is a far easier way to accomplish this end."

"What way," exclaimed the Pontiff, "speak, and more quickly. For over this do I labor, this do I desire, this is the one thing for which I should be willing to sell both body and soul."

And the other: "You can do all things. Whatsoever you order is accomplished. Why, therefore, do you not deprive the city of Rome and Italy of both the papacy and the empire? Why do you not transfer that empire to Cahors, our native place, that is to say, to Gascony?[3] It is not a difficult task; speak, and it

3. John XXII had been Jacques d'Euse, of Cahors. John's budget is worthy of note: library .17%, art .33%, stables .4%, alms 7.16%, upkeep and entertainment 12.7%, war 63.7%.

will be done. There is no need of arms, in which we are greatly their inferiors. By a single word you will triumph over your enemies. Thus, by transferring the very summit of power into our country, you will distinguish us with new honors, and you will deprive that hateful race of its double glory."

At these words the Pontiff raised his head and, smiling in the midst of his wrath, replied: "You have deceived me hitherto; I had not yet known you to rave like a madman. Do you not know, stupid one, that according to the way which you deemed to have so subtly devised, both I and my successors become merely bishops of Cahors, and that the emperor (whosoever he may be) becomes a prefect of Gascony? Do you not know that they who would rule at Rome in spiritual and in temporal matters would be, respectively, the real Pope and the real Emperor? And so, while thinking to overthrow the Italic name, you are elevating it to its former dignity. Therefore, while it is granted from on high, let us hold fast the reins of the Roman pontificate, and let us bend our every energy to this: that Italian hands may never, perchance, grasp what is theirs by right. But it is an uncertain matter how long this event can be delayed. Let us not haggle about mere names; for, whether we will it or no, the head and center of all things will still be Rome."

Upon hearing these words, that sagacious fool blushed scarlet. I, in truth, disapprove of the Pope's intentions, but am obliged to approve of his good sense; for, though he was consumed with undeserved hatred of us, he nevertheless remembered and knew full well whereon had been founded the lofty structure from the summit of which he exhibited his pride. He clearly realized that to impair the foundations would bring on ruin. He therefore decided that it was best to remain quiet and to enjoy the papacy in silence, as if over an object obtained by theft.

I do not know whether this tale has been recounted by others. I have given it in detail in order that, if you have already heard it, you may know that I, too, am acquainted with it; that if you have not yet heard it, in order that you may learn it from me, and that, being acquainted with the past, you may not be in ignorance of the present.

45. Ubi sunt?[1]

. . . Where now is Boniface VIII, the Roman pontiff, true wonder of peoples, of kings, and—it is said—of the world, whom, unless I am mistaken, some of you beheld?[2] Where are his successors, whom we have doubtless seen: John, Benedict, and the two Clements?[3] Where is the Roman Emperor, Henry?[4] Where is Philip, king of the Franks, called "the Fair" from his beauty? He, and his beautiful sons, who resembled him and succeeded him in order, were carried away by so untimely a death that theirs seems to have been not life but a dream.[5] Where is the other Philip, father of the present king and more fortunate?—for a grave holds the father, a prison the son.[6] Where is the king of Spain, once the terror of the Saracens and shield of the faith, but the object of westerners' insults?[7] Where, finally, is the glory of Gaul and the ornament of Italy, King Robert of Sicily? The ensuing storms of troubles show what sweet repose you had under his temporal rule, serving the eternal King.[8] And to avoid being prolix, I'll pass over not only those below kingly rank, but also most of the kings. Ask

1. From the *De Otio Religioso* ("On Monastic Freedom"), dedicated to the Carthusian monks at Montreux, among them Petrarch's younger brother Gherardo, with whom Petrarch had spent a happy visit early in 1347. The present selection dates, apparently, from some ten years later.
2. Boniface VIII, pope from 1294 to 1303.
3. John XXII (1316–34), Benedict XII (1334–42), Clement V (1305–14), Clement VI (1342–52). Innocent VI (1352–62) was pope at the time Petrarch wrote this.
4. Henry VII of Luxembourg.
5. Louis X (1314–16), Philip V (1316–22), and Charles IV (1322–28).
6. John II, son of Philip VI, was taken prisoner by the English in 1356 at Poitiers. He was later released as a result of the treaty of Brétigny, signed in May, 1360.
7. Probably Alfonso XI, king of Castile and León (1312–50), who stopped the Islamic invasions of Spain at the battle of Rio Salado in 1340.
8. Robert, as the sovereign of Provence, had afforded the monastery a measure of protection during his lifetime.

where they dwell: you will be shown little sepulchers, adorned by the talents of artists, perhaps even gleaming with gems and gold: not only is the life of men vainglorious, but their death as well. Likenesses of the dead will live in Parian stone, in accordance with the great poet's words: "They will fashion living features from marble."[9] But they themselves, pray tell, where are they? You will also be shown splendid epitaphs and high-sounding (but empty) inscriptions, to astound you when you read them. But tarry, I beseech you, while the door of the inner chamber is being opened: new spectacles take their place, a new wonder. Alas, what a meager pile of ash, what a huge quantity of worms and serpents! O unexpected change, O greatly altered appearance of things! Where now are the armed retinue, the flocks of girls, the royal Ganymede assigned to the cup? Where the artful cooks and the clever cleavers of fowl? Where are the beautiful wall hangings, the purple strewn beneath the feet, the roofs intagliated with ivory, the horses champing their golden bits? Where the carefully wrought furniture, the Corinthian vases, the Damascene works and animals standing out on golden vessels? Where are the couch and the gaming boards and the dwellings coated with cypress and ebony? Where the spectacles, the songs, the banquets drawn from the fruits of earth and sea, the wines imported from afar? Where are the enticements of pleasures and all those adornments for a vile little body, and the head gleaming with a diadem, and the tummy girt with a red belt, and delicate fingers shining from the spoils of India's shore and the carvers' genius? Finally, where the imperious spouse, where the "sons as plants grown up in their youth, and the daughters adorned like unto a temple,"[10] who with their caressing embrace and sweet kisses were recently fondling the neck of their father, who had not long to last? O lamentable and unhappy transformation! All has dissolved into worms and into serpents, and finally into nothing.[11]

9. Virgil, *Aeneid* VI, 848.

10. Psalms 143 [144], 12.

11. On the *De Otio Religioso* see Charles Trinkaus, "Humanist Treatises on the Status of the Religious: Petrarch, Salutati, Valla," *Studies in the Renaissance* XI (1964), 7–45.

46. Boccaccio Sends Petrarch a Copy of Dante[1]

Sure ornament of Italy, whose temples
The Roman leaders crowned, receive this work
Which pleases learned men, amazes common,
Its like composed in no prior age.
The verses of an exiled, uncrowned poet,
Resounding merely in his native tongue—
Let them not rouse your scorn. An unjust fortune
Had caused his exile; for the rest, he wished
To show posterity what modern verse could do.
This was his reason—though often savage men,   10
Raging with envy, have said that Dante did this
From utter ignorance. Perhaps you know
His studies drew him to the snowy heights,
Through nature's secret spots and hiding places,
And through the ways of heaven and earth and sea,
Aonian founts, Parnassus' peaks and caves,
To Julian Paris and the tardy Briton.
Hence virtue gave him the illustrious name
Of poet, theologian, and philosopher.
And he was almost made another glory   20
Of Florence; but a cruel, too hasty death
Forbade the laurel crown that he deserved.
If at first sight you think his Muse quite bare,
Unlock with all your mind the bar of Pluto,
The mount and throne of Jove, and you will see
His sense sublime is clothed with sacred shades,

1. A first version, composed between 1351 and 1353, was sent to Petrarch
with a copy of Dante. Boccaccio reworked the poem in 1359 and sent it along
with a letter that has been lost. For Petrarch's reply see the next selection.

DOMINVS IOHANNES BOCCACCIVS

The Bettmann Archive

5. Giovanni Boccaccio, by Andrea del Castagno.

And that on Nysa's peak the Muses move
God's lyre, and all things in a wondrous order
Are drawn. Gladly you'll say: "Another, Dante,
Will spring in time from him you praise and cherish,   30
Whom Florence, the great mother of poets, has borne
And now reveres, rejoicing; her son's name
Makes her name great among the world's great cities."
I pray you now, dear friend, our only hope,
Although your genius penetrates the sky
And though your name extends quite to the stars,
Receive, read through, and cherish and approve
Your fellow citizen, learned and a poet:
You'll do yourself, and win yourself, much favor.
Farewell, the City's glory and the world's.   40

47. Petrarch Disclaims All Jealousy of Dante[1]

There are many things in your letter which do not require
any answer; those, for example, which we have lately settled
face to face. Two points there were, however, which it seemed
to me should not be passed over in silence, and I will briefly
write down such reflections concerning them as may occur to
me. In the first place, you excuse yourself for seeming to praise
unduly a certain poet, a fellow-citizen of ours, who in point of
style is very popular, and who has certainly chosen a noble
theme. You beg my pardon for this, as if I regarded anything
said in his, or anyone else's praise, as detracting from my own.
You assert, for instance, that if I will only look closely at what
you say of him, I shall find that it all reflects glory upon me.

1. *Epistolae Familiares* XXI, 15 (from Milan, probably June, 1359), to
Giovanni Boccaccio. See Aldo S. Bernardo, "Petrarch's Attitude Toward
Dante," *PMLA* LXX (1955), 488–517.

You take pains to explain, in extenuation of your favorable
attitude towards him, that he was your first light and guide in
your early studies. Your praise is certainly only a just and
dutiful acknowledgment of his services, an expression of what
I may call filial piety. If we owe all to those who begot and
brought us forth, and much to those who are the authors of
our fortunes, what shall we say of our debt to the parents and
fashioners of our minds? How much more, indeed, is due to
those who refine the mind than to those who tend the body,
he will perceive who assigns to each its just value; for the one,
it will be seen, is an immortal gift, the other, corruptible and
destined to pass away.

Continue, then, not by my sufferance simply, but with my
approbation, to extol and cherish this poet, the guiding star of
your intellect, who has afforded you courage and light in the
arduous way by which you are pressing stoutly on towards a
most glorious goal. He has long been buffeted and wearied by
the windy plaudits of the multitude. Honor him now and exalt
him by sincere praise worthy alike of you and of him, and, you
may be sure, not unpleasing to me. He is worthy of such a
herald, while you, as you say, are the natural one to assume
the office. I therefore accept your song of praise with all my
heart, and join with you in extolling the poet you celebrate
therein.

Hence there was nothing in your letter of explanation to disturb me except the discovery that I am still so ill understood
by you who, as I firmly believed, knew me thoroughly. You
think, then, that I do not take pleasure in the praises of illustrious men and glory in them? Believe me, nothing is more
foreign to me than jealousy; there is no scourge of which I
know less. On the contrary, in order that you may see how far
I am from such feelings, I call upon Him before whom all
hearts are open to witness that few things in life have caused
me more pain than to see the meritorious passed by, utterly
without recognition or reward. Not that I am deploring my own
lot, or looking for personal gain; I am mourning the common
fate of mankind, as I behold the reward of the nobler arts
falling to the meaner. I am not unaware that although the rep-

utation that attaches to right conduct may stimulate the mind to deserve it, true virtue is, as the philosophers say, a stimulus to itself; it is its own reward, its own guide, its own end and aim. Nevertheless, now that you have yourself suggested a theme which I should not voluntarily have chosen, I shall proceed to refute for you, and through you for others, the commonly accepted notion of my judgment of this poet. It is not only false, as Quintilian says of the construction put upon his criticism of Seneca,[2] but it is insidious and, with many, out-and-out malevolent. My enemies say that I hate and despise him, and in this way stir up the common herd against me, for with them he is extremely popular. This is indeed a novel kind of perversity, and shows a marvelous aptitude for harming others. But truth herself shall defend me.

In the first place, there can be no possible cause for ill-will towards a man whom I never saw but once, and that in my very earliest childhood. He lived with my grandfather and my father, being younger than the former, but older than my father, with whom, on the same day and by the same civil commotion, he was driven from his country into exile. At such a time strong friendships are often formed between companions in misery. This proved especially true of these two men, since in their case not only a similar fate but a community of taste and a love for the same studies, served to bring them together. My father, however, forced by other cares and by regard for his family, succumbed to the natural influences of exile, while his friend resisted, throwing himself, indeed, with even greater ardor into what he had undertaken, neglecting everything else and desirous alone of future fame. In this I can scarce admire and praise him enough,—that neither the injustice of his fellow-citizens, nor exile, nor poverty, nor the attacks of his enemies, neither the love of wife, nor solicitude for his children, could divert him from the path he had once decided upon, when so many who are highly endowed are yet so weak of purpose that they are swerved from their course by the least disturbance. And this most often happens to writers of verse, for silence and quiet are especially

2. Quintilian **X**, 1, 125.

requisite for those who have to care not only for the thought and the words but the felicitous turn as well. Thus you will see that my supposed hate for this poet, which has been trumped up by I know not whom, is an odious and ridiculous invention, since there is absolutely no reason for such repugnance, but, on the contrary, every reason for partiality, on account of our common country, his friendship with my father, his genius, and his style, the best of its kind, which must always raise him far above contempt.

This brings us to the second reproach cast upon me, which is based upon the fact that, although in my early years I was very eager in my search for books of all kinds, I never possessed a copy of this poet's work, which would naturally have attracted me most at that age. While exceedingly anxious to obtain other books which I had little hope of finding, I showed a strange indifference, quite foreign to me, towards this one, although it was readily procurable. The fact I admit, but I deny the motives which are urged by my enemies. At that time I too was devoting my powers to compositions in the vernacular; I was convinced that nothing could be finer, and had not yet learned to look higher. I feared, however, in view of the impressionableness of youth and its readiness to admire everything, that, if I should imbue myself with his or any other writer's verses, I might perhaps unconsciously and against my will come to be an imitator. In the ardor of youth this thought filled me with aversion. Such was my self-confidence and enthusiasm that I deemed my own powers quite sufficient, without any mortal aid, to produce an original style all my own, in the species of production upon which I was engaged. It is for others to judge whether I was right in this. But I must add that if anything should be discovered in my Italian writings resembling, or even identical with, what has been said by him or others, it cannot be attributed to secret or conscious imitation. This rock I have always endeavored to avoid, especially in my writings in the vernacular, although it is possible that, either by accident or, as Cicero says, owing to similar ways of thinking, I may ignorantly have traversed the same path as others. If you ever believe me, believe me now; accept this as the real explanation of my conduct. Nothing can be more strictly true; and if my modesty and sense of propriety did not seem to you sufficient to vouch for this, my youthful pride at any rate certainly might have explained it.

Today, however, I have left these anxieties far behind, and, having done so, I am freed from my former apprehension, and can now unreservedly admire other writers, him above all. At that time I was submitting work of my own to the verdict of others, whereas now I am merely passing my own silent verdicts upon my fellows. I find that my opinion varies as regards all the rest, but in his case there can be no reason for doubt; without hesitation I yield him the palm for skill in the use of the vulgar tongue. They lie, then, who assert that I carp at his renown; I, who probably understand better than the majority of these foolish and immoderate admirers of his what it is that merely tickles their ears, without their knowing why, but cannot penetrate their thick heads, because the avenues of intelligence are obstructed. They belong to the same class that Cicero brands in his *Rhetoric,* who "read fine orations or beautiful poems, and praise the orators or poets, and yet do not know what it is that has aroused their admiration, for they lack the ability to see where the thing is that most pleases them, or what it is, or how it is produced."[3] If this happens with Demosthenes and Cicero, Homer and Virgil, among learned men and in the schools, how will it fare with our poet among the rude fellows who frequent the taverns and the public squares?

As for me, far from scorning his work, I admire and love him, and in justice to myself I may venture to add that if he had been permitted to live until this time he would have found few friends more devoted to him than myself, provided, of course, that I had found his character as attractive as his genius. On the other hand, there are none to whom he would have been more obnoxious than these same silly admirers, who, in general, know equally little about what they praise and what they condemn, and who so mispronounce and lacerate his verses that they do him the greatest injury that a poet can suffer. I might

---

3. *Rhetorica ad Herennium* IV, 2, 3.

even strive to the best of my powers to rescue him from this abuse, did not my own productions give me enough to think about. As it is, I can only give voice to my irritation, when I hear the common herd befouling with their stupid mouths the noble beauty of his lines.

Just here it may not be out of place to say that this was not the least of the considerations which led me to give up a style of composition to which I devoted myself in my early years. I feared for my writings the same fate which I had seen overtake those of others, especially those of the poet of whom we are speaking. I could not in my own case look for more musical tongues or more flexible minds among the common people than I noted in the rendering of those authors whom long favor and habit have made popular in the theaters and public squares. That my apprehensions were not idle is clear from the fact that I am continually tortured by the tongues of the people, as they sing the few productions which I allowed to escape me in my youth. I indignantly reject and hate what I once loved; and day by day walk the streets with vexation and execrate my own talents. Everywhere a crowd of ignorant fellows, everywhere I find my Damoetas ready at the street corner "to murder with his screeching reed" my poor song.[4]

However, I have already said more than enough concerning a trifling matter which I ought not to have taken so seriously, for this hour, which will never return, should have been devoted to other things. And yet your excuse did seem to me to have just a little in common with the accusations of these critics, some of whom are constantly asserting that I hate, some that I despise, this person,—whose name I have intentionally refrained today from mentioning, lest the mob, who catch up everything without understanding it, should cry out that I was defaming it. Others again claim that I am actuated by envy— men who are jealous of me and my fame; for although I scarcely am an object for envy, I yet have noticed late in life that there are those who entertain this feeling towards me, a thing that at one time I could not have believed possible. In answer to

4. Virgil, *Bucolics* III, 27.

this charge of envy brought against me, I might reply that, many years ago, in the ardor of youth, and with an approving conscience, I ventured to assert, not in any ordinary manner, but in a poem addressed to a certain illustrious person-age, that I envied no man.[5] Suppose, though, that I am not worthy of belief. Still, even then, what probability is there that I should be jealous of a writer who devoted his whole life to those things which with me were but the flower and first-fruits of my youth. What to him was, if not his only occupation, cer-tainly the supreme object of his life, to me was mere sport, a pastime, the first essay of my powers.

What occasion is there here for rancor? What ground is there for even a suspicion of jealousy? When you say, in praising him, that he might have devoted himself to another kind of composition, had he wished, I heartily agree with you. I have the highest opinion of his ability, for it is obvious from what he has done that he would have succeeded in anything he might have chosen to undertake. But suppose that he had turned his powers in another direction, and successfully—what then? What would there be in that to make me jealous? Why should it not rather be a source of satisfaction to me? Who indeed could excite envy in me, who do not envy even Virgil?—unless per-haps I should be jealous of the hoarse applause which our poet enjoys from the tavern-keepers, fullers, butchers, and others of that class, who dishonor those whom they would praise. But, far from desiring such popular recognition, I congratulate my-self, on the contrary, that, along with Virgil and Homer, I am free from it, inasmuch as I fully realize how little the plaudits of the unschooled multitude weigh with scholars. Should it be suggested that the citizen of Mantua is, when all is said, dearer to me than my fellow-citizen of Florence, I must urge that, although I will not deny that jealousy does flourish most rankly between neighbors, the mere fact of common origin cannot by itself justify such an inference. Indeed the simple fact of our belonging to different generations would make this latter sup-position absurd, for as one has elegantly said, who never speaks

5. *Epistolae Metricae* I, 6, to Giacomo Colonna.

otherwise than elegantly, "The dead are neither hated nor envied."[6]

You will accept my solemn affirmation that I delight in both the thought and style of our poet, nor do I ever refer to him except with the greatest admiration. It is true that I have sometimes said to those who wished to know precisely what I thought, that his style was unequal, for he rises to a higher plane of excellence in the vernacular than in poetry and prose. But you will not deny this, nor will it, if rightly understood, carry with it any disparagement of his fame and glory. Who, indeed—I will not say at the present time, when eloquence has so long been mourned as dead, but at the time when it flourished most—who, I say, ever excelled in all its various branches? Witness Seneca's *Declamations!*[7] No one dreams of attributing inexhaustible versatility even to Cicero, Virgil, Sallust, or Plato. Who would lay claim to a degree of praise which must be denied even to such genius? It is enough to have excelled in one kind of composition. This being true, let those be silent who attempt to twist my words into calumnies, and let those who have believed my calumniators read here, if they will, my opinion of them.

Having disposed thus of one matter which has been troubling me, I come now to a second. You thank me for my solicitude for your health. While you do this from courtesy, and in accordance with conventional usage, you well know that such acknowledgment is quite unnecessary. For who is ever thanked for his interest in himself, or his own affairs? and you, dear friend, are part and parcel of myself.

Although, next to virtue, friendship is the most sacred, the most God-like and divine thing in human intercourse, yet I think that it makes a difference whether one begins by loving or by being loved, and that those friendships should be more carefully fostered where we return love for love than where we simply receive it. I have been overwhelmed in a thousand instances by your kindness and friendly offices, but among them all there is one that I can never forget.

6. *Invective Against Sallust* II, 5 (wrongly attributed to Cicero).
7. By Seneca the rhetor (of whose existence Petrarch was unaware), father of Seneca the philosopher.

In days gone by, I was hurrying across central Italy in mid-winter; you hastened to greet me, not only with affectionate longings, which are the wings of the soul, but in person, impelled by a wondrous desire to behold one whom you had never yet seen, but whom you were nevertheless resolved to love. You had sent before you a piece of beautiful verse, thus showing me first the aspect of your genius, and then of your person. It was evening, and the light was fading, when, returning from my long exile, I found myself at last within my native walls. You welcomed me with a courtesy and respect greater than I merited, recalling the poetic meeting of Anchises and the King of Arcadia, who "in the ardor of youth, longed to speak with the hero and to press his hand."[8] Although I did not, like him, stand "above all others," but rather beneath, your zeal was none the less ardent. You introduced me, not within the walls of Pheneus, but into the sacred penetralia of your friendship. Nor did I present you with a "superb quiver and arrows of Lycia," but rather with my sincere and unchangeable affection. While acknowledging my inferiority in many respects, I will never willingly concede it in this, either to Nisus, or to Pythias, or to Laelius. Farewell.

48. Lament for the Loss of the Holy Land, and a Diatribe Against Contemporary Popes and Princes[1]

But here I am, contrary to my expectation, recalled once more to France, and while I am going about amongst the famous solitaries I seem to hear from afar a third Peter, as though he were crying out at my back that he ought not to be

8. A series of allusions to Virgil, *Aeneid* VIII, 163–66.

1. *De Vita Solitaria* II, ix (Zeitlin, pp. 237–52). Parts of this long digression were added considerably after the original date of composition: see notes 3 and 8 below.

passed over, and so I am constrained to stop. This is Peter the
Hermit who once led the solitary life in the region of Amiens,
where however he did not remain hidden. For when Christ was
beginning to grow indignant and wrathful at his own inheritance
having been so long trampled upon by his enemies and ours,
he did not reveal his wishes to any of those Christian kings
enamored of comfortable sleep on down and purple, nor to
Urban, the Pope of Rome,[2] who, though an earnest and accomplished man, was preoccupied, but to Peter, a poor, inactive
solitary, sleeping on a humble cot. He first inspired him to gird
himself in haste for the voyage across the sea in order that by
a direct view of the miseries he might be made more eager for
the pious business. When he had arrived at the place to which
he had been ordered, Peter was shocked by the wretched servitude of Simeon, who was then patriarch of Jerusalem, and of
the other faithful ones, and by the sad defilement of the holy
places. Groaning and praying, and passing nights in vigils on
the naked floor of the church, he was at length overcome by
sleep. And when he had fallen asleep, Christ again appeared
to him, ordering him to rouse the pastors and Catholic princes
for the vindication of his name. How devotedly he undertook
so great a mission and one so far beyond his strength, how
energetically and how faithfully he carried it out, Christ favor-
ing his pious exertions, and how fully he succeeded, it is not
now time to describe, especially as the thing is known even to
the general public through two volumes of considerable size
written in a passable style in the vulgar tongue. And since I
observe that in the case of this man too the minds of writers
are variously inclined, I follow in doubtful points those whom
I judge more worthy of trust and whom I think to be influenced
by an attention to facts rather than persons.

It were to be wished that the immediate issue had been the
permanent result, that the vengeance of Christ had been as enduring as it was fortunate, and that there had been no return
because of men's sins to former miseries after so victorious an
event. It is all the more disgraceful, inasmuch as to have lost

2. Urban II (1088–99), who in 1095 proclaimed the First Crusade.

again what was ours is more discreditable to us and more creditable to the enemy than not to have recovered it; it serves to diminish our hopes and to increase theirs for future control and is the occasion of their cruelty toward us. But now why do I weep or why do I complain over the manger, over Mount Calvary, the stone of the sepulchre, the Mount of Olives, the Valley of Judgment, and all the other places, singularly beloved of Christ, where he took humanity upon him and was brought forth into the light, where he cried on being born, where he crawled as a child, where he played as a boy, where he was taught as a man, where he gave up his living breath for us, where he lay in death and came to life again, whence he descended to hell, whence he rose to heaven, where at last he shall judge both the living and the dead with an irrevocable sentence? And now shall the Egyptian dog hold this land which was promised to our forefathers and snatched away from us, which was destined for us if we were men—the center of our hope, the pledge of our eternal home? Alas, what besides groans and complaints is left for a miserable man, when even our kings love nothing but pleasures and our popes nothing but riches, when the people either weep in their bondage or rage in their freedom, and everybody seeks his own interest, no one that of Christ, whose special patrimony is being destroyed while we are sitting idly by and looking on? What do I say, or why do I speak of these most active persons as idle? Verily while we are raging and meditating foolishness, while we are rolling about in filth and taken up with our pleasures, striving to keep them in our grasp as they flit by, while we are counting and hoarding the money of the poor, while we are building useless and tasteless towers in the latest Babylon so that our pride, in preparation for its fall, may mount to heaven, there is no one who will guard or vindicate the humble seat of Christ. Finally while we are laying siege against our brothers, we offer our side unguarded and unarmed to the impious enemy and supply him with an approach to the chamber of our king—an enormous crime and a lasting shame to our armies before which we impudently advance the banner of Christ in order thus magnificently to avenge the insults to him which he in fact might himself with a nod avenge, and is perhaps avenging with a hidden justice, looking down meanwhile from on high upon our faith.

But we are either listless, or consumed with the passions of our minds. Behold now how with insatiable lust and flaming hatred the kings and princes of the earth quarrel about some narrow strip of profane and barbaric soil. But suppose that they were in agreement, what public good were to be hoped from that? Never shall Herod and Pilate agree unless against the Lord and against Christ and his command. Probably they shall take their ease, and apply themselves to sleep and pleasure, and chase after disgraceful gains, and despoil their subjects in civic guise as they despoil them in military guise, for what is a necessity in time of war shall become a privilege in time of peace. Every one shall love his wife and children, no one God and his neighbor. There shall be as much thought for the body as disregard of the soul. They shall accumulate gold, jewels, and valuable furnishings, but they shall despise the ornaments of the virtues. They shall love their own fields, for these they shall not fear to fight and contend and die; but no one shall be moved by the loss of the entire Holy Land. Why, I ask, unless because what I have said is absolutely true, because the former seem to be matters of individual concern while the latter concern Christ? And so, despising the glory of our creator and redeemer, we seek our own, nor does it enter our minds that Lucifer once fell from heaven through the very conduct by which today we hope to ascend to heaven.

But if you are loth to put your faith in words, you will at least believe the facts, which, as it is said, are not in the habit of lying. Look about you, I pray, and survey the countries and ask what is happening among us. The Frenchman and the Briton are quarreling. Twenty-five years have revolved since Mars and Bellona instead of Christ and Mary have held sway over those kings,[3] and although the iron on both sides is already

3. Since the Hundred Years' War began in 1337, this sentence was probably written in 1362; but Petrarch's *quinque lustra* may not mean precisely twenty-five years. Presumably what follows was written between King John's capture in 1356 and his release in 1360. See Wilkins, *Petrarch's Eight Years*, pp. 233–34.

growing soft, their spirits of iron are not at all assuaged and the
rain of blood does not allay the great flames of their wrath.
Though it happened unexpectedly even among us, among our
grandfathers and great-grandfathers it was unheard of that a
much inferior enemy should drag away in chains one who but
now was by far the greatest of our kings, as if fortune could no
longer bear the weight of so great a kingdom. But for all that
there is no end to the matter, for the eldest son of the captured
king is again making trial of arms.[4] Therefore, as you see, the
war now rages with special fury, the royal armies now join
battle afresh, and the blood which should have been shed for
Christ is devoted to hatred.

The greater Spanish lord stands still and within his own
territory (alas, the shame!) allows the majesty of Christ to be
wickedly blasphemed on a narrow rock.[5] The one who occupies
our seacoast[6] thirsts for and thinks about nothing but the gold
in Venice and the blood of Genoa, being at the behest of avarice
the satellite of one and the enemy of the other, bound by one
party with gold, conquered by the other with steel. But the
remotest of the kings[7] has been deafened by the sound of the
ocean waves advancing and receding, and from his great distance he does not hear our sighs, but being buried in the extreme west has no care for what the East is doing.

This Caesar of ours snatched a crown and went away to
Germany,[8] content with his obscure land and the mere name
of the empire whose lowest members he embraces while dis-
daining the head. The man who we hoped would recover what
had been lost does not dare to preserve his own, and running

4. In 1358 John's son Charles V began preparations to renew the war,
and fighting broke out again in October, 1359.

5. Peter the Cruel (1350–69), son of Alfonso XI, was probably too occupied in the dynastic struggle with his half-brother to worry about driving
the Moors from Gibraltar. I have corrected Zeitlin's translation here.

6. Peter IV of Aragon, who in 1351 allied himself with Venice against
Genoa.

7. Peter I (1357–67) of Portugal.

8. On the dating of this passage, see Wilkins, *Petrarch's Eight Years*,
pp. 114–16. Most likely it was written in the second half of 1355, soon
after the flight of Charles IV from Italy. In 1356 the emperor received
Petrarch cordially in Prague, and their later relations were amicable.

away from the holy embraces of his spouse, though no one is
pursuing, he shudders at the face of fair Italy, as if anything
fairer existed under the heavens! I confess that my warm and
headlong faith, which has not been afraid to inveigh against the
very greatest, holds him blameworthy. He excuses himself and
swears he has vowed to the church not to spend more than one
day in Rome.[9] O infamous day, O shameful compact, O ye hosts
of heaven, is this a vow, is this religion, is this piety? A Roman
pontiff has so deserted his Rome that he does not wish it to be
visited by another and bargains about it with a Roman emperor. I do not know what to say here, and if I knew it would
be prudent to hold my peace, but there is one thing which in
my silence the facts should proclaim, that he who removes the
dweller from the city would bring in the ploughman there if
he could. Let him see how just is such a desire.

Germany has no other aim than to arm mercenary brigands
for the destruction of the state, and from her clouds she showers
down a continuous rain of iron upon our lands. It is deserved,
I do not deny, for it falls upon an abject people. Italy ruins
herself with her own laws, and when she does draw breath, the
love of gold, more potent than the love of Christ, seizes on the
minds of its people and scatters them over all the lands and
seas. Greece, turned away by her own errors or our pride,
despises the ancient fold and our pastures. It is a superfluous
labor to speak now of other kings and earthly lords and of our
Roman pontiffs. It is all common knowledge. Hence, indeed,
results the present state of Europe and hence it is painful to
proceed further in the description. But it behooves us to touch
the wounds which, though they are not at all far from the head
and vital members, have putrefied from their location and long
neglect.

Augustine, though he was born in Africa, says in his *Confessions*[10] that Homer was hard for him because of being written in a foreign language while Virgil was easy because he
wrote in his own, that is, the Latin language. But measure Africa

9. Petrarch was later to argue that Charles should obtain a dispensation
from this requirement.
10. I, 14, 23.

now and roam over it on the wings of thought from the bosom of the Nile to the Atlantic Ocean, and I believe you will not find any one there who understands or loves our literature, unless he chance to be some pilgrim, or merchant, or captive. Jerome, writing to Evander, also affirms that besides France and Britain, countries of our region, Africa and Persia and the East and India and all the barbaric lands worshipped Christ alone and observed the single true rule of life.[11] How far this holds at present it is not even expedient to mention. To touch on a later witness of our dishonor, does not Gregory somewhere give thanks and rejoice that in his time all of Asia adhered to the faith?[12] Now, alas, you may go through all the extensive windings of the oriental shore from the left bank of the Tanais to the right bank of the Nile, and you may examine the entire tract, its territory and its men, that lies between those far distant limits of the world and the surface of our own sea, and though some one may still be found there who has the name of Christ in his mouth, I believe there is no one who has the true faith of Christ in his heart, unless he belongs to the class of those that are held there by pilgrimage, traffic, or imprisonment

But let a fourth witness now come to the support of the clear truth. An authentic letter of Athanasius, sent to Jovinian Augustus, testified that in his time all the churches agreed in this true religion of Christ, not only those established in Spain and Britain, to begin from the remotest, but in France, Italy, Sardinia, Cyprus, Crete, and Dalmatia, and also in Cappadocia, and Mysia, and Macedonia, and in all Hellas, and in addition throughout Africa, Pamphilia, Lycia, Isauria, and in all Egypt and Libya and Pontus, and in the entire orient, except for a few Asian sectaries. And in this, he himself declares, he is not following rumor but reporting actual investigations, having by examination informed himself of everybody's opinion, and possessing written proof as well as the assurances of men. But if,

11. Jerome, *Epistulae* 149 (*ad Evangelum,* not *Evandrum*: cf. *Patrologia latina* 22, col. 1194).

12. Neither the citation nor the Gregory referred to has been identified, though Petrarch would seem to have in mind Gregory the Great.

perchance, the matter calls for additional witnesses, Ambrose, in the second book of the *Vocation of All Gentiles,* and after him Augustine himself, *On the Ninety-Fifth Psalm,* place the boundaries of the Christian faith more widely than those of the Roman Empire, observing in that connection that the yoke of a people ruling with iron could not have reached as far as the faith of Christ ruling by the cross. Inasmuch as they agree in saying this in relation to the real empire and not to what is now only the image and shadow of an empire, I could wish it might be true in our time as well. Then would not all Africa be sick, nor Persia, nor Syria, nor Egypt, nor well-nigh all of Asia, nor finally, what is more serious still, the greater part of Europe. For the ancient Roman Empire, as famous writers testify, lacked only a small portion of the East, while we, alas, lack nearly everything except a small portion of the West. I believe there is no person so wanting in faith and so dull that he does not realize how much credit and authority attaches to these writers individually as well as to them all collectively in the matter of this particular complaint. And what they all say, with something to boot, is compressed in very few words by Augustine not far from the beginning of his book on *The True Religion.* "In every part of the earth inhabited by man," he says, "the holy Christian practices are handed down"—a brief saying, but fraught with tears for us, by which we may easily measure all the vastness of our loss.

But why do I lean on the evidence of individuals? Let the ecclesiastical histories be perused. By how many names are we met there of Catholic leaders who assembled a thousand years ago from the furthest north and east and south to strengthen and popularize the holy teaching of Christ, where today there is not only no bishop but no Christian living! To pass over less serious cases and to be silent about other cities which had the same beginning and a similar end, the venerable town Nicaea itself where the foundation of the faith of the Apostles was compacted and strengthened with the mortar of powerful reasons by so many and such holy old men—workmen in behalf of truth—and all Bithynia as well of which it is a part, are now possessed by the enemies of the faith. Is this the way we

are ruled? Is this the care our princes have for the state? Is
this how we crave for others' possessions, that we may lose our
own? I might easily console myself in other respects with
silence and forgetfulness, but what shall I say to you, betrayed
and forsaken Jerusalem? Let us carry this wound, continually
fresh, in our eyes and faces; there is no way in which it can be
covered up and disguised, and we bear rather more easily the
burden of injury than of shame. Besides, is this our hope of
salvation? Is this our pursuit of glory? Are the holy places thus
being trampled on? While our members are inactive, is our
head being thus mangled with impunity by the Egyptian dog,
and are impious feet insulting the sanctuary of Jesus Christ,
while he himself because of our dishonor is suffering his injuries with patience or, as I have said, perhaps avenging them
in hidden ways? Amid so many and such general misfortunes,
is there any one who dares disparage the glory of the ancient
Romans and to pollute his mouth with such falsehoods? Alas,
deeply unworthy that we are! For us provision has been made
by the great favor of heaven, though our deserts are naught!
O truly gratuitous gifts of God! For here, when I am seized by
the agitation of my sorrow and the fever of my mind, my grief
grows bold and my indignation eloquent, and abundant matter
of complaint issues forth.

Say, father, for it pleases me to put the question, if Julius
Caesar should come back today from the lower regions, bringing with him his former spirit and power and if, living in Rome,
that is, his own country, he should acknowledge the name of
Christ, as he doubtless would, do you think that he would any
longer suffer the Egyptian thief, "the multitude so effeminate
of Pelusian Canopus,"[13] as the poet calls it, to possess not alone
Jerusalem and Judea and Syria but even Egypt and Alexandria,
when he remembered that he had once wrested kingdom,
spouse, and life from a legitimate king, and that at his own
peril he had conquered those lands in order to make a present
of them to Cleopatra? I do not inquire into the justice of the
performance, but I admire his force and energy of spirit and

13. Lucan VIII, 543.

declare it necessary to our own time. For with what ease would the action of the believer have restored his own to Christ, knowing he had received from him his soul and was destined to receive eternal glory, when he gave to a concubine such a prize for adultery? If Caesar Augustus, if both the Scipios, if the great Pompey, or a thousand others should come to life again in the same city, initiated in the holy rites of the Christian faith, would they suffer the name of their Christ to be held in contempt in the regions associated with their glory—the first one in Spain, where by the majesty of his name he composed the disorders which had troubled it for centuries, the next two in Africa which one of them made a tributary and the other quite destroyed, and the last in the northern and eastern regions where he bound with chains the necks of so many kings? If, wanting the light of true faith, they dared such great enterprises for an earthly country, what do you suppose they would not have dared prosperously, with Christ as leader, for their eternal country?

But our princes and exalted leaders of men, in their chamber braver than lions, in the field tamer than deer, dishonor masculine countenances with effeminate minds, being very alert for nocturnal wars but otherwise pacifically inclined, and spirited in nothing else than the pursuit of luxury and the hatred of virtue. Those whom they are unable to imitate and whom they ought at least to have revered or admired in silence, they persecute and disdain. But there is nothing unusual in finding that models of virtue are annoying to the enemies of virtue or that those who sympathize with Mahomet in many ways, should agree with him also in this. The latter, as I believe it is written, has blessed Mecca and Jerusalem among cities and cursed Rome and Antioch. It is worth while to inquire deliberately into the reasons of his blasphemies, but I find nothing at all to disturb me in his references to Mecca and Rome. For what novelty is it that an adulterous and licentious fellow should have enjoyed the city of Mecca, the profane dwelling-place of all impiety, the worthy lodging of a defiled and incestuous body? There the wicked, infamous robber is buried, though he is worthier to feed the bellies of wolves and crows. And that

butcher rests in the midst of his own people in the greatest
love and most undeserved respect, while the tomb of Christ,
alas the sorrow! is held without reverence by the enemy and
is approached only rarely and stealthily by the faithful, not
without serious danger and the dishonorable payment of tribute.
Moreover, what wonder is it that the creator of a wicked superstition should hate the gracious city that is hostile to his acts
and sprinkled with sacred blood of martyrs, and is the most
eminent stronghold of religion and faith, fearing it particularly
as the place whence in all likelihood should come destruction
to his own poisonous teaching, and recalling at the same time
all the ruin and heavy mischances that had fallen from that
quarter at different times on the Persians, Medes, Egyptians,
Chaldeans, and his Arab forefathers? The hatred inspired in
him by fear and distress is almost reasonable. I rather wonder
that the wildernesses of the Nile did not move him to hatred,
where he had heard of so many miracles and so many virtuous
deeds performed by the Anthonys and the Macarii through
the sole name of Christ. Indeed I have no doubt that he did
hate them, being an accomplished voluptuary and an instigator
of every obscene lust. What does puzzle the mind is the reason
of his love for Jerusalem and hatred of Antioch. But I am inclined to surmise that he remembered the first as the city in
which his adversary Christ—clearly an adversary, though perhaps he did not dare to abuse him openly because of the
majesty and glory of his name—had endured so many indigni-
ties, so many lashes, so cruel a death, and he was glad to love
it as the place which shared his hatred and envy of Christ,
even though the love which Christ's death instilled into his
savage breast ought to have been extinguished by the glorious
resurrection. But that the unreasonable and impious fellow,
blind with the lust of rule, failed to see. He hated Antioch, on
the other hand, because there the designation of Christianity
first arose, as is shown in the Acts of the Apostles,[14] and there
the Apostle Peter, the friend of Christ and the leader and stand-
ard-bearer of the Christian band, ascended the first pontifical

14. Acts 11, 26.

chair. It would seem then that one city disturbed him in that it approved Christ and the name of Christ, the other in that it supported the name and the vicar of Christ with renowned reverence. No place was more hateful to him, I suppppose, than Bethlehem. Yet he does not mention its name, being cunning with a native shrewdness of wit, though perhaps untaught, in order not to appear to betray too openly the reasons for his hatred. Thus much I may be allowed to offer as a diversion not unpleasant to myself and agreeable, I imagine, to the reader.

It is time to return to the point of our departure. Goaded by the sting of sorrow, I have with a glowing and flaming point impressed this indelible mark of infamy, which was all I could do, upon our peoples and princes who have involved themselves in so many useless, nay mischievous and impious concerns, and neglect this honorable and particularly obligatory duty to our home—I mean to our eternal home, Jerusalem, not the one here on earth but that of our mother which is situated in heaven on high, from which we are now exiled. The former bears but the image of the latter, and if it is estimated with reference to itself, it is not our country and merits the fate it has suffered, and is deserving of intenser hatred, since with sacrilegious daring and wicked unanimity it crucified its God who had come down to serve it in a lowly garb, though from the cloud of his flesh he shone with the splendor of many and great miracles. But that impiety, though destructive to herself, may be of advantage to the world, since by placing him on the cross it revealed him to the peoples for worship as though from a greater elevation.

Not for any country are all things to be dared, though those who have dared are exalted to the skies with many commendations. Among our own patriots who have shed their blood for their country, praise is given to Brutus and Mutius and Curtius and the Decii, the Fabii, and the Cornelii. Foreigners also meet with praise, for a like virtue deserves a commendation not unlike. Codrus and Themistocles are praised by Athens, Leonidas by Sparta, Epaminondas by Thebes, the brothers Philenus by Carthage, and other citizens by other states. If you ask my opinion about all of these, it is that our love should be for the celestial state, which is not disturbed by the agitations of tribunes, the uprisings of the populace, the arrogance of the senate, the envy of factions, or foreign and domestic wars; whoever sheds his blood for it is a good citizen and certain of his reward. Not that I think one's earthly country should on that account be forsaken, for which, if the situation requires it, we are even commanded to fight, yet only provided it is ruled by justice and lives under equitable laws, as was once the case with the Roman republic, according to the writings of Sallust, Livy, and many besides. Cicero in particular argues this point acutely and eloquently in his book on the Republic.[15] I might easily agree with the writers who maintain that Rome was just even when it imposed force upon the whole world and seemed to be most violent, on the ground that it was to the advantage of those very peoples who were coerced to be coerced, and that it might be salutary, though harsh to the taste, for the world to have a single head for its affairs, especially when it was a head of such supreme excellence. But there is this serious objection to such a view, namely, that while they maintained justice between men by means of those Roman arts described by the poet, assigning to each one his due, engrafting the laws of peace, forbearing the conquered, and warring down the proud,[16] and although, as Cicero notably remarks elsewhere, "As long as the empire of the Roman people maintained itself by acts of service, not of oppression, wars were waged in the interest of our allies or to safeguard our supremacy; the end of our wars was marked by acts of clemency or by only a necessary degree of severity; the senate was a haven of refuge for kings, tribes, and nations; and the highest ambition of our magistrates and generals was to defend our provinces and allies with justice and honor,"[17] and though it might be very true that "this could be called more accurately a protectorate of the world than a dominion"—although, I say, I might admit that the conduct of the Romans of that time was actuated by perfect justice and good will as regards men, yet toward God there can be no doubt they were unjust, for they deprived him of something not insignificant, namely of themselves, in the manner of fugi-

15. Known to Petrarch from Augustine, *De Civitate Dei* XIX, 21.
16. Cf. Virgil, *Aeneid* VI, 852–53.
17. Cicero, *De Officiis* II, 8, 26.

tive slaves making theft of themselves from their master, and, what is the most serious form of theft, offering to his enemies the worship due to him, which is doubtless a much greater injustice than if some ancestral estate or property were seized from a neighbor.

This passage is examined and curiously discussed by Augustine in his book on the celestial republic.[18] Suppose indeed a man should be born into a country corrupted with wicked manners, as are nearly all that you now see, should he be commended for having shed his blood for such a state? By no means. If at the risk of life a man sought to obtain for wicked and dishonest citizens impunity for their crimes, would you say he was deserving of praise and commemoration (though this has indeed happened to many of whom we read), would you say that his life was glorious? I call him wasteful of life and doubly dead, since he has thrown away at once his body and his soul, at once his temporal and eternal life. On the other hand, not to wander too far, if there is any piety or justice in us, what would it not be reasonable to dare and to do in behalf of the heavenly Jerusalem, in behalf of that eternal country which assures us of a blessed dwelling-place, without end, without toil, without trouble, without fear, without any vexation, in which there dwells nothing disgraceful, nothing impious, nothing unjust?

Truly, I have now journeyed as far from my beginning as Peter did from his home. The encounter of a single solitary old man gave me this courage to rebuke the princes and peoples of the West with our reproach in relation to the East. Would that my right hand were as effective in this as was Peter's tongue! That this wish is vain I am not at all sure; I rather fear lest I should be thought to have spoken with too much insistence and boldness by those who regard freedom of mind as recklessness, truth as madness, and every exhortation as an insult. But however the matter may be received, being now by these words and this digression eased of the heavy and annoying load of my grievances, I return to the path of the original narrative with greater alacrity.

18. *De Civitate Dei* XIX, 21.

49. He Turns from Profane to
   Religious Literature[1]

I noticed in a letter of yours that you were pleased at my mixture of sacred and secular themes, and that you thought Saint Jerome would have been likewise pleased. You mention the charm of variety, the beauty of structure, the force of association. What can I reply? You must make your own judgments, and certainly you are not easily or commonly deceived, except that well-wishers readily err, and often are eager to do so.

But putting all this to one side, let me speak of myself and of my new but serious enthusiasm, which turns my thoughts and my writings to sacred literature. Let the supercilious laugh, who are revolted by the austerity of holy words, as the modest garb of a chaste matron repels those who are used to the flaunting colors of light women. I think that the Muses and Apollo will not merely grant me permission, they will applaud, that after giving my youth to studies proper to that age, I should devote my riper years to more important matters. Nor am I to be criticized, if I, who so often used to rouse by night to work for empty fame and celebrate the futile lauds of men, should now arise at midnight to recite the lauds of my creator, and devote the hours proper to quiet and repose to him who shall neither slumber nor sleep while he keepeth Israel; nor is he content with universal custodianship, but he watches over me personally and is solicitous for my welfare. I am clearly conscious of this, and all men capable of gratitude must feel the same. He cares for each individual as if he were forgetful of mankind *en masse;* and so he rules the mass as if he were careless of each individual. Thus I have it firmly in mind that if it be heaven's will I shall spend the rest of my life in these

1. *Epistolae Familiares* XXII, 10 (from Milan, September 18, perhaps 1360), to Francesco Nelli.

studies and occupations. In what state could I better die than
in loving, remembering, and praising him, without whose constant love I should be nothing, or damned, which is less than
nothing? And if his love for me should cease, my damnation
would have no end.

I loved Cicero, I admit, and I loved Virgil. I delighted in
their thought and expression so far that I thought nothing could
surpass them. I loved many others also of the troop of great
writers, but I loved Cicero as if he were my father, Virgil as
my brother. My admiration, my familiarity with their genius,
contracted in long study, inspired in me such love for their
persons that you may think it hardly possible to feel a like
affection for living men. Similarly I loved, of the Greeks, Plato
and Homer. When I compared their genius with that of our
own masters I was often in despair of sound judgment.

But now I must think of more serious matters. My care is
more for my salvation than for noble language. I used to read
what gave me pleasure, now I read what may be profitable.
This is my state of mind, and it has been so for some time. I
am not just beginning this practice, and my white hair warns
me that I began none too soon. Now my orators shall be Ambrose, Augustine, Jerome, Gregory; my philosopher shall be
Paul, my poet David. You remember that years ago, in the
first eclogue of my *Bucolicum carmen* I contrasted him with
Homer and Virgil, and I left the victory among them undecided.
But now, in spite of my old deep-rooted habit, experience and
the shining revelation of truth leave me in no doubt as to the
victor. But although I put the Christian writers first, I do not
reject the others. (Jerome said that he did so, but it seems to
me from the imitative style of his writing that he actually approved them.)[2] I seem able to love both groups at once, provided that I consciously distinguish between those I prefer for
style and those I prefer for substance. Why should I not act
the prudent householder, who assigns part of his furniture for
use and another for ornament, who appoints some of his slaves

2. On Jerome's sometimes ambiguous attitude toward pagan literature,
see Philip Levine, "The Continuity and Preservation of the Latin Tradition," in *The Transformation of the Roman World,* ed. Lynn White, Jr.
(Berkeley and Los Angeles, 1966), pp. 219–21.

to guard his son, and others to provide the son with sport? Both gold and silver are kinds of money, and you must know their value and not confound them. Especially since those ancient writers demand nothing of me except that I do not let them fall into oblivion. Happy that I have spent upon them my early studies, they now let me give all my time to more important matters.

Since I had already come of myself to this conclusion, I shall now so act the more confidently thanks to your encouragement. If circumstances require, I shall practice, for style, Virgil and Cicero, and I shall not hesitate to draw from Greece whatever Rome may seem to lack. But for the direction of life, though I know much that is useful in the classics, I shall still use those counselors and guides to salvation, in whose faith and doctrine there can be no suspicion of error. First among them in point of merit will David always be to me, the more beautiful for his naivety, the more profound, the more vigorous, for his purity. I want to have his Psalter always at hand during my waking hours where I may steal a glance at it; and I want to have it beneath my pillow when I sleep and when I come to die. I think that such an outcome will be no less glorious for me than was the act of Plato, greatest of philosophers, in keeping the *Mimes* of Sophron under his pillow.

Farewell, and remember me.

50. To Homer[1]

Long before your letter reached me I had formed an intention of writing to you, and I should really have done it if it had not been for the lack of a common language. I am not so fortunate

---

1. From *Epistolae Familiares* XXIV, 12, in response to a long letter sent, purportedly, from the shade of Homer. Its author was probably Pietro da Muglio, professor of letters at the University of Bologna: see Roberto Weiss, "Notes on Petrarch and Homer," *Rinascimento* IV (1953), 263–75 (esp. 267–70).

as to have learned Greek, and the Latin tongue, which you once spoke, by the aid of our writers,[2] you seem of late, through the negligence of their successors, to have quite forgotten. From both avenues of communication, consequently, I have been debarred, and so have kept silence. But now there comes a man who restores you to us, single-handed, and makes you a Latin again.[3]

Your Penelope cannot have waited longer nor with more eager expectation for her Ulysses than I did for you. At last, though, my hope was fading gradually away. Except for a few of the opening lines of certain books, from which there seemed to flash upon me the face of the friend whom I had been longing to behold, a momentary glimpse, dim through distance, or, rather, the sight of his streaming hair, as he vanished from my view—except for this no hint of a Latin Homer had come to me, and I had no hope of being able ever to see you face to face. For as regards the little book that is circulated under your name,[4] while I cannot say whose it is I do feel sure that it is yours only as it has been culled from you and accredited to you, and is not your real work at all. This friend of ours, however, if he lives, will restore you to us in your entirety. He is now at work, and we are beginning to enjoy not only the treasures of wisdom that are stored away in your divine poems but also the sweetness and charm of your speech. One fragment has come to my hands already, Grecian precious ointment in Latin vessels. . . .[5]

[The major portion of Petrarch's letter is here omitted.]

A word now in reference to your complaint that the valley of Fiesole and the banks of the Arno can furnish only three men who know you and love you. You ought not to wonder at this. It is enough; indeed, it is a very great deal, more than I

2. The earliest monument of Latin literature was Livius Andronicus' translation of the *Odyssey,* which was used as a schoolbook even in Horace's day.

3. At the instance of Petrarch and Boccaccio, a Calabrian, Leontius Pilatus, was in Florence translating Homer into Latin prose.

4. A metrical abridgment of the *Iliad* by Silius Italicus.

5. By this time Pilatus had probably made for Petrarch a preliminary translation of the first five books of the Iliad.

should have expected, to discover three Pierian spirits in a
city so entirely given up to gain. But even if you think otherwise you need not be discouraged; it is a large and populous
place, and if you seek you will find there a fourth. And to these
four I could once have added a fifth,[6] a man who well deserves
to be honored thus, for the laurels of Peneus bind his brow—
or of Alpheus rather. But alas! the great Babylon beyond the
Alps has contrived to steal him away from us. To find five such
men at one time and in one city, is that, think you, a little
thing? Search through other cities. Your beloved Bologna that
you sigh for, hospitable though she is to all who are of studious
mind, has yet but one such person, though you seek in every
corner and crevice. Verona has two; Sulmona one; and Mantua
one, if the heavens have not tempted him quite away from the
things of earth, for he has left your banner and enlisted under
that of Ptolemy. Rome herself, the capital of the world, has
been drained of such citizens almost to a man, strange though
it seems. Perugia did produce one, a man who might have
made a name for himself; but he has neglected his opportuni-
ties, and turned his back not on Parnassus only but on our
Apennines and Alps as well, and now, in old age, is leading a
vagabond life, in Spain, toiling as a copyist to earn his daily
bread. And other cities have given birth to others, but all of
these whom I have known have before now left this mortal home
and migrated to that continuing city which one day shall receive us all. . . .

For a long while I have been talking to you just as if you
were present; but now the strong illusion fades away, and I
realize how far you are from me. There comes over me a fear
that you will scarcely care, down in the shades, to read the
many things that I have written here. Yet remember that you
wrote freely to me.

And now farewell, forever. To Orpheus, and Linus, and Euripides, and all the others, I beg you to give my kindest greet-
ings, when you come again to your abode.

Written in the world above; in the *Midland* between the

6. Surely Zanobi da Strada. The Sulmonese must be Barbato.

famous rivers Po and Ticino and Adda and others, whence some
say our *Milan* derives its name; on the ninth day of October,
in the year of this last age of the world the 1360th.

51. Ravages of the War in France[1]

Astonishment is the product of inexperience. We marvel at
the strange, not at the familiar. Do not marvel then at all, for
the objects of your wonder are essentially trite and common-
place. Human affairs are forever changing; and as with all else
military glory is transient; it shifts its favor from one race to
another. The one thing stable in all we see is instability; the
one surety is in error, the one repose in perpetual movement.
You need not look afar for examples; merely contemplate your
times and your country. In my youth the Britons, who were
called Angli or English, were considered the most cowardly of all
barbarous peoples; now they have become the most bellicose.
They have routed the French, long crowned with martial glory,
in such frequent, unhoped-for victories,[2] that those who once

1. *Epistolae Familiares* XXII, 14, dated February 27, 1361, while Petrarch was en route back from France to Milan, but never sent (for lack of
a messenger). Addressed to Pierre Bersuire (also known as Petrus Ber-
chorius and Pierre de Poitiers), the author of the *Ovidius Moralizatus,* who
about 1342 had used a passage from Book III of the *Africa* as the basis of
his descriptions of classical gods. See E. H. Wilkins, "Descriptions of Pagan
Divinities from Petrarch to Chaucer," *Speculum* XXXII (1957), 511–22.
    Before King John might reenter Paris, he had to pay the English 600,000
écus, a sum the French were unable to furnish. Since Galeazzo Visconti
wished an alliance with the French royal family, he bought the dower rights
of the princess Isabelle (then eleven years old), who in October, 1360,
married Galeazzo's eight-year-old son, Gian Galeazzo, in Milan. To congratulate King John on his return to Paris, Galeazzo sent a mission with
Petrarch as orator. Petrarch's oration was delivered on January 13, to a
very receptive audience, for the king was highly interested in what he had
to say about Fortune; and even after Petrarch's return to Milan John wrote
urging the Visconti to send him back to Paris.
    2. E.g., at Sluis (1340), Crécy (1346), and Poitier (1356), the last the
occasion of John's capture.

could not make head against even the vile Scots captured the wretched, undeserving French king, whom I cannot recall without a sigh, and they laid waste his whole kingdom with fire and sword. Thus when recently I journeyed there on an official mission I could hardly be persuaded that it was the same land I had seen before. Everywhere was dismal abandonment, grief, destruction, weedy, untilled fields, ruined, deserted houses, except for those protected by the walls of cities and strongholds. Everywhere appeared the melancholy vestiges of the English passage, the recent, horrible wounds of their devastation. Nay more; Paris itself, the capital, was surrounded, up to its gates, with a burned and wasted land. It seemed to tremble with horror at its adversity, and even the Seine that penetrates its walls seemed to mourn in terror the city's fate. . . .

Northern Italy: 1361-74

52. Dedication and Preface[1]

Writing some years ago to Socrates I complained that that
year 1348 had, by the death of my friends, robbed me of nearly
all pleasure in life. And I well remember how I had mourned
them with grief, tears, and lamentations. Now what shall I say
of this year 1361, which has reft away, among so many, my one
dearest friend, Socrates? I shan't mention the others who have
vanished, lest the sad memories of this year of the plague
should reawaken my grief. This year has not merely equaled,
it has surpassed the devastations of that earlier year, especially
here in northern Italy. It has almost utterly wasted this blooming, crowded city of Milan, which had previously escaped the
pestilence. I would not again be forced to laments unsuitable
to my age and my studies. I then permitted myself many free-
doms which I now deny myself. I hope fortune will not further
force me to tears. I shall stand upright if I can; if not, fortune
will lay me low dry-eyed and silent. Groans and moans are
more shameful than destruction.

I come to the point. I dedicated to Socrates my *Letters on
Familiar Matters*. Its bulk was great; it would be still greater

1. *Epistolae Seniles* I, 1, to Francesco Nelli. Written in Padua in the
autumn of 1361 and actually sent some time later. Petrarch had left Milan
for Padua in June, and two months later learned of Socrates' death. In the
early autumn a letter from Cardinal Talleyrand informed him that Innocent
VI wished Petrarch to take the position of papal secretary left vacant by
the death of Zanobi da Strada. Petrarch refused, suggesting Boccaccio or
Nelli, who had left Florence for Naples to enter the service of Niccolò
Acciaiuoli. (Later in the year Niccolò invited Petrarch himself to settle
there.)

if I had so permitted it. Now I see fulfilled what I had foreseen; the end of my letter writing will be the end of my life.
Whatever letters I may henceforth write, tempted by friends
or compelled by circumstances, I have decided to dedicate to
you.[2] (True, in the press of my affairs, I seek rather to lighten
my burdens than to add to them.) I know that you are fonder
of prose than of verse. I don't know how much writing, or how
much of my life, is still to come; however little it be, accept
it in good part; though it be trifling, it is all yours. And do not
take it ill that I have given you second place; do not imagine
that I loved Socrates better than you. Remember that when I
began that collection I did not yet know you—though there
are many letters to you therein. I had not yet given you the
name of Simonides.

So please accept this present, whatever it may turn out to be.
It is something like an empty net I cast before you. You may
appreciate it the more since it comes late. For the gifts of old
men are rarer and longer pondered than are those of the
young.

53. Religion Does Not Require Us to Give Up Literature[1]

Your letter, my brother, filled me with the saddest forebodings. As I ran through it amazement and profound grief struggled for the supremacy in my heart, but when I had finished,
both gave way to other feelings. As long as I was ignorant of
the facts, and attended only to the words, how indeed could I

2. There is, however, no absolute chronological line between the two
collections, since the *Familiares* contain a few letters written before, and
the *Seniles* a few written after, the year 1361.
1. From *Seniles* I, 5 (from Padua, May 28, 1362), to Giovanni Boccaccio.

read, with dry eyes, of your tears and approaching death? For at first glance I quite failed to see the real state of affairs. A little thought, however, served to put me in quite a different frame of mind, and to banish both grief and surprise.

But before I proceed I must touch upon the matter to which you refer in the earlier part of your letter. You dare not deprecate, you say with the utmost deference, the plan of your illustrious master—as you too humbly call me—for migrating to Germany, or far-off Sarmatia (I quote your words), carrying with me, as you would have it, all the Muses, and Helicon itself, as if I deemed the Italians unworthy longer to enjoy my presence or the fruits of my labor. You well know, however, that I have never been other than an obscure and lowly dweller on Helicon, and that I have been so distracted by outside cares as to have become by this time almost an exile. I must admit that your method of holding me back from such a venture is more efficacious than a flood of satirical eloquence would have been. I am much gratified by such tokens of your esteem, and by the keen interest you exhibit. I should much prefer to see signs of exaggerated apprehension on your part (*omnia tuta timens,*[2] as Virgil says) than any suggestion of waning affection.

I have no desire to conceal any of my plans from you, dear friend, and will freely tell you the whole secret of my poor wounded heart. I can never see enough of this land of Italy; but, by Hercules! I am so utterly disgusted with Italian affairs that, as I recently wrote to our Simonides, I must confess that I have sometimes harbored the idea of betaking myself—not to Germany, certainly, but to some secluded part of the world. There I might hope to escape this eternal hubbub, as well as the storms of jealousy to which I am exposed not so much by my lot in life (which to my thinking might rather excite contempt than envy) as by a certain renown which I have acquired in some way or other. Thus secluded I should have done what I could to live an upright life and die a righteous death. This design I should have carried out had not fortune prevented.

2. "Though safe, fearing everything" (*Aeneid* IV, 298).

But as to turning my thoughts northward, that was by no means done with the intention which you imagine. I did not think of seeking repose in that barbarous and uninviting land, with its inclement sky. I was only submitting, from motives of respect and propriety, to the solicitations of our Emperor, who had repeatedly urged me to come and see him, with such insistence that my refusal to visit him, for a short time at least, might have been regarded as an exhibition of pride and rebellion, or even as a species of sacrilege. For, as you have read in Valerius, our ancestors were wont to regard those who could not venerate princes as capable of any form of crime. But you may dismiss your fears, and cease your laments; for—to my not very great regret—I have found this road, too, blocked by war. Anomalously enough, I am glad not to go where I should with even greater gladness have gone if I had been able. To have wished to go is enough to satisfy both my ruler's desires and my own scruples; for the rest fortune was responsible. . . .

Neither exhortations to virtue nor the argument of approaching death[3] should divert us from literature; for in a good mind it excites the love of virtue, and dissipates, or at least diminishes, the fear of death. To desert our studies shows want of self-confidence rather than wisdom, for letters do not hinder but aid the properly constituted mind which possesses them; they facilitate our life, they do not retard it. Just as many kinds of food which lie heavy on an enfeebled and nauseated stomach furnish excellent nourishment for one who is well but famishing, so in our studies many things which are deadly to the weak mind may prove most salutary to an acute and healthy intellect, especially if in our use of both food and learning we exercise proper discretion. If it were otherwise, surely the zeal of certain persons who persevered to the end could not have roused such admiration. Cato, I never forget, acquainted himself with Latin literature as he was growing old, and Greek when he had really become an old man. Varro, who reached his hun-

---

3. On his deathbed a certain Peter of Siena had asserted that Boccaccio had only a few years left to live and should renounce the study of poetry.

dredth year still reading and writing, parted from life sooner than from his love of study. Livius Drusus, although weakened by age and afflicted with blindness, did not give up his interpretation of the civil law, which he carried on to the great advantage of the state. . . .

Besides these and innumerable others like them, have not all those of our own religion whom we should wish most to imitate devoted their whole lives to literature, and grown old and died in the same pursuit? Some, indeed, were overtaken by death while still at work reading or writing. To none of them, so far as I know, did it prove a disadvantage to be noted for secular learning, except to Jerome, whom I mentioned above; while to many, and Jerome himself not least, it was a source of glory. I do not forget that Benedict was praised by Gregory for deserting the studies which he had begun, to devote himself to a solitary and ascetic mode of life. Benedict, however, had renounced, not the poets especially, but literature altogether. Moreover, I very much doubt if his admirer would have been himself admired had he proceeded to adopt the same plan. It is one thing to have learned, another to be in the process of learning. It is only the hope of acquisition which the boy renounces—quite a different thing from the learning itself, which an older person gives up; the former but turns away from an obstacle, while the latter sacrifices an ornament. The trials and uncertainties of acquisition are alone surrendered in one case; in the other the man sacrifices the sure and sweet fruit of long, laborious years, and turns his back upon the precious treasure of learning which he has gathered together with great effort.

While I know that many have become famous for piety without learning, at the same time I know of no one who has been prevented by literature from following the path of holiness. The apostle Paul was, to be sure, accused of having his head turned by study,[4] but the world has long ago passed its verdict upon this accusation. If I may be allowed to speak for myself,

4. Acts 26, 24.

it seems to me that, although the path to virtue by the way of ignorance may be plain, it fosters sloth. The goal of all good people is the same, but the ways of reaching it are many and various. Some advance slowly, others with more spirit; some obscurely, others again conspicuously. One takes a lower, another a higher path. Although all alike are on the road to happiness, certainly the more elevated path is the more glorious. Hence ignorance, however devout, is by no means to be put on a plane with the enlightened devoutness of one familiar with literature. Nor can you pick me out from the whole array of unlettered saints, an example so holy that I cannot match it with a still holier one from the other group.

But I will trouble you no longer with these matters, as I have already been led by the nature of the subject to discuss them often. I will add only this: if you persist in your resolution to give up those studies which I turned my back upon so long ago, as well as literature in general, and, by scattering your books, to rid yourself of the very means of study—if this is your firm intention, I am glad indeed that you have decided to give me the preference before everyone else in this sale. As you say, I am most covetous of books. I could hardly venture to deny that without being refuted by my works. Although I might seem in a sense to be purchasing what is already my own, I should not like to see the books of such a distinguished man scattered here and there, or falling, as will often happen, into profane hands.[5] In this way, just as we have been of one mind, although separated in the flesh, I trust that our instruments of study may, if God will grant my prayer, be deposited all together in some sacred spot where they may remain a perpetual memorial to us both. I came to this decision upon the day on which he died[6] who I hoped might succeed me in my studies. . . .

5. Boccaccio survived the crisis and kept his books, which in his will of 1374 he bequeathed to Father Martino da Signa—and, after Martino's death, to the monastery of Santo Spirito in Florence.
6. On July 14, 1361, Petrarch learned that his son Giovanni had died of the plague in Milan a few days earlier.

54. He Offers His Library to Venice[1]

Francesco Petrarca desires, if it shall please Christ and St. Mark, to bequeath to that blessed Evangelist the books he now possesses or may acquire in the future, on condition that the books shall not be sold or in any way scattered, but shall be kept in perpetuity in some appointed place, safe from fire and rain, in honor of the said saint and as a memorial of the giver, as well as for the encouragement and convenience of the scholars and gentlemen of the said city who may delight in such things. He does not wish this because his books are very numerous or very valuable,[2] but is impelled by the hope that hereafter that glorious city may, from time to time, add other works at the public expense, and that private individuals, nobles, or other citizens who love their country, or perhaps even strangers, may follow his example and leave a part of their books, by their last will, to the said church. Thus it may easily fall out that the collection shall one day become a great and famous library, equal to those of the ancients. The glory which this would shed upon this State can be understood by learned and ignorant alike. Should this be brought about, with the aid of God and of the famous patron of your city, the said Francesco would be greatly rejoiced, and glorify God that he had been permitted to be, in a way, the source of this great benefit. He may write

1. This is the minute (probably prepared by his friend Benintendi dei Ravagnani, Chancellor of the Republic) based on Petrarch's proposal (the earliest recorded) for the foundation of a *"bibliotheca publica."* On September 4, 1362, the grand council accepted the offer of "Master Francesco Petrarca, whose glory is such throughout the entire world that no one, in the memory of man, could be compared with him in all Christendom, as a moral philosopher and a poet."

2. In the course of his life Petrarch assembled a collection of some two hundred volumes—a considerable personal library at that time.

at greater length if the affair proceeds. That it may be quite clear that he does not mean to confine himself in so important a matter to mere words, he desires to accomplish what he promises, etc.

In the meantime he would like for himself and the said books a house, not large, but respectable, in order that none of the accidents to which mortals are subject shall interfere with the realization of his plan. He would gladly reside in the city if he can conveniently do so, but of this he cannot be sure, owing to numerous difficulties. Still he hopes that he may do so.[3]

55. The Censorious Florentines[1]

Frederick—the last of that name to rule the Roman Empire, in the age preceding our own[2]—a very judicious prince, was German in origin, Italian in abode, so that by nature and contact he had become fully acquainted with the ways and characters of each people We hear that he was wont to say these two were the foremost peoples in the whole world, but very dissimilar, for the merits of both should be rewarded but

3. Although Petrarch lived in Venice five years, his books never did form the basis of a public library there (such an establishment had to wait until Cardinal Bessarion laid the basis of the Biblioteca Marciana in 1469). Petrarch eventually gathered his books at Arquà; and after his death it was to Padua that Salutati and others sent for copies. Since Petrarch's last patron, Francesco da Carrara, was on bad terms with Venice, it is understandable that the books were never delivered to Saint Mark's. Francesco seems to have kept some and sold many. When in 1388 he was forced to cede all his possessions to Gian Galeazzo Visconti, the books were carried to Pavia; and in 1499 the French transported them to Blois, whence they made their way to Paris. Others are scattered over all of western Europe.

1. From *Epistolae Seniles* II, 1 (from Venice, March 13, 1363), a long letter to Giovanni Boccaccio in which Petrarch defends himself against his critics.

2. Frederick II (1194–1250), king of Sicily (1197–1250), German king (1212–50) and Holy Roman Emperor (1220–50).

punishment worked differently in each case. Reward roused both to excellence, but Italians became better if indulged, recognizing their own fault and the forbearance of their leader, whereas Germans swelled up if unpunished, imputing compassion to fear: the more you overlooked, the bolder they would become. And so it was often not only safe but expedient to go easy on Italians, but it was very dangerous even to defer giving Germans the punishment due them. For the rest, Italians should be treated with respect, Germans with familiarity: the former took joy in honors, the latter in affectionate communion, and by these practices the one group and the other were drawn into amity and loyalty. One should avoid personal friendships with Italians because they are inquisitive and too sharp concerning the faults of others, and judge everything—not only what is real, but what they have conceived a false opinion of—in such a way that they mock anything that happens differently from how they think it should. Each one has such self-confidence that he considers himself a capable critic of everything. On the contrary one should give one's self over to the social intercourse of the Germans, who pass no judgments on friends, and wish nothing in friendship except to be loved, and believe familiarity is the best proof of love.

I have related all this so that you might see what so great a man observed about our friendships and our passion for making judgments. I'm not discussing how true his opinion is, but I think I can assert this in all truth: if he were saying this not about Italians but just about our fellow citizens, nothing truer or weightier could be affirmed. Theirs are not friendships but censorships, not gentle and mild but inexorable and bitter. There is not one of them, even though in mode of life he be softer than Sardanapalus, who in passing judgment is not far sterner than Fabricius or Cato. And—to pass over their judgments of other things which regard me less—they judge letters as if nothing could be said properly that does not fill their wide, capacious ears, and soothe them when they are rough, and please them when they are hostile, and refresh them when they are weary, and charm them when they are voluptuous—a task difficult for a Cicero or a Virgil, or, as I rather think, impossible for either. I suppose they have not read what was said by that author (most of whose writings do not please me—but this does very much): "He does badly who is clever at the expense of another's book."[3] And how much worse does he do who is very clever at the expense of another's work, and scrupulous to the point of loathing and hatred, while in regard to his own he is not only dull but silent, speechless, lifeless.

For my part, as much as I can, I rejoice in our geniuses. Those few little unadorned verses,[4] having crossed the Apennines, and the Po, and the Alps, and the Danube, found a censurer nowhere, I hear, except in my native land. But—O geniuses more sharp than sound, more acute than mature! —what fire burns you, what poison infects you, what spur goads you on? The fury of raging Aetna or of Charybdis, the crash of the wild sea or the thunder, does not sound so dreadful to you as the name of a fellow citizen of yours. For it is not a matter of me alone: whoever strives to remove himself from the general herd is a public enemy. Why, for heaven's sake? Or perhaps that saying of Seneca's is true in your case: "It is expedient for you that no one seem good, as if the virtue of another were a reproach to the faults of all."[5] Believe me, my friend who share with me this indignity and injustice: we were born in a city where to praise one is to reproach the many, especially if it comes close to their sluggishness—whence they hate nothing more than their own fellow citizens, if they have attained any excellence. For what cause, do you suppose?—except that those eager to hide find the light more displeasing the closer it comes. Do you wish this made clearer than day to you? Think how often—in our memory, and in that of our fathers and grandfathers—when they were engaged in serious wars, although they always had at home a good supply of brave men well versed in warfare they went now to Cisalpine Gaul, now to Picenum and other lands for their military leaders, choosing to be defeated under the command of others rather than to win

3. Martial, preface to *Epigrammaton* Liber I.
4. The description of Mago's death.
5. *De Vita Beata* 19, 2.

under their own.[6] So great a source of shame is success gained by a leader of their own that they prefer for the enemy to obtain victory over themselves than for a fellow citizen to obtain glory over the enemy. . . .

56. Venetian Celebrations of Victory in Crete[1]

Being present in spirit, and your body being not far distant, you could almost have heard the roar of the crowd, you could almost have seen the smoke and breathed the dust of the games. And you may have had reports by word of mouth to supplement the news of day-long and night-long celebrations. Nevertheless I think my description will be welcome, though not matching the splendid reality, which your illness prevented you from witnessing. For, I ask you, what finer sight can be imagined, what more suitable celebration, than an honorable city rejoicing, not for damage done to its neighbor, not for civic dissensions or aggressions, as happens elsewhere, but for justice alone? The august city of Venice rejoices, the one home today of liberty, peace, and justice, the one refuge of honorable men, the one port to which can repair the storm-tossed, the tyrant-hounded craft of men who seek the good life. Venice—rich in gold but richer in fame, mighty in her resources but mightier in virtue, solidly built on marble but standing more solid on a foundation of civil concord, ringed with salt waters but more secure with the salt of good counsel. Do not think

6. Petrarch could be alluding to Pietro Rossi da Parma (1336–37), Malatesta III da Rimini (1341), Pandolfo Malatesta (1359), and Rodolfo da Varano (1362), who were among the many foreign captains employed by Florence.

1. *Epistolae Seniles* IV, 3 (from Venice, August 10, 1364), to Pietro da Muglio, who was Salutati's teacher of rhetoric at Bologna. Pietro was at this time in Padua.

that Venice exults merely for the recovery of the island of
Crete, which, though great in antiquity, is poor in great spirits—
and all great things are small in comparison with virtue. Venice
rejoices at the outcome, which is as it should be—the victory
not of its arms but of justice. For it is no remarkable achievement for men of might, with the power of Venice and a great
leader, and with mastery of sea and land warfare, to have vanquished a swarm of unarmed, cowardly, runaway Greeklings.
The important thing is that even in our age fraud yields so
speedily to fortitude, vices succumb to virtue, and God still
watches over and fosters man's affairs. "I am the Lord, and I
change not,"[2] he says. And again: "I am that I am."[3] He would
not partake of truth and perfection if there were any change in
him. He is ever what he was; the Psalmist did not lightly attribute to him this quality.[4] Moreover, what he was and what he
is will be forever. Indeed "was" and "will be" hardly apply to
him; he "is" only. And if anyone should doubt this on the ground
that men's affairs often seem to be neglected, whether for man's
manifest sins or from the obscurity of God's judgments, this
swift, bloodless, easy victory must disabuse him. It was indeed
so great that one will now hear in Venice, concerning the Cre-
tans, what was once said in Rome of the Illyrians, that "their
war was finished before it was begun."[5] Hence our just joy and
triumph.

It would take too long for my burdened and all too incompetent pen to describe all the rejoicings. I shall give you merely
a summary. On the fourth of June of this year 1364, at about
the sixth hour of the day, I happened to be standing at my
window, looking out at the sea, with a brother in God, now the
beloved Archbishop of Patras.[6] He is to proceed at the beginning of autumn to his seat, but out of his constant love for
me and by the favor of circumstance he is spending the summer
in his own house (which is formally known as my house).

2. Malachi 3, 6.
3. Exodus 3, 14.
4. Cf. Psalms 33, 4 [34, 3].
5. Florus I, 29 (-II, 13).
6. Bartolomeo Carbone dei Papazurri.

While we were watching, one of those long ships called galleys, garlanded with blooming branches, rowed in at the harbor mouth. This unexpected sight stilled our conversation. We conceived the hope that the vessel brought good news. It crossed the harbor under full sail; happy sailors and young men crowned with leaves made joyful signals and from the bow waved banners aloft. They hailed the fatherland victorious, though why we did not yet know. Now the watchman on the city's highest tower signaled the arrival of the strange ship. Out of curiosity, at no command, the whole population ran down to the shore. When the ship came closer and details were visible, we recognized the enemy's flags hanging from the stern, and no doubt remained that she brought news of victory. We hoped for word of a captured city or of the winning of a single battle, not for the war's ending; our minds did not grasp the facts. But when the messengers landed and made their report to the Council, we had glad news beyond our hope and expectation. The enemies were conquered, killed, captured, or in flight, our citizens were released from their bonds, the cities had returned to their duty, our yoke was laid again on Crete, we had suspended operations, the war was ended without slaughter, and peace was gained with our glory.

When the report was made, the doge Lorenzo, noble in name as in fact[7] (unless my love for him deludes me), memorable for his elevated mind, his courtly manners, his zeal for virtue, and above all for his unusual piety and patriotism, convinced as he is that nothing can succeed unless it is based on religion, decreed a universal thanksgiving and praise of God. This took place throughout the city, but noteworthily in the basilica of the blessed Mark the Evangelist. I think there is nothing more beautiful on earth. There was done everything that man can do for God's honor. The rites were sumptuously celebrated, and there was a mighty procession around the church. Not only the populace and all the clergy were present, but there were high prelates from afar, who happened to be in the city or who

7. Lorenzo Celso, doge from 1361 to 1365. In Latin *celsus* means "lofty," "noble."

were attracted by eagerness to participate or by the news of the great ceremony.

When religion had amply received its due, everyone turned to games and spectacles. It would be tiresome to enumerate all the different kinds of games, their forms, costs, solemnity, and decorum such that, remarkably enough, there was nowhere confusion and ill feeling. Everything breathed joy, courtesy, concord, love. Such a lofty mood pervaded the city that modesty and sobriety, far from disappearing, ruled everywhere and prevented excesses in the celebrations. These continued in various forms through many festive days, and concluded with two great functions. I don't know the Latin names for them, so I shall describe them.

The first was a race; the second a contest, or joust. In the first the contestants dash down a straight course; in the second they dash against each other. In both the participants are mounted; in the first the riders do not clash but give a warlike note by brandishing spear and shield and carrying fluttering silk banners. The second is a sort of duel in armor. In the first reigns the utmost of elegance, with a minimum of peril. The second is a mock conflict; the French call it, not very properly, *jeu de lance;* this would better fit the first game, for in that they play, and in the second they fight. In both I realized something I should hardly have accepted on others' testimony, but I must credit my own eyes: this people possesses a rare eminence, not only, as everyone is aware, in nautical and seafaring skills but in military exercises. They display the arts of horsemanship and of weapon-handling, *élan* and endurance, enough to rank them with the fiercest fighters on earth.

Both performances were held in that great square, which I doubt has any match in this world, in front of the marble and gold façade of the temple. No outsider took part in the first contest. Twenty-four noble youths, handsome and splendidly clad, were chosen for this part of the ceremony. And Tommaso Bombasi was summoned from Ferrara. Let me record for the benefit of our sons—if my words are to persist at all among them—that he has the same standing in the Venetian state as the actor Roscius had in Rome, and he is as close a friend of mine as Roscius was to Cicero (although this comparison of persons is far from exact).[8] Anyway, under his direction the performance was staged so skillfully that you would have said the riders were flying angels. It was a marvelous sight to see all these gallant youths, dressed in purple and gold, checking and spurring their fleet-footed steeds adorned with glittering trappings so that they seemed hardly to touch the ground. They followed their captain's orders so exactly that at the moment one reached the goal another sprang from the mark, and another made ready for his race. With this alternation of uniform riders there was a constant race. One man's finish was another man's starting point; when one stopped another began; so that, though many coursed in full view, you would have said at the end that just one man had ridden the whole way. Now you would see the spear points flash through the air, now the purple banners fluttering in the breeze. The size of the multitude is hard to reckon and hard to believe; both sexes and every age and station were represented. The doge himself with a great band of the leading men occupied the loggia above the church vestibule; at their feet, below this marble tribune, the crowd was massed. This is where the four gilded bronze horses stand, the work of some ancient unknown but illustrious sculptor. On their high place they look almost alive, whinnying and stamping. To avoid the heat and dazzle of the descending summer sun, the loggia was everywhere protected with varicolored awnings.

I was invited, as I had often been similarly honored. I sat at the right of the doge. I was delighted with the spectacle during two days; but thereafter I excused myself, on the ground of my occupations, which are well known. Down below there was not a vacant inch; as the saying goes, a grain of millet couldn't have fallen to earth. The great square, the church itself, the towers, roofs, porches, windows were not so much filled as jammed with spectators. An inestimable, an incredible throng covered the face of the earth. Under our eyes the swarming,

8. At his death Petrarch left his lute to Tommaso Bombasi, "that he might play it, not for the vainglory of this fleeing world, but in praise of God everlasting" (see Mommsen, *Medieval and Renaissance Studies,* pp. 217–18).

well-mannered offspring of the flourishing city augmented the joy of the festival. The general gaiety was reflected and redoubled by one's recognition of it on one's neighbor's face.

On the right a great wooden grandstand had been hastily erected for this purpose only. There sat four hundred young women of the flower of the nobility, very beautiful and splendidly dressed. They watched the daily spectacles, and early and late they adorned brilliant receptions for invited guests. Nor should I overlook the presence of certain high noblemen from Britain, kinsmen of the king, who had journeyed here by sea to celebrate our victory, and who were reposing after the hardships of ship life.

The equestrian games ended after a good many days. The only prize awarded was that of honor; and this was so equally distributed that one might rightly say that every man was victor, no man vanquished. But prizes were offered in the other game, in which the outcomes were more variable and the danger greater, and in which some foreigners came to take part. A heavy crown of pure gold, sparkling with gems, was granted to the victor; a silver-mounted sword belt of splendid workmanship went to solace him who merited the glory of second place. A challenge in military form and in Italian, authenticated with the doge's seal, had been sent to the provinces near and far, by which all those who were tempted by such glory were summoned to that tourney on horseback. Many indeed assembled not only of different cities but of different languages, who possessed military training, confidence in their own merit, and hope of distinction.

When the races were over, the jousts began on the fourth of August and lasted four successive days with such splendor that the memory of man records nothing comparable since the founding of the city. On the last day, by the decision of the doge, of the senators, of the visiting military men, and noteworthily of our general, author (after God) of our victory, and of all our joy, the first prize was awarded to one of our citizens, the second to a visitor from Ferrara. This was the end of our games, but not of our joy and of our successes. And let this be also the end of this letter, in which I have tried to present to your eyes and ears what illness deprived you of, in order that you may know the succession of affairs here and recognize that in a maritime people there may exist a soldiery spirit, and a sense of magnificent display, and mettlesome character, and contempt for lucre, and a lust for glory. Farewell.

57. Encouragement for Boccaccio and a Diatribe Against Ignoramuses of Several Sorts[1]

"I have somewhat to say unto thee," if a poor sinner may use the words of his Savior, and this something for which you are listening, what should it be but what I am wont to tell you? So prepare your mind for patience and your ears for reproaches. For, although nothing could be more alike than our two minds, I have often noticed with surprise that nothing could be more unlike than our acts and resolutions. I frequently ask myself how this happens, not only in your case but in that of certain others of my friends, in whom I note the same contrast. I find no other explanation than that our common mother, nature, made us the same, but that habit, which is said to be a second nature, has rendered us unlike. Would that we might have lived together, for then we should have been but one mind in two bodies.

You may imagine now that I have something really important to tell you, but you are mistaken—and, as you well know, a thing must be trivial indeed which the author himself declares to be unimportant, for our own utterances are so dear to us that scarcely anyone is a good judge of his own performances, so prone are we to be misled by partiality for ourselves and

1. *Epistolae Seniles* V, 2 (from Venice, August 28, 1364), to Giovanni Boccaccio.

our works. You, among many thousands, are the only one to be
betrayed into a false estimate of your compositions by aversion
and contempt, instead of inordinate love—unless, mayhap, I
am myself deceived in this matter, and attribute to humility
what is really due to pride. What I mean by all this you shall
now hear.

You are familiar, no doubt, with that widely distributed and
vulgar set of men who live by words, and those not their own,
and who have increased to such an irritating extent among us.
They are persons of no great ability, but of retentive memories;
of great industry, too, but of greater audacity. They haunt the
antechambers of kings and potentates, naked if it were not
for the poetic vesture that they have filched from others. Any
especially good bit which this one or that one has turned off,
they seize upon, more particularly if it be in the mother tongue,
and recite it with huge gusto. In this way they strive to gain
the favor of the nobility, and procure money, clothes, or other
gifts. Their stock-in-trade is partly picked up here and there,
partly obtained directly from the writers themselves, either by
begging, or, where cupidity or poverty exists, for money. This
last case is described by the satirist: "He will die of hunger if
he does not succeed in selling to Paris his yet unheard *Agave*."[2]

You can easily imagine how often these fellows have pestered
me, and I doubt not others, with their disgusting fawning. It is
true I suffer less than formerly, owing to my altered studies, or
to respect for my age, or to repulses already received; for, lest
they should get in the habit of annoying me, I have often sharply
refused to aid them, and have not allowed myself to be affected
by any amount of insistence. Sometimes indeed, especially when
I knew the applicant to be humble and needy, a certain bene-
volent instinct has led me to assist the poor fellow to a living,
with such skill as I possessed. My aid might be of permanent
use to the recipient, while it cost me only a short hour of work.
Some of those whom I had been induced to assist, and who had
left me with their wish fulfilled, but otherwise poor and ill-clad,
returned shortly after arrayed in silks, with well-filled bellies

---

2. Juvenal, *Satires* VII, 87.

and purses, to thank me for the assistance which had enabled them to cast off the burden of poverty. On such occasions I have sometimes been led to vow that I would never refuse this peculiar kind of alms; but there always comes a moment, when, wearied by their importunities, I retract the resolve.

When I asked some of these beggars why they always came to me, and never applied to others, and in particular to you, for assistance, they replied that so far as you were concerned they had often done so, but never with success. While I was wondering that one who was so generous with his property should be so niggardly with his words, they added that you had burnt all the verses which you had ever written in the vulgar tongue. This, instead of satisfying me, only served to increase my astonishment. When I asked the reason of your doing this, they all confessed ignorance and held their tongues, except one. He said that he believed—whether he had actually heard it somewhere or other, I do not know—that you intended to revise all the things which you had written both in your earlier days, and, later, in your prime, in order to give your works, in this revision, the advantage of a mature—I am tempted to say hoary—mind. Such confidence in the prolongation of our most uncertain existence, especially at your age,[3] seemed to both of us exaggerated. Although I have the greatest confidence in your discretion and vigor of mind, my surprise was only increased by what I had heard. What a perverted idea, I said, to burn up what you wished to revise, so as to have nothing left for revision!

My astonishment continued until at last, on coming to this city, I became intimate with our Donato,[4] who is so faithful and devoted a friend of yours. It was from him that I learned recently, in the course of our daily conversation, not only the fact which I had already heard, but also the explanation of it, which had so long puzzled me. He said that in your earlier years

3. Boccaccio was born in 1313, and his age might not strike us as terribly advanced; but see the interesting article by Creighton Gilbert, "When Did a Man in the Renaissance Grow Old?" *Studies in the Renaissance* XIV, 7–32.

4. Donato Albanzani.

you had been especially fond of writing in the vulgar tongue, and had devoted much time and pains to it, until in the course of your researches and reading you had happened upon my youthful compositions in the vernacular. Then your enthusiasm for writing similar things suddenly cooled. Not content simply to refrain from analogous work in the future, you conceived a great dislike to what you had already done and burned everything, not with the idea of correcting but of destroying. In this way you deprived both yourself and posterity of the fruits of your labors in this field of literature, and for no better reason than that you thought what you had written was inferior to my productions. But your dislike was ill-founded and the sacrifice inexpedient. As for your motive, that is doubtful. Was it humility, which despised itself, or pride, which would be second to none? You who can see your own heart must judge. I can only wander among the various possible conjectures, writing to you, as usual, as if I were talking to myself.

I congratulate you, then, on regarding yourself as inferior to those whose superior you really are. I would far rather share that error than his who, being really inferior, believes himself to be on a higher plane. This reminds me of Lucan of Cordova, a man of the ardent spirit and the genius which pave the way alike to great eminence and to an abyss of failure. Finding himself far advanced in his studies while still young, he became, upon turning over in his mind his age and the successful beginnings of his career, so puffed up that he ventured to compare himself with Virgil. In reciting a portion of a work on the Civil War, which was interrupted by his death, he said in his introductory remarks, "Do I in any way fall short of the *Culex?*"[5] Whether this arrogant speech was noticed by any friend of the poet, or what answer he received, I do not know; for myself, I have often, since I read the passage, inwardly replied indignantly to this braggart: "My fine fellow, thy performance may indeed equal the *Culex,* but what a gulf between it and the *Aeneid!*" But why, then, do I not praise your humility, who

5. *The Gnat,* a poem ascribed to Virgil by several ancient writers. This incident is recorded in Suetonius' *Life of Lucan.*

judge me to be your superior, and praise it the more highly in contrast with the boast of this upstart, who would believe himself superior, or at least equal, to Virgil?

But there is something else here which I would gladly discover, but which is of so obscure a nature that it is not easily cleared up with the pen. I will, however, do the best I can. I fear that your remarkable humility may after all be only pride. This will doubtless seem to many a novel and even surprising name for humility, and if it should prove offensive I will use some other term. I only fear that this signal exhibition of humility is not altogether free from some admixture of haughtiness. I have seen men at a banquet, or some other assembly, rise and voluntarily take the lowest place, because they had not been assigned the head of the table, and this under cover of humility, although pride was the real motive. I have seen another so weak as even to leave the room. Thus anger sometimes, and sometimes pride, leads men to act as though one who did not enjoy the highest seat, which in the nature of things cannot be assigned to more than a single individual, was necessarily unworthy of any place except pehaps the lowest. But there are degrees of glory as well as of merit.

As for you, you show your humility in not assuming the first place. Some, inferior to you both in talents and style, have laid claim to it, and have aroused our indignation, not unmixed with merriment, by their absurd aspirations. Would that the support of the vulgar, which they sometimes enjoy, weighed no more in the marketplace than with the dwellers on Parnassus. But not to be able to take the second or third rank, does not that smack of genuine pride? Suppose for the moment that I surpass you, I, who would so gladly be your equal; suppose that you are surpassed by the great master of our mother tongue; beware lest there be more pride in refusing to see yourself distanced by one or the other, especially by your fellow-citizen, or, at most, by a very few, than in soliciting the distinction of the first place for yourself. To long for supremacy may be regarded as the sign of a great mind, but to despise what only approaches supremacy is a certain indication of arrogance.

I have heard that our Old Man of Ravenna, who is by no means a bad judge in such matters, is accustomed, whenever the conversation turns on these matters, to assign you the third place. If this displeases you, and if you think that I prevent your attaining to the first rank—though I am really no obstacle —I willingly renounce all pretensions to precedence, and leave you the second place. If you refuse this I do not think that you ought to be pardoned. If the very first alone are illustrious, it is easy to see how innumerable are the obscure, and how few enjoy the radiance of glory. Consider, moreover, how much safer, and even higher, is the second place. There is someone to receive the first attacks of envy, and, at the risk of his own reputation, to indicate your path; for by watching his course, you will learn when to follow it, and when to avoid it. You have someone to aid you to throw off all slothful habits through your effort to overtake him. You are spurred on to equal him, and not be forever second. Such an one serves as a goad to noble minds and often accomplishes wonders. He who knows how to put up with the second place will ere long deserve the first, while he who scorns the second place has already begun to be unworthy even of that. If you will but consult your memory, you will scarcely find a first-rate commander, philosopher, or poet, who did not reach the top through the aid of just such stimulus.

Furthermore, if the first place is to most persons a source of complacent satisfaction with themselves, and of envy on the part of others, it is certainly also liable to produce inertia. The student as well as the lover is spurred on by jealousy: love without rivalry, and merit without emulation are equally prone to languish. Industrious poverty is much to be preferred to idle opulence. It is better to struggle up a steep declivity with watchful care than to lie sunk in shameful ease; better and safer to trust to the aid of active virtue than to rely upon the distinction of an idle reputation.

These are good reasons, it seems to me, for cheerfully accepting the second place. But what if you are assigned to the third or the fourth? Will this rouse your anger? or have you forgotten the passage where Seneca defends Fabianus Papirius against

Lucilius?[6] After assigning Cicero a higher rank, he remarked: "It is no slight thing to be second only to the highest." Then, naming Asinius Pollio next to Cicero, he added: "Nor in such a case is the third place to be despised." Lastly, placing Livy in the fourth rank, he concluded, "What a vast number of writers does he excel who is vanquished by three only, and these three the most gifted!" Does not this apply very well to you, my dear friend? Only, whatever place you occupy, or whomsoever you may seem to see ahead of you, it cannot, in my judgment, be I who precede you. So, eschew the flames, and have mercy on your verses.

If, however, you and others are, in spite of what I say, thoroughly convinced that I must, willy-nilly, be your superior in literary rank, do you really feel aggrieved, and regard it as a shameful thing to be ranked next to me? If this be true, permit me to say that I have long been deceived in you, and that neither your natural modesty nor your love of me is what I had hoped. True friends place those whom they love above themselves. They not only wish to be excelled, but experience an extreme pleasure in being outstripped, just as no fond author would deny that his greatest pleasure consisted in being surpassed by his son. I hoped and hope still that I am inferior to you. I do not claim to be like a dear son to you, or to believe that my reputation is dearer to you than your own. I remember, though, that you, in a moment of friendly anger, once reproached me for this. If you were really sincere, you ought to grant me the right of way with joy. Instead of giving up the race, you should press after me with all your might, and so prevent any other competitor from thrusting himself between us and stealing your place. He who sits in the chariot or runs by his friend's side does not ask who is first, but is only anxious that they two shall be as near as possible. Nothing is sweeter than the longed-for closeness of companionship. Love is everything, precedence next to nothing, among friends. The first are last and the last first, for all are really one in friendship.

So much for the case against you. Let us now turn to the

6. Seneca, *Epistulae Morales*, 100, 9.

excuses for your conduct. In spite of your own explanation and that which comes to me through such a very good friend of yours, I have tried to discover some higher motive for your action than that which you mention; for the same act may be good or bad according to the motives which dictate it. I will tell you, then, what has occurred to me.

You did not destroy your productions, in a manner so unfair both to you and to them, through false pride, which is quite foreign to your gentle character; nor because you were jealous of someone else, or dissatisfied with your own lot. You were actuated by a noble indignation against the emptiness and vanity of our age, which in its crass ignorance corrupts or, far worse, despises everything good. You wished to withdraw your productions from the judgment of the men of today, and, as Virginius once slew his own daughter to save her from shame, so you have committed to the flames your beautiful inventions, the children of your intellect, to prevent their becoming the prey of such a rabble. And now, my dear friend, how near the truth have I guessed? I have indeed often thought of doing the same for my own compositions in the vulgar tongue, few as they are; and it was my own experience which suggested this explanation of your conduct. I should perhaps have done so, had they not been so widely circulated as to have long ago escaped my control. And yet, on the other hand, I have sometimes harbored quite the opposite design, and thought of devoting my whole attention to the vernacular.

To be sure, the Latin, in both prose and poetry, is undoubtedly the nobler language, but for that very reason it has been so thoroughly developed by earlier writers that neither we nor anyone else may expect to add very much to it. The vernacular, on the other hand, has but recently been discovered, and, though it has been ravaged by many, it still remains uncultivated, in spite of a few earnest laborers, and still shows itself capable of much improvement and enrichment. Stimulated by this thought, and by the enterprise of youth, I began an extensive work in that language. I laid the foundations of the structure, and got together my lime and stones and wood. And then I began to consider a little more carefully the times in which we live, the fact that our age is the mother of pride and indolence, and that the ability of the vainglorious fellows who would be my judges, and their peculiar grace of delivery is such that they can hardly be said to recite the writings of others, but rather to mangle them. Hearing their performances again and again, and turning the matter over in my mind, I concluded at length that I was building upon unstable earth and shifting sand, and should simply waste my labors and see the work of my hands levelled by the common herd. Like one who finds a great serpent across his track, I stopped and changed my route—for a higher and more direct one, I hope. Although the short things I once wrote in the vulgar tongue are, as I have said, so scattered that they now belong to the public rather than to me, I shall take precautions against having my more important works torn to pieces in the same way.

And yet why should I find fault with the unenlightenment of the common people, when those who call themselves learned afford so much more just and serious a ground for complaint? Besides many other ridiculous peculiarities, these people add to their gross ignorance an exaggerated and most disgusting pride. It is this that leads them to carp at the reputation of those whose most trivial sayings they were once proud to comprehend, in even the most fragmentary fashion. O inglorious age! that scorns antiquity, its mother, to whom it owes every noble art—that dares to declare itself not only equal but superior to the glorious past. I say nothing of the vulgar, the dregs of mankind, whose sayings and opinions may raise a laugh but hardly merit serious censure. I will say nothing of the military class and the leaders in war, who do not blush to assert that their time has beheld the culmination and perfection of military art, when there is no doubt that this art has degenerated and is utterly going to ruin in their hands. They have neither skill nor intelligence, but rely entirely upon indolence and chance. They go to war decked out as if for a wedding, bent on meat and drink and the gratification of their lust. They think much more of flight than they do of victory. Their skill lies not in striking the adversary, but in holding out the hand of submission; not in terrifying the enemy, but in pleasing the eyes of their mistresses.[7] But even these false notions may be excused in view of the utter ignorance and want of instruction on the part of those who hold them.

I will pass over the kings, who act as if they thought that their office consisted in purple and gold, in scepter and diadem, and that, excelling their predecessors in these things, they must excel them likewise in prowess and glory. Although they were put upon the throne for the single purpose of ruling (whence their title, *rex*, is derived), they do not in reality govern the people over whom they are placed, but, as their conduct shows, are themselves governed by their passions. They are rulers of men, but, at the same time, slaves of sloth and luxury. Still ignorance of the past, the ephemeral glory that fortune bestows and the vanity that always attends undue prosperity, may serve to excuse in some measure even these. But what can be said in defence of men of education who ought not to be ignorant of antiquity and yet are plunged in this same darkness and delusion?

You see that I cannot speak of these matters without the greatest irritation and indignation. There has arisen of late a set of dialecticians, who are not only ignorant but demented.[8] Like a black army of ants from some old rotten oak, they swarm forth from their hiding-places and devastate the fields of sound learning. They condemn Plato and Aristotle, and laugh at Socrates and Pythagoras. And, good God! under what silly and incompetent leaders these opinions are put forth! I should prefer not to give a name to this group of men. They have done nothing to merit one, though their folly has made them famous. I do not wish to place among the greatest of mankind those whom I see consorting with the most abject. These fellows

7. Cf. chapter XII of *The Prince*.

8. With the following pages compare Petrarch's invective, *On His Own Ignorance and That of Many Others,* translated by Hans Nachod in *The Renaissance Philosophy of Man,* ed. Ernst Cassirer *et al.* (Phoenix paperback), pp. 47–133.

have deserted all trustworthy leaders, and glory in the name of those who, whatever they may learn after death, exhibited in this world no trace of power, or knowledge, or reputation for knowledge. What shall we say of men who scorn Marcus Tullius Cicero, the bright sun of eloquence? Of those who scoff at Varro and Seneca, and are scandalized at what they choose to call the crude, unfinished style of Livy and Sallust? And all this in obedience to leaders of whom no one has ever heard, and for whom their followers ought to blush! Once I happened to be present when Virgil's style was the subject of their scornful criticism. Astonished at their crazy outbreak, I turned to a person of some cultivation and asked what he had detected in this famous man to rouse such a storm of reproach. Listen to the reply he gave me, with a contemptuous shrug of the shoulders: "He is too fond of conjunctions." Arise, O Virgil, and polish the verses that, with the aid of the Muses, thou didst snatch from heaven, in order that they may be fit to deliver into hands like these!

How shall I deal with that other monstrous kind of pedant, who wears a religious garb, but is most profane in heart and conduct; who would have us believe that Ambrose, Augustine, and Jerome were ignoramuses, for all their elaborate treatises? I do not know the origin of these new theologians, who do not spare the great teachers, and will not much longer spare the Apostles and the Gospel itself. They will soon turn their impudent tongues even against Christ, unless he, whose cause is at stake, interferes and curbs the raging beasts. It has already become a well-established habit with these fellows to express their scorn by a mute gesture or by some impious observation, whenever revered and sacred names are mentioned. "Augustine," they will say, "saw much, but understood little." Nor do they speak less insultingly of other great men.

Recently one of these philosophers of the modern stamp happened to be in my library. He did not, like the others, wear a religious habit, but, after all, Christianity is not a matter of clothes. He was one of those who think they live in vain unless they are constantly snarling at Christ or his divine teachings.

When I cited some passage or other from the Holy Scriptures, he exploded with wrath, and with his face, naturally ugly, still further disfigured by anger and contempt, he exclaimed: "You are welcome to your two-penny church fathers; as for me, I know the man for me to follow, *for I know him whom I have believed.*"[9] "You," I replied, "use the words of the Apostle. I would that you would take them to heart." "Your Apostle," he answered, "was a sower of words and a lunatic." "You reply like a good philosopher," I said. "The first of your accusations was brought against him by other philosophers,[10] and the second to his face by Festus, Governor of Syria.[11] He did indeed sow the word, and with such success that, cultivated by the beneficent plough of his successors and watered by the holy blood of the martyrs, it has borne such an abundant harvest of faith as we all behold." At this he burst forth into a sickening roar of laughter. "Well, be a 'good Christian'! As for me, I put no faith in all that stuff. Your Paul and your Augustine and all the rest of the crowd you preach about were a set of babblers. If you could but stomach Averroes you would quickly see how much superior he was to these empty-headed fellows of yours." I was very angry, I must confess, and could scarcely keep from striking his filthy, blasphemous mouth. "It is the old feud between me and other heretics of your class. You can go," I cried, "you and your heresy, and never return." With this I plucked him by the gown, and, with a want of ceremony less consonant with my habits than his own, hustled him out of the house.[12]

There are thousands of instances of this kind, where nothing will prevail—not even the majesty of the Christian name nor reverence for Christ himself (whom the angels fall down and worship though weak and depraved mortals may insult him),

9. II Timothy 1, 12.

10. Acts 17, 18.

11. Acts 26, 24: "And as he thus spake for himself, Festus said with a loud voice, Paul, thou art beside thyself; much learning doth make thee mad."

12. For an interpretation of Renaissance humanism which is based largely on such texts, see the recent essay by Rocco Montano, "The Renaissance? *What* Renaissance?" *Umanesimo* I (May, 1967), 1–10.

nor yet the fear of punishment or the armed inquisitors of heresy. The prison and stake are alike impotent to restrain the impudence of ignorance or the audacity of heresy.

Such are the times, my friend, upon which we have fallen; such is the period in which we live and are growing old. Such are the critics of today, as I so often have occasion to lament and complain—men who are innocent of knowledge or virtue, and yet harbor the most exalted opinion of themselves. Not content with losing the words of the ancients, they must attack their genius and their ashes. They rejoice in their ignorance, as if what they did not know were not worth knowing. They give full rein to their licence and conceit, and freely introduce among us new authors and outlandish teachings.

If you, having no other means of defence, have resorted to the fire to save your works from the criticism of such despotic judges, I cannot disapprove the act and must commend your motives. I have done the same with many of my own productions, and almost repent me that I did not include all, while it was yet in my power; for we have no prospect of fairer judges, while the number and audacity of the existing ones grow from day to day. They are no longer confined to the schools, but fill the largest towns, choking up the streets and public squares. We are come to such a pass that I am sometimes angry at myself for having been so vexed by the recent and warlike and destructive years, and having bemoaned the depopulation of the earth. It is perhaps depopulated of true men, but was never more densely crowded with vices and the creatures of vice. In short, had I been among the Aediles, and felt as I do now, I should have acquitted the daughter of Appius Claudius.[13] But now farewell, as I have nothing more to write to you at present.

13. She was fined for speaking against the Roman people.

58. The Charms of Pavia[1]

You have done well to visit me by letter, since you either
would not or could not come to see me in person. On hearing
that you had crossed the Alps to see the Babylon of the West,
worse than the ancient city of that name because nearer to us,
I was in a constant state of anxiety until I learned of your safe
return. For I well know the difficulties of the route, having
traversed it frequently, and I thought, too, of your heaviness
of body, and of your seriousness of mind, so favorable to scholarly leisure and so averse to the responsibilities which you had
assumed. Worried by these considerations, I enjoyed no peace,
day or night, and I thank God that you are back safe and sound.
The greater the perils of the sea that you have escaped, the
greater is my gratitude for your return.

But, unless you were in a very great hurry, it would have
been very easy for you, on reaching Genoa, to have turned this
way. It would have required but two days to come to see me—
whom indeed you see always and wherever you go—and you
would also have seen this city of Ticinum, on the banks of the
Ticino, which I believe you have never visited. It is now called
Pavia, which the grammarians tell us means admirable, or
wonderful. It was long the celebrated capital of the Lombards.
Still earlier than their time I find that Caesar Augustus took
up his quarters here, on the eve of the German war. I suppose
he wished to be nearer the scene of action. He had sent his
step-son on into Germany, where he was performing the most
glorious deeds of prowess. From here Augustus could observe
the campaign as from a watch-tower, stimulating the leader,
and ready, should one of the reverses so common in war occur,

1. From *Epistolae Seniles* V, 1 (December 22, 1365), to Giovanni
Boccaccio.

to bring to his succor all the imperial forces, as well as the majesty of his own name.

You would have seen where the Carthaginian leader gained his first victory over our generals, in a conflict during which the Roman commander was snatched from the enemy's weapons and saved from imminent death by his son, scarcely more than a boy—a striking presage that the lad would himself one day become a great leader.[2] You would have seen where St. Augustine is buried, and where Boethius found a fitting place of exile in which to spend his old age and to die. They now repose together in two urns, under the same roof with King Liutprand, who transferred the body of St. Augustine from Sardinia to this city.[3] This is indeed a pious and devout concourse of illustrious men. One might think that Boethius followed in the footsteps of St. Augustine, during his life, by his spirit and writings, especially those on the Trinity, which he composed after the example of Augustine, and in death, because his remains share the same tomb. You would wish that your mortal remains might have been destined to lie near such good and learned men. Finally, you would have seen a city famous in the mouths of men for its age. It is true that no reference to it occurs, so far as I can recollect, earlier than the period of the second Punic war, of which I just spoke. Indeed, if my memory does not play me false, even in connection with that period Livy only mentions the river and not the town. However, the similarity of the names—the river, *Ticinus,* and the town, *Ticinum*—might easily lead to the confusion of one with the other.

But I will leave to one side all such doubtful matters and confine myself to what is certain. You would find the air of the place very salubrious. I have now spent three summers here, and I do not remember to have experienced ever anywhere else such frequent and plentiful showers with so little thunder and lightning, such freedom from heat, and such steady, refreshing breezes. You would find the city beautifully situated. The Ligurians, of old a notable race and to this day a very powerful people, occupy the greater part of northern Italy, and the city

2. The future Scipio Africanus (Livy XXI, 46).
3. It was Boethius' body that Liutprand so transferred.

lies in the midst of their territory. Commandingly situated on a slight elevation, and on the margin of gently sloping banks, it raises its crown of towers into the clouds, and enjoys a wide and free prospect on all sides, one which, so far as I know, is not exceeded in extent or beauty by that of any town which lies thus in a plain. By turning one's head ever so little one can see in one direction the snowy crest of the Alps, and in the other the wooded Apennines. The Ticino itself, descending in graceful curves and hastening to join the Po, flows close by the walls, and as it is written, makes glad the city by its swift waters. Its two banks are joined by as fine a bridge as you would wish to see. It is the clearest of streams, both in reputation and in fact, and flows very rapidly, although just here, as if tired after its long journey and perturbed by the neighborhood of a more famous river, it moves more deliberately, and has been deprived of some of its natural purity by the brooks which join it. It is, in short, very much like my Transalpine Sorgue, save that the Ticino is larger, while the Sorgue, on account of the nearness of its source, is cooler in summer and warmer in winter.

You would see, also, one of those works in which you have such an interest, and in which I, too, take the greatest delight— an equestrian statue gilded bronze. It stands in the middle of the marketplace, and seems to be just on the point of reaching, with a spirited bound, the summit of an eminence. The figure is said to have been carried off from your dear people of Ravenna. Those best trained in sculpture and painting declare it to be second to none.

Lastly, in order of time, though not of importance, you would see the huge palace, situated on the highest point of the city; an admirable building, which cost a vast amount. It was built by the princely Galeazzo, the younger of the Visconti, the rulers of Milan, Pavia, and many neighboring towns, a man who surpasses others in many ways, and in the magnificence of his buildings fairly excels himself. I am convinced, unless I be misled by my partiality for the founder, that, with your good taste in such matters, you would declare this to be the most noble production of modern art.

So if you had come you would not only have seen your friend, which I hope, and indeed know, would have been most agreeable to you, but you would have been delighted also by the spectacle, not, as Virgil says,[4] of wonderful little things, but of a multitude of great and glorious objects. I must confess that in my own case these objects are a source of supreme pleasure, and would keep me here, were it not that other interests call me away. I leave here shortly, but very gladly return to pass the summer months—if fate grant me more summer months. . . .

59. Freedom and Necessity[1]

I have noticed from your letters sent to a friend that you are very solicitous for me over the matter of liberty. This spirit of yours is pleasing to me, I confess, but nothing new. However, lay aside your fear and be persuaded that thus far, even while seeming to be subject to a harsh yoke, I have always been the freest of men—and, I should add, will be, if any knowledge of the future were certain. Nevertheless I shall strive, I hope successfully, not to learn servility as an old man, and to be free in spirit everywhere, although one must in body and other things be subject to superiors—whether to one, as I am, or to many, in your case. Mine may not be the more burdensome sort of yoke: I believe I endure a man more easily than a tyrannous people. Unless this had always been the case, so that I was free everywhere, life would have failed me long since (or certainly the serenity and pleasantness of life)—and you are my best witness to the contrary. I should certainly be unable long to serve any mortal, except of my own accord and at love's command. What then? You know the ways of men and the difficulties of life and the snares of circumstance, whose

4. *Georgics* IV, 3 (about the works of bees).
1. *Epistolae Seniles* VI, 2 (probably 1366), to Giovanni Boccaccio.

perplexities arithmetic does not number nor geometry measure nor astrology explore; they are perceived by those who walk among them with eyes open. Wherefore I have always been pleased by, and often praised, that wise Hebrew's brief but weighty and sententious saying: "All things are difficult."[2] Yes, all things, even those which seem very easy. But none is more difficult than to live, especially to live long. Every hour and every moment brings something new, every step is slippery and full of sharp stones, to tread on which is painful, to avoid difficult.

But where am I being carried, wasting time over the difficulties of circumstances? The subject is unlimited, and you know it as well as I do, perhaps better. I'll say no more on it.

Certainly the elder Africanus, as you see, by a long abode lost his value in the eyes of the Romans.[3] What do you suppose happens to lesser men in the eyes of others? Believe me, to many, and especially to the ill, an occasional change of scene is advantageous; and it is a mark not of inconstancy but of wisdom to turn one's sails in accord with the variation of the winds and the tempest of affairs. All things cannot be entrusted to a letter; but if you knew everything I do, you would advise, I am sure—I do not say that I depart—but that I at some time take care of life's unpleasantnesses by a change of places. Pray God, then, that the end of this tale of ours, which is called life, will be good and pleasing to him. For the rest, do not give up hope of my choosing the better course, or the lesser evil, so long as the light of heaven illumines my eyes and shows the way.

There remains for you to know that your Homer—now Latin and renewing my love for the sender and my sorrowful memory of the translator—has finally reached us and filled me and all the inhabitants of this library, whether Greek or Latin, with a wonderful joy and delight.[4] Farewell, my beloved brother.

2. Ecclesiastes 1, 8.
3. Cf. Livy XXXV, 10, 6.
4. See Agostino Pertusi, *Leonzio Pilato fra Petrarca e Boccaccio* (Venice and Rome, 1964); and D. S. Carne-Ross, "The Means and the Moment," *Arion* 7 (Winter, 1968), 549–57.

60. Literary Imitation[1]

... An imitator must see to it that what he writes is similar, but not the very same; and the similarity, moreover, should be not like that of a painting or statue to the person represented, but rather like that of a son to a father, where there is often great difference in the features and members, and yet after all there is a shadowy something—akin to what our painters call one's *air*—hovering about the face, and especially the eyes, out of which there grows a likeness that immediately calls the father up before us. If it were a matter of measurement every detail would be found to be different, and yet there certainly is some subtle presence there that has this effect. In much the same way we writers, too, must see to it that along with the similarity there is a large measure of dissimilarity; and further-more such likeness as there is must be elusive, something that it is impossible to seize except by a sort of still-hunt, a quality to be felt rather than defined. In brief, we may appropriate another's thought, and may even copy the very colors of his style, but we must abstain from borrowing his actual words. The resemblance in the one case is hidden away below the surface; in the other it stares the reader in the face. The one kind of imitation makes poets; the other apes. It may all be summed up by saying with Seneca, and with Flaccus before him,[2] that we must write just as the bees make honey, not keeping the flowers but turning them into a sweetness of our own, blending many very different flavors into one, which shall be unlike them all, and better. . . .

1. From *Epistolae Familiares* **XXIII**, 19 (from Pavia, October 28, 1366), in which Petrarch tells Boccaccio about Giovanni Malpaghini, who in two years' service had copied the *Familiares*. This is the gist of advice Petrarch had given Giovanni, who was not only a fine copyist but a would-be poet.
2. Cf. Horace, *Odes* IV, ii, 27–32; and Seneca, *Epistulae Morales* 84, 5, 6.

61. Then and Now[1]

... When near puberty we were sent from Carpentras—again together: for what have we done separately during a great part of our lives?—to study law at Montpellier, at that time a most flourishing town, where we spent another four years. It was then in the power of the king of Majorca, except for a small corner subject to the king of France, who—as the nearness of the very powerful is always dangerous—soon drew to himself lordship over the whole town.[2] What tranquillity was there also at that time, what peace, what wealth of merchants, what a swarm of students, what a supply of teachers! We know, and the citizens who have seen both times perceive, how greatly all these are lacking there now, how greatly altered are things public and private.

From there we went to Bologna, than which I think there is nothing freer or more pleasant in the whole world. You remember clearly the gatherings of students, the row of seats, the watchful attention, the majesty of the teachers: you would suppose that the ancient lawyers had come back to life! There is almost none of them there today: in place of so many and so great geniuses a single ignorance has taken possession of that city. . . .

1. From *Epistolae Seniles* X, 2 (from Venice, 1367), a long, gloomy autobiographical letter to Guido Sette, who was born in 1304, became bishop of Genoa in 1358, and died November 20, 1367.
2. Montpellier was under the jurisdiction of the king of Aragon from 1204 until 1349, when it passed from the Aragonese king of Majorca (James III) to Philip VI of France. Petrarch studied there from 1316 to 1320.

62. A Boat Trip down the Po in Wartime[1]

. . . I left Padua on 25 May and reached Pavia six days later at about 9 A.M. Not to bother with details, I should have returned promptly had it not been for an injury to my bad leg, which has been unlucky since boyhood. As in the past, the affliction lasted quite a long time, and forced me into the unwelcome hands of the doctors, and still keeps me under care. And the war then raging blocked the overland road, and one could not find at any price a boat that would venture the perilous journey. Still, though the Po valley was ablaze with war, I hoped that the waterway might be freer of roving brigands. If I could escape these I was afraid of nothing. I thought my stand, my love of peace and hatred of all war, were well known to both sides. So indeed it turned out, that after more than a full month of hunting for a boat and surmounting various difficulties, I finally found a skipper less timorous than the rest. Seeing me so confident, he dismissed his fears. I boarded the craft amid general surprise, and to the tune of some very sharp scoldings. But by God's guidance all turned out well. We met everywhere armed fleets on the water and embattled soldiery on the banks. Our sailors and servants trembled and turned pale; I alone, whether from courage or foolhardiness, went everywhere intrepidly and unarmed. I was not merely

1. From *Epistolae Seniles* XI, 2 (from Padua, July 21, 1368), to Francesco Bruni, a young Florentine with whom Petrarch began corresponding in 1361. As papal secretary, Bruni had in 1366 relayed to Urban V a letter from Petrarch that may have played some part in the Pope's decision to leave for Rome the following spring.

In the spring of 1368 Petrarch went from Venice to Padua, and thence with Francesco da Carrara to Udine to greet Charles IV, who, allied with enemies of the Visconti, had entered Italy with his troops. On returning to Padua Petrarch was then asked by Galeazzo Visconti to come immediately to Pavia, to take part in negotiating a peace treaty.

untouched, I was honored; and everyone agreed that I alone could have made that journey in safety. When I attributed my safety to my insignificance, as small animals penetrate where large creatures cannot pass, everyone cried with one voice that no creatures great or small could be found that would not be suspect and ill received by one party or the other. I am no Varro, and no doubt I am saying more than is needful because I am sure you will read this with pleasure. But where the soldiers would capture and kill everyone and certainly rob them, I had my vessel so loaded down with wine and fat birds and fruit and all sorts of things that I was delayed not by the warriors' ferocity but by their generosity. All of this I attribute not to any merits of mine but to divine favor, which bestowed on me a pacific character, which is to be read clearly on my face for all to recognize.[2]

63. His Birthplace a Shrine[1]

. . . I was born in Arezzo, in that interior street commonly called Garden Lane. There was sown, there sprang the arid flower, the insipid fruit that was I. My parents were Florentines, but driven into exile in that same storm that expelled the better part of the citizens, as so often happens in our cities. Bologna rescued some survivors of our shipwreck, Arezzo took others

2. In 1365, 1366, and 1367, Petrarch had spent the first part of the year in Venice, the second in Pavia; but on their mission to Udine Francesco da Carrara (the son of Giacomo) apparently convinced Petrarch to settle in Padua, for he never returned to Venice. Padua may have been attractive to him for several reasons: he still had his tenancy in the cathedral close; Francesco was likely to be the friendliest of patrons; and Petrarch perhaps still longed for a home in the country, such as he found at Arquà, on land given him by Francesco (he moved in March, 1370). On Petrarch's relationship with Francesco (to whom he dedicated the *De Viris Illustribus*) see Mommsen, "Petrarch and the Decoration of the Sala Virorum Illustrium in Padua," *Medieval and Renaissance Studies*, pp. 130–74.

1. From *Epistolae Seniles* XIII, 3 (from Arquà, September 9, 1370), to Giovanni Fei of Arezzo.

to its great heart. Here let me insert a story which I hope you will read with pleasure. In the Jubilee year I was returning from Rome and was about to traverse Arezzo. Certain noble fellow citizens of yours, judging me worthy of an escort, met me outside the city walls. They conducted me, unsuspecting, to that little street, and to my amazement they pointed out the house where I was born. It was certainly not very big or magnificent, but what you might expect as an exile's refuge. They told me one thing that, as Livy says, filled me with more wonder than credence;[2] they said that the owner had planned to enlarge the house, but that he was forbidden by public ordinance to make any changes whatever from the state of the house when that poor little homunculus and great sinner entered there into this laborious and wretched existence! Thenceforth your citizens point it out proudly;[3] and Arezzo shows more regard for an outsider than Florence to its own son. . . .

64. His Poor Health[1]

. . . Since this humble concern has touched your noble spirit, so that you wish to know how I am, know that I am utterly uncertain about the state of my body—and not I alone, but all us mortals who live here—but that I am the more uncertain the more visibly I struggle every day with death itself. Whether it overwhelms me speedily, as it has threatened four times now in the space of one year, or whether it delays a little longer, it will surely not be put off long. For all things I thank my Christ equally; for he himself knows what is advantageous for me, and will himself do it. Whether indeed it is better to die

2. Cf. Livy I, 1.
3. Though the original house no longer exists, the present-day "Casa del Petrarca" may stand on the same site.
1. From *Epistolae Seniles* XIII, 9[8] (from Arquà, June 9, 1371), to Pandolfo Malatesta, lord of Fano, Pesaro, and Rimini since 1364. For his wedding in 1362 Petrarch had written a long letter amounting almost to a treatise on matrimony.

The Bettmann Archive

6. Petrarch's house at Arqua. Engraving.

or to live God knows; "I think no man knows," as Cicero quotes the dying Socrates.[2] I define my own case this way: Neither you, best of men, nor any of those to whom I am dear, should think or wish for anything but a good end. And certainly it is now time; it profits not to live to the point of distaste—enough is enough.

Live happily and mindful of me. Farewell.

65. Better Peace Before War than After[1]

I received your note, full of affection and solicitude, like your other letters; I thank you; I am in your debt. Do not worry, and don't interrupt your worthy labors. My family, for which I feared much more than for myself, has fortunately escaped the thunderbolts of Mars, and is here with me, thank God. I have nothing else to write you about; but it occurs to me that, to fill out the page, I might put in a somewhat comic story, perhaps new to you, about a fool and his far from foolish remark. It was when the great troubles between the Florentines and the Pisans were raging. (These occur almost annually, thanks to the sins of both sides.) The army of Florence was marching out of the gates; and a certain fool, who wandered nearly naked about the streets, was struck by the sight. He asked what it was all about. A bystander answered: "Don't you know, fool, that war has been declared against the Pisans?"

Said the fool: "And after this war there will be peace?"

"How can you think of peace, you idiot? Now the great war is just beginning."

"I still wonder," said the fool. "Won't there be a peace sometime after this war?"

2. *Tusculan Disputations* I, 41, 99.
1. *Epistolae Seniles* XIII, 18 (from Padua, November 22, 1372), to Gasparo Squaro dei Broaspini of Verona. On October 3, warfare had begun between Venice and Padua, making it advisable for Petrarch to leave Arquà; so on November 15 he moved into Padua, taking his books with him.

"Well, certainly. No war lasts forever. Of course there will be peace sometime; but now there is war."

"Well, then," said the fool, "wouldn't it be better to make the peace now, before the war begins to rage?"

What shall I say to that? Merely, if it were permissible, that the fool was very wise. Would that our warmakers might ponder his words! So might a war never be begun, or it might be ended before we should sink under war's ravages and calamities, after which indeed peace will come. That peace will be good, though it be all too late; it would be much the best, if it could come in time. But men's ears are shut against wise counsels. The ultimate triumph of war, they say, is total madness. And surely the cause of all our evils is man's sin. We shall see this clearly at the war's end. Till then we can merely await God's will. Farewell.

66. Latin Writers Versus Aristotle[1]

. . . So great is his ardor and his impulse to disparage that he does not consider what he is saying. "Where, pray tell," he asks, "can we read Cicero's *Physics,* Varro's *Metaphysics?*" O stupid inquiry! The insolent barbarian is delighted by Greek

1. From the *Invectiva Contra Eum qui Maledixit Italiae* ("Invective Against Him Who Slandered Italy"), written as a letter from Padua (dated March 1, 1373) to Uguccione da Thiene. Before Urban V left Avignon in 1367 Charles V of France had sent an embassy to urge that he not leave France. When Petrarch learned that the orator, Ancel Choquart, had not only exalted France but disparaged Italy, in the spring of 1368 he wrote to Urban to combat Choquart's arguments. (Comparing the intellectual achievements of France and Italy, he observed that all of the four Doctors of the Church were Italian, two by birth and two by study or residence). Although Choquart died in late 1368 or early 1369, a year later Jean de Hesdin composed against Petrarch an invective that reached him early in 1373, via Uguccione. One assertion in Petrarch's reply is that none of the renowned men of the University of Paris was French—in fact, many were Italian: Peter Lombard, Thomas Aquinas, Bonaventura da Bagnoreggio, and Egidio Romano.

names, and says this as if Aristotle, the author of those books,
were a Gaul. I have read the book of a certain little brother,[2]
entitled *Prosodion*. In this little grammatical treatise he im-
pertinently oversteps his bounds, and drunk with a groundless
love for his country says that Aristotle was Spanish—the same
Aristotle whom that frenetic fellow probably makes Gallic. For
what else is the point of his words against Italian and Roman
Cicero, unless he is holding up against him that Gaul who never
saw Gaul, I'm sure, or heard of it, since he was Greek or Macedonian, from Stagira? The Gaul does indeed admit—not, I
think, sincerely, but from a certain Gallic sense of courtesy—
that "Italy is a great and good part of the world" (I quote his
words). Let us therefore render thanks unto the Gaul—or
rather to the truth, which forces him to admit what it annoys
him to hear from another, and to praise strongly what he hates
very much. He admits in addition that some of our writers
composed many books useful for human life, "but nevertheless
to be esteemed much less than Aristotle." A wondrous sort of
battle! Here I thought I had undertaken war with one man;
but now that he is worn out, his step unsteady, he throws in
my way another, stronger opponent, as if to catch me off guard.
For what does the *Ethics* of Aristotle have in common with the
ignorance of the Gauls? Even grant that Aristotle is superior:
what is this to the Gauls?—unless intense hatred ascribes to
itself whatever it takes away from an enemy.

However, I am not swayed by this strong warrior he has
brought in from abroad. I persist in my opinion, which, I think,
is supported by experience and by the truth. Since my subject
forced me to discuss this a while back at great length,[3] I shall
touch on it now only briefly. I know that Aristotle's *Ethics* and
his other books were the products of a lofty genius. However,
as regards the concern of moral philosophy—that is, that we
become good, as Aristotle himself defines it[4]—I deny that any
secular books should be (I won't say preferred) placed on a
level with the books of our writers. Cicero confirms this sure

2. Unidentified.
3. In the *De Ignorantia,* composed in 1367 and published January, 1371.
4. *Nicomachean Ethics* II, 2, 1 (1103 B).

truth in many places, but in one especially: "It has always been my judgment," he says, "that our countrymen have always discovered everything on their own more wisely than the Greeks, or improved what they received from them—at least whatever they considered worth elaboration."[5] This then is also my judgment (and it is not on that account less true because it is perhaps unacceptable to a Gaul): Aristotle is more informative, Cicero affects our spirits more; in the moral writings of the former there is more acumen, in those of the latter more efficacy. Aristotle teaches more carefully what virtue is; Cicero urges its cultivation more powerfully. Let the Gaul himself decide which is more useful to men's life. And with Cicero I place Seneca, about whom Plutarch—a great man, and a Greek —willingly admits there was no one in Greece who could be compared with him as a moral writer.[6] But the Gaul will rush to say he was of Spanish origin. I shall answer that in excellence and abode, and moreover in style and studies, he is Roman; and that it is enough for me that he assuredly was not Gallic, just as my adversary finds it sufficient that Aristotle was not Italian.

Cicero did not write the *Physics*. I add: nor the *Ethics*. Varro did not write the *Metaphysics*. I add: nor the *Problems*. For we are neither Greeks nor barbarians, but Italians and Latins. But Cicero wrote the books of *Moral Duties*—that is his *Ethics*. He wrote about private matters, or about his own household— that is his *Economics*. He wrote about the commonwealth and about military matters—that is his *Politics*. But the little Gaul loves Greek titles, and although perhaps he has no Greek or Latin learning, he thinks himself something great while he belches "Physics" and spits out "Metaphysics." Cicero did not write the *Physics,* but he wrote about the laws, about the Academy, and a book concerning the praise of philosophy, by which Augustine frankly declares himself to have been helped to the right way of life and to zeal for the truth.[7] Which he never said

5. *Tusculan Disputations* I, 1.
6. This judgment appears in neither Plutarch nor pseudo-Plutarch.
7. On the effect of Cicero's *Hortensius* see *Confessions* III, 4, 7.

about Aristotle. Whether he said it about any of the Gallic
philosophers, I do not know; perhaps my adversary knows, since
he hunts watchfully for praises of Gaul. Cicero did not write
the *Physics;* but he wrote on the being of the world, the nature
of the gods, divination, fate, old age, friendship, consolation,
the ends of goods and evils, the best sort of speech, two volumes
of rhetoric, three of letters, and countless orations, whose eloquence has never had an equal. The Gaul is astounded at the
foreign names, although I have touched on just a few of many
and there is much greater splendor in their contents than their
titles. What does he mean, Varro did not write the *Metaphysics?*
A prodigious accusation against a learned man! But he wrote
twenty-five books about human matters, sixteen about divine.
"But in these last he compiled many false things inconsistent
with worship of the true divinity." Let our Gaul give thanks
to the divine providence and mercy that saved him from
those old errors for a better age and a knowledge of the true
God. For he is well aware that he had as his own ancestors
Druid priests overwhelmed by many names of false gods and
by the vainest superstition, who affirmed that all Gauls were
descended from Dis. And this empty assertion obtained general belief. For in no way could the truth about divine things
appear to them, for whom the true sun of justice had not yet
shone.

Geniuses shone forth, however, amidst the errors, and their
eyes were no less lively on that account, although surrounded
by darkness; so that we owe them not hatred for their error
but pity for their undeserved lot.[8] And that they served idols,
as Jerome says, should be attributed not to obstinacy of mind
but to ignorance. Great they surely were, but placed in the
depths; we are inconsiderable, but thanks to God we have been

8. Cf. Dante, *Inferno* IV. In his defense of poetry (*Invective Contra
Medicum,* III), Petrarch had quoted Augustine's citation of Romans 1,
19–20: "Because that which may be known of God is manifest in them;
for God hath shewed it unto them. For the invisible things of him from
the creation of the world are clearly seen, being understood by the things
that are made, even his eternal power and Godhead." Of course, Paul's
conclusion is: "so that they are without excuse."

set on high.[9] For them there was the dead of night; for us, shining midday. Because without merit, we cannot be called better on account of this; but we can certainly be called more fortunate. And this is my understanding not just about the two I have in hand, but about all the philosophers and poets of the gentiles, between whose mind's eye and the object of truth there intervened an impenetrable cloud. . . .

67. On Boccaccio's *Decameron*[1]

Your book, written in our mother tongue and published, I presume, during your early years, has fallen into my hands, I know not whence or how. If I told you that I had read it, I should deceive you. It is a very big volume, written in prose and for the multitude. I have been, moreover, occupied with more serious business, and much pressed for time. You can easily imagine the unrest caused by the warlike stir about me, for, far as I have been from actual participation in the disturbances, I could not but be affected by the critical condition of the state. What I did was to run through your book, like a

9. Cf. John of Salisbury, *The Metalogicon,* trans. Daniel D. McGarry (Berkeley and Los Angeles, 1955), p. 167: "Bernard of Chartres used to compare us to dwarfs perched on the shoulders of giants. He pointed out that we see more and further than our predecessors, not because we have keener vision or greater height, but because we are lifted up and borne aloft on their gigantic stature." See R. Klibansky, "Standing on the Shoulders of Giants," *Isis* **XXVI** (1936), 147–49. For later humanist conceptions of progress, see Hans Baron, "The *Querelle* of the Ancients and the Moderns as a Problem for Renaissance Scholarship," *Journal of the History of Ideas* **XX** (1959), 3–22; and E. H. Gombrich, "The Renaissance Conception of Artistic Progress and Its Consequences," in *Norm and Form* (London, 1966), pp. 1–10.

1. From *Epistolae Seniles* XVII, 3, written late in the winter or early in the spring of 1373 (before *Seniles* XVII, 2) from Padua, to Giovanni Boccaccio. (All four letters in Book XVII were addressed to Boccaccio; apparently none reached him.)

traveller who, while hastening forward, looks about him here and there, without pausing. I have heard somewhere that your volume was attacked by the teeth of certain hounds, but that you defended it valiantly with staff and voice. This did not surprise me, for not only do I well know your ability, but I have learned from experience of the existence of an insolent and cowardly class who attack in the work of others everything which they do not happen to fancy or be familiar with, or which they cannot themselves accomplish. Their insight and capabilities extend no farther; on all other themes they are silent.

My hasty perusal afforded me much pleasure. If the humor is a little too free at times, this may be excused in view of the age at which you wrote, the style and language which you employ, and the frivolity of the subjects, and of the persons who are likely to read such tales. It is important to know for whom we are writing, and a difference in the characters of one's listeners justifies a difference in style. Along with much that was light and amusing, I discovered some serious and edifying things as well, but I can pass no definite judgment upon them, since I have not examined the work thoroughly.

As usual, when one looks hastily through a book, I read somewhat more carefully at the beginning and at the end. At the beginning you have, it seems to me, accurately described and eloquently lamented the condition of our country during that siege of pestilence which forms so dark and melancholy a period in our century.[2] At the close you have placed a story which differs entirely from most that precede it, and which so delighted and fascinated me that, in spite of cares which made me almost oblivious of myself, I was seized with a desire to learn it by heart, so that I might have the pleasure of recalling it for my own benefit, and of relating it to my friends in conversation. When an opportunity for telling it offered itself shortly after, I found that my auditors were delighted. Later it suddenly occurred to me that others, perhaps, who were unacquainted with our tongue, might be pleased with so charming a story, as it had delighted me ever since I first heard it some

2. The Black Death of 1348.

years ago, and as you had not considered it unworthy of pre-
sentation in the mother tongue, and had placed it, moreover,
at the end of your book, where, according to the principles of
rhetoric, the most effective part of the composition belongs. So
one fine day when, as usual, my mind was distracted by a variety
of occupations, discontented with myself and my surroundings,
I suddenly sent everything flying, and, snatching my pen, I
attacked this story of yours. I sincerely trust that it will gratify
you that I have of my own free will undertaken to translate
your work, something I should certainly never think of doing
for anyone else, but which I was induced to do in this instance
by my partiality for you and for the story. Not neglecting the
precept of Horace in his *Art of Poetry*,[3] that the careful translator should not attempt to render word for word, I have told
your tale in my own language, in some places changing or even
adding a few words, for I felt that you would not only permit,
but would approve, such alterations. . . .[4]

68. Petrarch's Intention to Work Until the Last[1]

. . . I certainly will not reject the praise you bestow upon
me for having stimulated in many instances, not only in Italy
but perhaps beyond its confines also, the pursuit of studies such
as ours, which have suffered neglect for so many centuries; I am,

3. Lines 131–35.
4. Petrarch's Latin adaptation of the tale of patient Griselda forms the
major portion of the letter. On the *fortuna* of this translation in the fourteenth century, see J. B. Severs, *The Literary Relationships of Chaucer's
"Clerkes Tale"* (New Haven: Yale University Press, 1942), pp. 21–37.
(Though Chaucer was in Italy in 1373, it seems unlikely that he went to
Padua.)
1. From *Epistolae Seniles* XVII, 2 (from Padua, April 28, 1373), to
Boccaccio.

indeed, almost the oldest of those among us who are engaged in the cultivation of these subjects.[2] But I cannot accept the conclusion you draw from this, namely, that I should give place to younger minds, and, interrupting the plan of work on which I am engaged, give others an opportunity to write something, if they will, and not seem longer to desire to reserve everything for my own pen. How radically do our opinions differ, although, at bottom, our object is the same! I seem to you to have written everything, or at least a great deal, while to myself I appear to have produced almost nothing.

But let us admit that I have written much, and shall continue to write—what better means have I of exhorting those who are following my example to continued perseverance? Example is often more potent than words. The aged veteran Camillus, going into battle like a young man, assuredly aroused more enthusiasm in the younger warriors than if, after drawing them up in line of battle and telling them what was to be done, he had left them and withdrawn to his tent.[3] The fear you appear to harbor, that I shall cover the whole field and leave nothing for others to write, recalls the ridiculous apprehensions which Alexander of Macedon is reported to have entertained, lest his father, Philip, by conquering the whole world, should deprive him of any chance of military renown.[4] Foolish boy! He little realized what wars still remained for him to fight, if he lived, even though the Orient were quite subjugated; he had, perhaps, never heard of Papirius Cursor, or the Marsian generals. Seneca has, however, delivered us from this anxiety, in a letter to Lucilius, where he says, "Much still remains to be done; much will always remain, and even a thousand years hence no one of our descendants need be denied the opportunity of adding his something."[5]

You, my friend, by a strange confusion of arguments, try to

2. Cf. Boccaccio's letter to Jacopo Pizzinga (1372), partially translated in *The Portable Renaissance Reader*, ed. J. B. Ross and M. M. McLaughlin (Viking), pp. 123–26.

3. Livy VI, 24.

4. Livy IX, 17 ff.

5. *Epistulae Morales* 64, 7.

dissuade me from continuing my chosen work by urging, on the one hand, the hopelessness of bringing my task to completion, and by dwelling, on the other, upon the glory which I have already acquired. Then, after asserting that I have filled the world with my writings, you ask me if I expect to equal the number of volumes written by Origen or Augustine. No one, it seems to me, can hope to equal Augustine. Who, nowadays, could hope to equal one who, in my judgment, was the greatest in an age fertile in great minds? As for Origen, you know that I am wont to value quality rather than quantity, and I should prefer to have produced a very few irreproachable works rather than numberless volumes such as those of Origen, which are filled with grave and intolerable errors.[6] It is certainly impossible, as you say, for me to equal either of these, although for very different reasons in the two cases. And yet you contradict yourself, for, though your pen invites me to repose, you cite the names of certain active old men—Socrates, Sophocles, and, among our own people, Cato the Censor—as if you had some quite different end in view. How many more names you might have recalled, except that one does not consciously argue long against himself! Searching desperately for some excuse for your advice and my weakness, you urge that perhaps their temperaments differed from mine. I readily grant you this, although my constitution has sometimes been pronounced very vigorous by those who claim to be experienced in such matters; still, old age will triumph.

You assert, too, that I have sacrificed a great deal of time in the service of princes. But that you may no longer labor under a delusion in this matter, here is the truth. I have lived nominally with princes; in reality, the princes lived with me. I was present sometimes at their councils, and, very rarely, at their banquets. I should never have submitted to any conditions which would, in any degree, have interfered with my liberty or my studies. When everyone else sought the palace, I hied me to the woods, or spent my time quietly in my room, among my books. To say that I have never lost a day would be false. I

6. On Renaissance reassessments of Origen, see E. Wind, "The Revival of Origen," *Studies in Art and Literature for Belle da Costa Greene* (Princeton, 1954), pp. 412–424.

have lost many days (please God, not all) through inertia, or sickness, or distress of mind—evils which no one is so fortunate as to escape entirely. What time I have lost in the service of princes you shall hear, for, like Seneca,[7] I keep an account of my outlays.

First, I was sent to Venice to negotiate a peace between that city and Genoa, which occupied me for an entire winter month.[8] Next I betook myself to the extreme confines of the land of the barbarians,[9] and spent three summer months in arranging for peace in Liguria, with that Roman sovereign who fostered —or I had better say deferred—the hope of restoring a sadly ruined Empire. Finally, I went to France to carry congratulations to King John on his deliverance from an English prison; here three more winter months were lost. Although during these three journeys I dwelt upon my usual subjects of thought, nevertheless, since I could neither write down my ideas nor impress them on my memory, I call those days lost. It is true that when I reached Italy, on my return from the last expedition, I dictated a voluminous letter on the variableness of fortune to a studious old man, Peter of Poitiers; it arrived too late, however, and found him dead. Here, then, are seven months lost in the service of princes; nor is this a trifling sacrifice, I admit, considering the shortness of life. Would that I need not fear a greater loss, incurred long ago by the vanity and frivolous employments of my youth!

You add, further, that possibly the measure of life was different in olden times from what it is in ours, and that nowadays we may regard men as old who were then looked upon as young. But I can only reply to you as I did recently to a certain lawyer in this university, who, as I learned, was accustomed to make that same assertion in his lectures, and excuse the sloth

---

7. *Epistulae Morales* 1, 4.

8. After a disastrous defeat off Sardinia by a Venetian and Catalan fleet (August, 1353), the Genoese decided to offer lordship of Genoa to the Archbishop Giovanni Visconti, who early in 1354 sent a mission to Venice. Petrarch acted as orator and talked privately with the doge, Andrea Dandolo, with whom he had corresponded previously.

9. To Prague, in 1356, to ask the emperor to act on behalf of Galeazzo and Bernabò Visconti, who were being hard pressed by various enemies. It was on this occasion that Charles made Petrarch a Count Palatine.

of our contemporaries. I sent by one of his students to warn him against repeating the statement, unless he wished to be considered an ignoramus. For more than two thousand years there has been no change in the length of human life. Aristotle lived sixty-three years. Cicero lived the same length of time; moreover, although he might have been spared longer had it pleased the heartless and drunken Antony, he had some time before his death written a good deal about his unhappy and premature decline, and had composed a treatise on *Old Age*, for the edification of himself and a friend. Ennius lived seventy years, Horace the same time, while Virgil died at fifty-two, a brief life even for our time. Plato, it is true, lived to be eighty-one; but this, it is said, was looked upon as a prodigy, and because he had attained the most perfect age the Magi decided to offer him a sacrifice, as if he were superior to the rest of mankind. Yet nowadays we frequently see in our cities those who have reached this age; octogenarians and nonagenarians are often to be met with, and no one is surprised, or offers sacrifices to them. If you recall Varro to me, or Cato, or others who reached their hundredth year, or Gorgias of Leontium who greatly exceeded that age, I have other modern instances to set off against them. But as the names are obscure I will mention only one, Romualdo of Ravenna, a very noted hermit, who recently reached the age of one hundred and twenty years, in spite of the greatest privations, suffered for the love of Christ, and in the performance of numerous vigils and fasts such as you are now doing all in your power to induce me to refrain from. I have said a good deal about this matter in order that you may neither believe nor assert that, with the exception of the patriarchs, who lived at the beginning of the world, and who, I am convinced, developed no literary activity whatever, any of our predecessors enjoyed greater longevity than ourselves. They could boast of greater activity, not of a longer life —if, indeed, life without industry deserves to be called life at all, and not a slothful and useless delay.

By a few cautious words, however, you avoid the foregoing criticism, for you admit that it may not be a question of age after all, but that it may perhaps be temperament, or possibly climate, or diet, or some other cause, which precludes me from doing what the others were all able to do. I freely concede this, but I cannot accept the deduction you draw from it, and which you support with laboriously elaborate arguments; for some of your reasons are, in a certain sense, quite opposed to the thesis you would prove. You counsel me to be contented—I quote you literally—with having perhaps equalled Virgil in verse (as you assert) and Cicero in prose.[10] Oh, that you had been induced by the truth, rather than seduced by friendship, in saying this! You add that, in virtue of a senatus consultum following the custom of our ancestors, I have received the most glorious of titles, and the rare honor of the Roman laurel. Your conclusion from all this is that, with the happy results of my studies, in which I rival the greatest, and with my labors honored by the noblest of prizes, I should leave off importuning God and man, and rest content with my fate and the fulfilment of my fondest wishes. Certainly I could make no objection to this if what your affection for me has led you to believe were true, or were even accepted by the rest of the world; I should gladly acquiesce in the opinions of others, for I should always rather trust their judgment than my own. But your view is not shared by others, and least of all by myself, who am convinced that I have rivalled no one, except, perhaps, the common herd, and rather than be like it I should choose to remain entirely unknown. . . .

69. *"Valete amici, valete epistole"*[1]

. . . I know now that neither of two long letters that I wrote to you have reached you. But what can we do?—nothing but submit. We may wax indignant, but we cannot avenge ourselves. A most insupportable set of fellows has appeared in northern

10. This is a major theme in Salutati's praises of Petrarch.
1. The conclusion of *Epistolae Seniles* XVII, 4 (from Arquà, June 4, 1374), sent to Giovanni Boccaccio along with copies of the letters he had sent a year previously. This is Petrarch's last letter.

Italy, who nominally guard the passes, but are really the bane of messengers. They not only glance over the letters that they open, but they read them with the utmost curiosity. They may, perhaps, have for an excuse the orders of their masters, who, conscious of being subject to every reproach in their restless careers of insolence, imagine that everyone must be writing about and against them; hence their anxiety to know everything. But it is certainly inexcusable, when they find something in the letters that tickles their asinine ears, that instead of detaining the messengers while they take time to copy the contents, as they used to do, they should now, with ever increasing audacity, spare their fingers the fatigue, and order the messengers off without their letters. And, to make this procedure the more disgusting, those who carry on this trade are complete ignoramuses, suggesting those unfortunates who possess a capacious and imperious appetite together with a weak digestion, which keeps them always on the verge of illness. I find nothing more irritating and vexatious than the interference of these scoundrels. It has often kept me from writing, and often caused me to repent after I had written. There is nothing more to be done against these letter-thieves, for everything is upside down, and the liberty of the state is entirely destroyed.

To this obstacle to correspondence I may add my age, my flagging interest in almost everything, and not merely satiety of writing but an actual repugnance to it. These reasons taken together have induced me to give up writing to you, my friend, and to those others with whom I have been wont to correspond. I utter this farewell, not so much that these frivolous letters shall, at last, cease to interfere, as they so long have done, with more serious work, but rather to prevent my writings from falling into the hands of these paltry wretches. I shall, in this way, at least escape their insolence, and when I am forced to write to you or to others I shall write to be understood and not to please. I remember already to have promised, in a letter of this kind, that I would thereafter be more concise in my correspondence, in order to economize the brief time which remained to me. But I have not been able to keep this engagement. It seems to me much easier to remain silent altogether with one's friends than to be brief, for when one has once begun, the desire to continue the conversation is so great that it were easier not to begin than to check the flow.

Valete amici, valete epistole.[2]

70. Envoi[1]

My lot has been to live amidst a storm
Of varying, disturbing circumstances.
For you, perhaps—if, as I hope and wish,
You'll live long after me—a better age
Awaits, for this Lethean lethargy
Will not go on forever. Our descendants
Perhaps—the darkness having been dispersed—
Can come again to the old radiance.

2. "Farewell friends, farewell letters." Although these words may have appeared at the end of the letter Petrarch sent to Boccaccio, they were more likely added when he prepared the text for inclusion in the *Seniles.* In either case, they may well be the last words he ever wrote, for on July 18 he suffered another of the attacks to which he had been subject for years, this time a fatal one.

1. *Africa* IX, 451–57, from Petrarch's address to his poem. On Petrarch's view of history, see Mommsen, *Medieval and Renaissance Studies,* pp. 106–29; and Hans Baron, *From Petrarch to Leonardo Bruni,* esp. pp. 23–30. On Petrarch as the beginning of the better age he had hoped for (in the view of Boccaccio and Bruni), Hans Baron, *The Crisis of the Early Italian Renaissance* (revised one-volume edition, Princeton, 1966), esp. pp. 260–62. Bruni's important *Life of Petrarch* is translated in *The Three Crowns of Florence: Humanist Assessments of Dante, Petrarca and Boccaccio,* ed. and trans. David Thompson and Alan F. Nagel (forthcoming Harper Torchbook).

Basic Bibliography

A number of specialized studies (mostly in English) are cited in the notes to individual selections. For the historical context see Robert E. Lerner, *The Age of Adversity: The Fourteenth Century* (Cornell University Press paperback); and Lynn Thorndike, "Dates in Intellectual History: The Fourteenth Century," *Journal of the History of Ideas,* Supplement I (1945).

Some Recent Books in English

1. Hans Baron, *From Petrarch to Leonardo Bruni: Studies in Humanistic and Political Literature* (Chicago and London, 1968).

2. Aldo S. Bernardo, *Petrarch, Scipio and the "Africa": The Birth of Humanism's Dream* (Baltimore, 1962).

3. Morris Bishop, *Petrarch and His World* (Bloomington, Ind., 1963).

4. Theodor E. Mommsen, *Medieval and Renaissance Studies,* ed. Eugene F. Rice, Jr. (Ithaca, N. Y., 1959, 1966).

5. B. L. Ullman, *Studies in the Italian Renaissance* (Rome, 1955).

6. J. H. Whitfield, *Petrarch and the Renascence* (reprint: New York, 1965).

7. E. H. Wilkins, *The "Epistolae Metricae" of Petrarch* (Rome, 1956).

8. ———, *Life of Petrarch* (Chicago, 1961: also Phoenix Book).

9. ———, *The Making of the "Canzoniere" and Other Petrarchan Studies* (Rome, 1951).

10. ———, *Petrarch's Correspondence* (Padua, 1960).

11. ———, *Petrarch's Eight Years in Milan* (Cambridge, Mass., 1958).

12. ———, *Petrarch's Later Years* (Cambridge, Mass., 1959).

13. ———, *Studies in the Life and Works of Petrarch* (Cambridge, Mass., 1955).

INDEX

WIDENER UNIVERSITY
WOLFGRAM
LIBRARY
CHESTER, PA

70 71 72 73   12 11 10 9 8 7 6 5 4 3 2 1

Format by C. Linda Dingler
Composed by Westcott & Thomson, Incorporated
Printed and bound by Murray Printing Company
HARPER & ROW, PUBLISHERS, INCORPORATED